literary | atheism

PETER LANG
New York • Washington, D.C./Baltimore • Bern
Frankfurt am Main • Berlin • Brussels • Vienna • Oxford

ACKNOWLEDGMENTS

I am especially grateful to Gerhard Joseph, Naomi Lebowitz, and Ruth Newton, whose constructive editing of the entire manuscript at an early stage and whose fine understanding of its intentions made possible the development of this book. I am very glad also to acknowledge the help of colleagues and friends who importantly influenced some part or aspect of the work: H. Porter Abbott, Daniel Gerould, N. John Hall, Jan Heissinger, Norman Kelvin, Louis Menand, Burton Pike, Ruth Prigozy, and Joan Richardson. The pages on Samuel Beckett in Chapter Two were published, in somewhat different form, in REVIEW 22 (2000), and I thank its editor, James O. Hoge, for permission to use the material here.

David J. Gordon

literary | atheism

PETER LANG
New York • Washington, D.C./Baltimore • Bern
Frankfurt am Main • Berlin • Brussels • Vienna • Oxford

Library of Congress Cataloging-in-Publication Data

Gordon, David J.
Literary atheism / David J. Gordon.
p. cm.
Includes bibliographical references and index.
1. Religion and literature. 2. Literature, Modern—History
and criticism. 3. Atheism in literature. I. Title.
PN49 .G633   809'.93382118—dc21   2002006240
ISBN 0-8204-6214-4

Die Deutsche Bibliothek-CIP-Einheitsaufnahme

Gordon, David J.:
Literary atheism / David J. Gordon.
–New York; Washington, D.C./Baltimore; Bern;
Frankfurt am Main; Berlin; Brussels; Vienna; Oxford: Lang.
ISBN 0-8204-6214-4

Cover design by Lisa Barfield

The paper in this book meets the guidelines for permanence and durability
of the Committee on Production Guidelines for Book Longevity
of the Council of Library Resources.

© 2002 Peter Lang Publishing, Inc., New York

All rights reserved.
Reprint or reproduction, even partially, in all forms such as microfilm,
xerography, microfiche, microcard, and offset strictly prohibited.

Printed in the United States of America

In memory of my father, Rabbi Julius Gordon

CONTENTS

Acknowledgments ix

Introduction 1

Chapter One: Modern Atheism 11

Chapter Two: Seven Literary Atheists 59

Chapter Three: Literature and Religion 125

Chapter Four: From Sacred Writing to Heightened Reading 173

Works Cited 193

Index 205

INTRODUCTION

"Both fundamentalists and neo-skeptics reject or ignore...what has made perspective into such a powerful cognitive metaphor: the tension between subjective point of view and objective verifiable truth....If this tension can only be kept open, the notion of perspective will cease to be a stumbling block between scientists and social scientists and become instead a space...where we can converse, discuss, and disagree."
Carlo Ginzburg, *Wooden Eyes*

The word atheism—derived from the ancient Greek *atheos*, without God—has always implied a reaction against a particular theism. It was because their bold questioning seemed to undermine the official gods of the state and thus endanger public order that Anaxagoras and Protagoras were forced to flee Athens, and a similar suspicion at the trial of Socrates contributed to his condemnation. But in general the Greeks said to have been atheists demoted rather than abandoned their gods. Even Democritus and Epicurus, who denied any intervention by the gods in the creation of the cosmos, found a place for them within the scheme of nature. Lucretius' *On the Nature of Things*, our source of knowledge about Epicurus, begins, for example, with an invocation to "Venus the life-giver" and teaches us not to deny the existence of gods but to cast off dependence upon them. That is to say, the "atheist" cosmogonists of ancient Greece found, as did Plato and Aristotle, that gods in some measure explained their universe and were morally convenient as well. Plato specified several kinds of atheism—outright denial of the gods along with skepticism about their relevance to human actions and about the efficacy of prayer—but did so in a spirit of inquiry. Like Aristotle he supposed that divinity was at work in the movement of heavenly bodies and that public worship of the gods contributed to social order. Greek religion overall was not centered on belief in the creedal sense we associate with Christianity but on ritual observance and the welfare of the polis.

The ancient Hebrews, lacking the rationalist tradition of the Greeks and the tolerance of other religions bred by polytheism, did not even possess the concept of atheism. The apparently startling statement found at the beginning of Psalms 14 and 53—"The fool hath said in his heart, There is no God"—did not mean for them what it seems to mean for us. The fool is not denying divine existence but defying divine retribution; he is "corrupt" and "abominable" because he is ungrateful to God and disobeys God's law. There are other challenges to God throughout the Hebrew Bible, most memorably in the Book of Job, but in none is God's existence questioned, only his justice. The vanity of life evoked in Ecclesiastes is not inconsistent, as the concluding verses testify, with the lesson that we should "Fear God, and keep his commandments."

In the first centuries of the Common Era, both Christians and Jews were called atheists by their pagan contemporaries, a clear indication of the word's political significance. Then in the long stretch of time during which Europe was dominated by Christianity, from the fourth to the seventeenth century, the Church stigmatized deviation from its doctrines as heresy, and regarded Jews, Muslims, and pagans as infidels or heathens, but it had no need to compete with secularism, as in the modern world, for the non-ecclesiastical authority of the medieval world did not stand outside the Christian authority, whatever tensions existed between them. Finally in the Renaissance this cohesion really did begin to crack. It is not fanciful to date modern atheism from the time that a charge of "heresy" begins to sound quaint. Against a seventeenth-century background we may describe John Milton's deviations from Christian doctrine as "heresies" without provoking demurral, but, against a late eighteenth and early nineteenth-century background, William Blake's revisions of Christian doctrine seem to require a quite different kind of word, like originality.

The emergence of modern atheism is best understood as a two-phase phenomenon. The first spans a period from the time of Descartes, *circa* 1630, to about 1770, from the newly formulated precedence of the natural over the supernatural to the first overt avowals of nonbelief in a purposeful higher intelligence that created the universe and cares for man. The second and (for this study) more crucial phase sets in after the Enlightenment, after the inward turn pursued by Kant and the Romantics had begun to persuade many thoughtful people that a transcendent and caring deity was an idea rather than a being and had to be evaluated accordingly.

I maintain that most educated post-Enlightenment persons are agnostic in their objective knowing, for they live in a scientific age and respect the kind of thinking that seeks methodical results based on verifiable evidence. From that standpoint, there is nothing to be learned about a supernatural world, no evidence of a supernatural being. I separate agnosticism, then, from convinced belief or disbelief, both products of subjective knowing. Of course these modes of cognition are never in practice quite distinct from one another. The thinking of scientists and scholars is energized by feeling, and the feeling of believers, moralists, and poets is influenced by their perception of the world about them. When the word God is imaginatively kindled, the line between what is *thought* and *felt* to be true can be difficult to draw. Nonetheless, what is new for educated post-Enlightenment persons, and usually clear enough despite the overlapping of thought and feeling, is the very distinction between objective and subjective standpoints, the purposes of science and scholarship on the one hand and those of religion and the arts on the other.

Although it is possible to describe matters of *fact* objectively, this study adopts the position that *moral* truth can never be absolute and universal, can never be truth that everyone understands alike. But this position (defended in our day by Richard Rorty and Stanley Fish, and traceable to Nietzsche), is not relativism—or is so, as Fish explains, only if relativism means the intelligent practice of trying to understand an adversary's point of view, *not* if it means ceasing to prefer one's own convictions.[1] Because of this ambiguity I would rather use the Nietzschean term perspectivism, which, according to Alexander Nehamas, "holds that I can both believe that your views are false" and understand your need to believe them.[2] Perspectivism is also better able to do the work of differentiating kinds of believing—enabling us, for example, to say with Wittgenstein that we don't believe what persons of faith say they believe and yet do not contradict them, because one kind of believing is not the same as the other.[3]

Like Carlo Ginzburg, I will use the concept of perspectivism to distinguish two modes of understanding, subjective and objective, *within an individual*. We can warm to the idea of God and yet, on a second or "higher" level, remain coolly agnostic. Aroused by a situation or a text, we can commit ourselves to an absolute moral judgment and yet stand back as well, take into account the judgments of others, and thereby arrive at a relativistic verdict. There is a difference, in other words, between direct moral judgment and second-level judgment *of* moral judgment. Taken together, they lead to a distinction between subjective and objective points of view, a distinction that allows "absolute" and "relative" judgments to coexist. But if the minds of individuals are thus divisible, it does not mean that their thinking must be torn by conflict. We are usually well able to shuttle from one perspective to the other, though perhaps not without some internal effort. I take it then as a *psychological fact* and not a *logical problem* that one person, at the same time, can feel passionately and think skeptically, can be moved toward (or against) God and yet consider herself an agnostic.

Only when truth based on emotional conviction competitively claims to *displace* truth arrived at by impersonal method and verifiable evidence does it become troublesome. When a highly individual writer tells us what God *is*—when a Tolstoy tells us that God is the name of his desire—he need not, despite the apodictic statement, be defining God for everyone but only for himself. The practice of imaginative theologians is similar, only somewhat less individual. Jacques Maritain, Karl Barth, and Martin Buber, although their tone is dogmatic, may be understood as defining God not for everyone but for a particular group—Catholics, Protestants or Jews. Thus, theists need not be considered naïve because their convictions are forceful and because they are attached to them. It would be enough that their work implicitly acknowledges that one person's or one group's theology is not binding on everyone. If, however, allowance is explicitly *not* made for the reader to make such an inference, I must conclude that the writer is in the grip of a myth without knowing it.

It is true that, at critical historical moments, a strong leader may erase the subjective-objective distinction in order to kindle the desire for revolutionary change, as when Martin Luther King, Jr. in 1954 identified the justice of his cause with the very justice of God. But intolerance toward opposing viewpoints, especially when backed up by appeals to the authority of God, does typically lead to violence. The moral battling today between Islamic and Western militancy, based on the strong conviction all around that The One True God Is On Our Side, gives little promise of peaceful resolution, and cries out for more finely shaded understanding.

Linking the modern objective perspective with agnosticism restricts the meaning of both theism and atheism. Belief or disbelief in God is then necessarily based on emotional conviction, and enlightened theists and atheists will understand, perhaps reluctantly, that their beliefs, supported by whatever they call evidence, are rooted in subjectivity. Miguel de Unamuno makes this point, and all the more strikingly because he thinks unbelief is a product of despair. Stressing the phrase "in his heart" in the psalmist's verse about the wicked fool's scorn of God, he indicates that reasoning about God is unimportant because it is only in the heart that one can really repudiate or embrace Him.[4]

The Enlightenment paved the way for science as we know it today, but, in doing so, aroused distrust of the imagination and of psychological phenomena in general. The Romantic reaction to the Enlightenment provided a valuable corrective. Kant allowed God to be understood not as a heavenly being but as an idea (albeit a universal one) and the Romantics modified Kant's position by saying that this understanding could not be universal because it was a product of individual feeling and imagination. Theism after the Enlightenment began to be understood as an enabling mythology, and atheism began necessarily to mean not a logical denial of God's supernatural existence but opposition to an influential myth perceived as oppressive. And the dominant theological myth in Western societies continues to be the personal and providential deity of the Judeo-Christian tradition. In *The Rebel*, Albert Camus observed, I think correctly, that atheism is inseparable from the idea of a personal god in the history of Christianity.[5]

This study will de-emphasize the common distinction between believers and unbelievers and bring forward a distinction between theists or atheists who are *naïve* and those who are *sophisticated*. The naïve group are convinced that the existence of God can be proved or disproved by objective evidence whereas the sophisticated group are able to acknowledge that their God is to be understood intellectually as myth or metaphor. The first group, then, are dogmatic. Whether theist or atheist, they are likely to scorn agnostics as wishy-washy people who lack the courage of their convictions. The second group do not confuse objective and subjective perspectives. Whether theist or atheist, they can enter into—and retreat from—the spirit of texts that represent supernatural intervention in human affairs. They know that the God idea they contend with is not an absolute but is always mediated by social and psychological circumstances, whatever its strength.

My particular interest in these pages is the sophisticated or literary atheist. Such a person can be described as not believing in the ghosts of religion yet to some degree, as a participant in her culture, continuing to be haunted by them. Like Samuel Beckett's Hamm, who impugns God as a "bastard [who] doesn't exist," the literary atheist is typically ironical, an unbeliever who must acknowledge some sort of residual presence. Because the word atheist sounds assertive, I had thought of substituting "antitheist," a word that usefully implies not denial of, but opposition to, God. Yet "antitheist" is itself assertive, and in a misleading way, for it suggests that one can scorn a culture's strong myth from the outside, without personal involvement. It suffers, too, by its lack of familiarity, which makes it more difficult for me to engage the extensive literature of unbelief. So I have settled on the phrase "literary atheism." The phrase is meant to indicate that, in adopting an objective point of view, one *is* distanced from this cultural myth (hence many scientists find it easy to describe themselves as agnostics or atheists) while from the subjective point of view necessarily adopted in imaginative writing one *cannot* be so distanced.

In making a distinction between subjective and objective perspectives, I am by no means endorsing an obsolete dualism of mind and body. William James explained some time ago that scientific thinking abstracts one aspect of consciousness from the whole of it, which is "practically necessary and indispensable," but, philosophically, scientific thinking is not separate from other kinds of thinking—ethical, religious, or aesthetic.[6] Mary Midgley in *Science and Poetry* provides further clarification: "The words *mind* and *body* do not name two separate kinds of stuff" but "aspects of ourselves" or "points of view." She warns that, if like some scientists we see the world we live in, including mind, only in physical or material terms, we cannot "fit together...ourselves as subjects and ourselves as objects."[7] One thing I mean to say by calling these aspects or viewpoints perspectives is that science on the one hand and religion and literature on the other are, whatever the strain between them, interrelated. The strain cannot be removed altogether, but knowledge from one perspective alone will always be partial.

In this study I regularly call the sophisticated modern atheist a literary atheist because contending with an idea inside oneself seems to me a characteristic activity of the literary imagination. This is where the poet lives and moves and has his being. I doubt that many sophisticated believers would like to be called literary theists, the counterpart of literary atheists, although both are in fact wrestling with ideas and images. But I am arguing that, in the post-Enlightenment world, what is conventionally called atheism—reasoned, categorical denial of the existence of God—is at best naïve, and that the only atheism worthy of serious discussion consists not of dismissing what is after all an active myth but rather of opposing it, making literary use of it. I know that some sophisticated nonbelievers do not like the atheist label in any form because they sense rightly enough that it is forcing them to take a position on a badly framed question. Since, however, they have no difficulty entering into the spirit of texts that involve either belief or unbelief, I hope they will welcome a phrase like literary atheism.

We must, however, recognize the fact that there is an area between poetic and religious belief in which skepticism and conviction jostle one another.

The poet must in some sense believe in his fictions in order to compose them effectively, as the poets Robert Frost and Wallace Stevens well knew, and doubtless Christian (or other) believers need to forget at times the sliding nature of the language that expresses their faith, defined by St. Paul as "the assurance of things hoped for, the conviction of things not seen."[8] Thus the relation between literature and religion is complex. And it has been further complicated in recent decades by the influence of scientific speculation and its competing and compelling narratives about human origins and ends. The triangular pressure of literature, religion, and science is a topic that will receive consideration in these pages.

While working on this book I have been asked two questions more than any others: "Are *you* an atheist?" and "What has the literary imagination got to do with atheism?" I trust I have implied my answers to them. As to the first question, the answer is that my objective view of the existence of God is best described as agnostic but that my imaginative, passionate understanding is potentially either theistic or atheistic. Imaginatively I am readily engaged by strong religious literature, but am at least as attracted to strong writers who adopt a rebellious, antitheistic stance. What I distrust is subjective conviction presented as objective truth, and I would uncover the absolutism hidden in concepts that religion typically puts its stamp upon, such as God, moral truth, and the sacred text.

My answer to the second question adjudicates the three outlooks alluded to: the scientific/scholarly, the theological/religious, and the literary/artistic. (Philosophy, especially ethics or moral philosophy, belongs in this picture too but is difficult to place because it fits any of the three depending on its shading.) Literature is allied to religion in its dependence on myth, but is closer to the scientific habit of mind, which works with hypotheses, in that it knows itself to be myth. A potential danger in religious imagining is refusing to acknowledge that it is basically a form of poetry. A potential danger in scientific imagining, not an inherent one but one that has become more noticeable recently, is a tendency to see the truth it deals with as the only kind worth bothering about, hence to condescend to the truth-claims of art and religion or to absorb them in a unified view of knowledge. By virtue of its peculiar flexibility as it moves between intellect and emotion, the literary imagination, which in this study will be understood as a general activity of mind as well as a specific agent of art, can play an important critical role in relation to several kinds of absolutistic thinking that rely on the premise of divine authority.

A reformulation of atheism makes possible, in the first half of this book, a fresh look at dozens of writers who oppose a major myth in imaginatively interesting ways. In the second half, which brings forward some social and political aspects of my subject, it supports an inquiry into the absolutism that too often characterizes the influence of religion upon literature, science, and secular society. The literary atheist functions as a critic of books but also as a general educator, suspicious of authority that derives from "God" and, for the sake of promoting greater self and social understanding, ready to question our investment in such authority.

NOTES

To avoid excessive documentation, I have, throughout this book, not provided notes for quotations whose sources are widely accessible or that are adequately identified in the text.

1. Stanley Fish, "Condemnation Without Absolutes," *New York Times* (15 October 2001), A19.
2. Alexander Nehamas, *The Art of Living: Socratic Reflections from Plato to Foucault* (Berkeley: University of California Press, 1998), 147–49.
3. Ludwig Wittgenstein, *Lectures & Conversations on Aesthetics, Psychology and Religious Belief*, compiled by Yorick Smythies, Rush Rhees, and James Taylor, ed. Cyril Barrett (Berkeley: University of California Press, 1972), 56.
4. Miguel de Unamuno, *The Tragic Sense of Life in Men and Peoples*, trans. J. E. Crawford Flitch (London: Macmillan, 1926), 184.
5. Albert Camus, *The Rebel: An Essay on Man in Revolt*, trans. Anthony Bower (New York: Vintage, 1962), 28.
6. William James, *Principles of Psychology* (Cleveland: World Publishing Company, [1890] 1948), 6–7.
7. Mary Midgley, *Science and Poetry* (London: Routledge, 2001), 10.
8. I choose here the translation of Pauline faith in the New Revised Standard Version (hereafter NRSV) rather than the more familiar King James translation ("substance of things hoped for, evidence of things not seen" [Hebrews 11:1]) because the phrase "evidence of things not seen" has become somewhat ambiguous in the tussle between science and religion that will concern us in Chapter Three. Science as science finds insufficient evidence to postulate the existence of God, but it regularly makes inferences from available evidence concerning "things not seen."

CHAPTER ONE
Modern Atheism

"God is not a being outside me, but merely a thought in me."
Immanuel Kant, "Opus Postumum"

In the 1940s the historian Lucien Febvre published a memorable study about unbelief in sixteenth-century France, arguing that Rabelais was not an atheist because he *could not* have been. Not only were social customs still embraced by Christian rule but the conceptual vocabulary required to support unbelief—including terms like materialism, rationalism, and laws of nature—was not yet in place.[1] While respecting Febvre's bold claim, subsequent historians have rightly modified it, for the sixteenth was also the first of the modern centuries in which atheism became a subject of debate.[2] The revival of classical learning led people's minds beyond the confines of Christianity; the Protestant Reformation promoted individual judgment about religious as well as other issues; and the spirit of rationalism that led to dramatic developments in seventeenth-century science and philosophy was already in the air.

The word atheist entered the English language in the 1540s, and by the end of the century it was applied broadly, although no one accepted the label as self-description. Marlowe and Raleigh were rumored to be atheists. Thomas Nashe proclaimed "that the ambitious, the greedy, the gluttons, the vainglorious and prostitutes were all atheists." The hypocrite and the arrogant sinner might also be so charged. In general "atheist" was an accusation ready for anyone whose language or behavior was disturbingly liberal or libertine, as well as for those who questioned tenets of Christian doctrine.[3]

The underlying issue was the security of religious institutions. The custodians of Christianity worried mainly about those who lived as though God did not exist, and worried too about those whose words could weaken particular beliefs that propped the Church's authority, such as the providence of God, the immortality of the soul, the truth of the Gospels. Carlo Ginzburg has written a fascinating, full-length study of such a person in Italy, a person as sincere as he was socially obscure,[4] and similar testimonies mounted as the century turned. In the course of the seventeenth century some thoughtful skeptics were attracted to the emerging philosophy of deism, which tried to preserve what seemed compatible with reason (the creative and providential nature of God) and to belittle what did not (revealed truth, mainly the divinity of Jesus).

Imaginative writers, however, were sometimes fascinated by atheism because they understood, in the words of Pierre Charron, a disciple of Montaigne, that "it requires a strong soul to resolutely divest oneself of the apprehension and belief in God."[5] Francis Bacon, in "Of Atheism" and "Of Superstition," expressed a similar thought, conceding to atheists a disturbing measure, if not a sufficiency, of philosophic acuity. The dramatist and poet, then, might endow with charisma a villain bold enough to proclaim his irreligion openly. Marlowe's Machiavel, at the start of *The Jew of Malta*, boasts, "I count religion but a childish toy." Shakespeare's most fascinating villains, Iago and Edmund, are contemptuous of all pieties. And Milton's Satan repudiates Heaven on a heroic scale and is allowed to evoke some measure of pathos by virtue of his very separation from God.

The emergence of conceptual atheism in the seventeenth and eighteenth centuries will be traced through a line of major thinkers from Descartes to Diderot, including Spinoza, Hobbes, Newton, Locke, Voltaire, and Hume. None of them was strictly an atheist but each weakened traditional theology, particularly the "cosmological" and "teleological" arguments based on the perceived logical necessity of a first cause and of a supreme, purposeful intelligence. After writers like Hume and Diderot had exerted their influence, the idea of a supernatural creator and caretaker became less awesome, even when the deity's mere existence was conceded. Post-Enlightenment atheism is built upon their critical work.

But lest we think of the undermining of theology as the work of only a few bold thinkers, it is important to add, before we turn to them, that the drift toward atheism in the seventeenth and eighteenth centuries was abetted by orthodox believers themselves, who were constrained by the rationalistic spirit of the age to argue the case *for* God on philosophic grounds where they were sure to get the worst of it. This paradoxical thesis has been well and fully argued in two studies, *At the Origins of Modern Atheism* by Michael J. Buckley, and *Atheism in France, 1650–1729: The Orthodox Sources of*

Unbelief by Alan Charles Kors. Kors studied what he called "the generation of disbelief by orthodox culture itself," and Buckley declared: "in failing to assert its own competence, in commissioning philosophy in its defense, religion shaped its own eventual negation."[6] Heinrich Heine long ago made the same point concisely, looking back on the Enlightenment from close range: "As soon as religion seeks help from philosophy, its doom is inevitable."[7] For intellectuals, however, the growing spirit of rationalism during this period may have been impossible to escape. In the sixteenth century, John Calvin could or would see no conflict between science and scripture. In the seventeenth, George Herbert accepted Bacon's distinction between God's word and God's works, but Pascal felt obliged to express his faith in terms of mathematical probability, and John Milton made his God argue the case for divine justice like a schoolmaster.

From Descartes to Diderot

For most of the major figures involved in the line of thought to be traced here, the main issue was the primary reality of substance (which Descartes thought of as either mental or corporeal, the first being more certain), a naturalistic emphasis that undermined, perhaps unintentionally, supernatural religion. Descartes' systematic doubt, which aimed to achieve a mathematical kind of certainty, was launched in reaction to Montaigne's more humane skepticism aimed only at the presumptuousness of reason regarding religion and belief. The fact that Descartes was eventually led by his method to repostulate the existence of God was less important than that his starting point was human reason, the famous *cogito*, departing from the old assumption that human existence was a consequence of divine intention. Substance, he wrote in *Principles of Philosophy*, "exists in such a way as to depend on no other thing for its existence."[8] His argument that God's existence is necessarily to be inferred from the fact that our minds contain the idea of perfection (a version of the scholastic ontological argument) does not then privilege divine initiative, and becomes an important step toward Newton's demonstration, *contra* Aristotle, that the laws governing the movement of matter are mathematical and do not require supernatural explanation. In general, Descartes' thinking had little use for the caring, heavenly divinity of traditional Judeo-Christianity, and thus his influence moved his age toward what came to be termed natural theology.

Descartes himself was not called an atheist, perhaps because his argument did not point at religion, but Spinoza and Hobbes, who followed him, were so stigmatized. Spinoza in fact was excommunicated by the Jews of Amsterdam after he refused to keep quiet, and one can see why, for his pantheistic philosophy, despite its emphasis on God (the German Romantics were to call him admiringly *der Gott betrunkene Mensch*), clearly subverted their tradition. He sought to demonstrate that rational laws upheld the entire substance of the natural world and that God was to be identified with those laws. Thus a *supernatural* event, like a miracle, would establish God's *non*-existence. Immanence in Spinoza's philosophy was total, absorbing all trace of divine transcendence and all trace as well of an anthropomorphic deity. It envisioned the complete harmony of what exists at the expense of a personal God concerned with man and, of course, at the expense of scripture, whose main purpose, Spinoza believed, was to make men not religious but obedient. Although his ideas were bound to shock orthodox believers, his way of combining natural law and divine presence, of sanctifying the intelligibility of the natural world, has proved attractive down the years both to poets with a taste for science like Goethe and scientists with a taste for poetry like Einstein.

Hobbes argued for a mechanistic view both of mind and of society, and indeed his "theology" is little more than an extension of this view. He went so far (in *Leviathan*) as to link religion with credulity and to name all gods "creatures of fancy." Writing in the midst of the English Civil War, he was concerned primarily to bolster the authority of the State. Christianity was reconceived as civil religion, whose authority was to be respected as an aspect of the sovereign's. Thus, as one scholar put it, "Hobbes had some favorable words for the deity but the drift of his argument went the other way."[9] It is not surprising that he was persistently suspected of atheism, though he lived and died peacefully. A measure of prudent dissimulation perhaps entered also into his official theism, as it surely did in the more overtly heterodox views of Voltaire, Hume, and Diderot.

Newton's discovery that the motions of both heavenly and earthly bodies were governed by the same encompassing law, implying that nature herself obeys reason, made its discoverer "the patron saint of the Enlightenment," for it "could serve the *philosophes* as a model for remaking human society."[10] But, although Newton had at a stroke overturned the long-standing tradition of Aristotelian cosmology, his God was not quite the remote Watchmaker, who wound up the universe and let it run on its own, that Voltaire's popularization turned it into. In the words of Dorinda Outram, his cosmos of mathematical law was "not only originally set in motion by its creator, but also required considerable intervention from him to correct irregularities and supply energy,"[11] an argument to prop Christian belief that has been revived in our day by the philosopher Alvin Plantinga.

Newton's fellow Englishman, John Locke, in his significantly titled "The Reasonableness of Christianity" as well as in *An Essay on Human Understanding* and his several essays on toleration, also helped to shape the Enlightenment tradition by modifying the seventeenth-century's idealization of reason. He shifted the register of the word reason from rationalism to reasonableness and good sense—that is, to a universal standard based on the intuitive knowledge we have of our own existence. This was a standard flexible enough in application to accommodate "degrees of assent," hence to permit a measure of compromise in the always controversial areas of politics and religion. He urged toleration of beliefs because they were involuntary, and he deemed liberty of conscience desirable, ideas that would mean much to the American Founding Fathers. He was not quite prepared to attack revelation (or welcome atheists), but his denial of innate ideas, his rejection of the Cartesian hypothesis of soul or mind (the same word, *âme*, in French) as separate from body, did constitute yet another step away from traditional theology and religion, making him an important influence on deism if not quite a deist himself.

In France too there were compromises between belief and unbelief, although a stronger anti-clerical tradition made for a sharper, more ironic skepticism, as we see in the representative case of Voltaire, whose deism is fairly well defined by the way he begins his entry in the *Philosophical Dictionary* for "Superstition," calling by that name "almost everything that goes beyond the worship of a supreme Being and the submission of one's head to its eternal demands." As the entry on "Atheism" shows, he was more than a little beguiled by the strongly skeptical thinking of Pierre Bayle, who thought that faith was *not* consistent with reason and who even speculated that a society made up of atheists might be workable. Voltaire backed away from full agreement on this question, and even described atheism as "a monstrous evil…almost always fatal to virtue," but he considered "fanaticism…a thousand times more disastrous, for atheism inspires no sanguinary passion." The whole entry suggests that his real scruple about atheists was that they were too eager for explanation where none could be found, and so resorted to belief in materialism and "necessity."[12]

Voltaire was impressed by the scandalous posthumous "Testament" of a *curé* named Jean Meslier, which found Christian doctrines unproved, absurd, and offensive, and saw in nature only blind mechanism. But in helping to arrange for its publication in 1729, he chose to tone down the sharp edges, in effect making Meslier a deist like himself. Voltaire's anti-clericalism is still legendary (*écrasez l'infâme!*), and his hostility sometimes spilled onto the Bible and the Bible's God: "*Je veux aimer ce Dieu, je cherche en lui mon père:/ On me montre un tyran que nous devons haïr.*"[13] But he was not so much anti-theological as impatient with the obscurities of theological argument wherever he found them. The famous ending of *Candide* implies the moral range of his deism pretty well: God exists but is far away, and man's business in the world is to replace prayer and devotion with useful industry.

The purest skeptic of the Enlightenment period was surely David Hume, to the extent that he can hardly be labeled theist, deist *or* atheist. In fact, Hume described the difference between atheist and theist as a matter of degree, the one insisting on the difficulty of belief, the other on its necessity.[14] Eschewing a charge of atheism was doubtless prudent but it was also, I think, a matter of principle, for, without a visible ax to grind, Hume shredded whatever theological arguments lay at hand, especially the influential argument from design. The strong essay on "Miracles" undermines a pillar of revealed religion, and in the *Dialogues Concerning Natural Religion* even deism is left without much support.

Hume's skepticism was the more thorough because he did not share the confidence in progress that animated the *philosophes* across the Channel. He did not write polemic or wish to attack the institution of religion, which like Hobbes he seems to have found useful for maintaining order. Indeed, his skepticism was so pure that he understood its limits, observing nicely that "philosophy would render us entirely pyrrhonian were not nature too strong for it."[15] That is, our satisfaction in living does not depend on logical demonstrations concerning such matters as the existence of God. In general, Hume sought to show not so much the error but the weakness of the supporting arguments, their remoteness from any pretense of certainty. "The whole of Natural Theology," he concluded, "resolves itself into one simple, though somewhat ambiguous, at least undefined proposition, *That the cause or causes of order in the universe probably bear some remote analogy to human intelligence.*"[16] The deity, though not denied, is thus stripped of human interest. In a letter denying he is an atheist, Hume asserts that the deity "is not the natural Object of any Passion or Affection. He is no Object either of the

Senses or Imagination, & very little of the Understanding, without which it is impossible to excite any Affection."[17] Diderot expressed a similar idea more ironically in a letter to Voltaire, describing the existence of God as one of those "*très sublime et très inutiles vérités*" that he would love to discuss with his correspondent but cannot declare publicly because of social considerations.[18]

Hume's skepticism did not bring to a halt reasoned defense of the argument from design, as is evident from the popularity of William Paley's resourceful books, *Evidences for Christianity* (1794) and *Natural Theology* (1802), but it was the strongest counter-argument that could be made until Darwin came along and showed that there was a strong *naturalistic* argument that *could* explain design.

In mid eighteenth-century France for the first time, comments Michael Buckley, atheism became "a signature and a boast."[19] The story is told that, while dining at the lavish table of Baron d'Holbach, Hume remarked skeptically that he had never met any actual atheists. Holbach waved his arm about the table and replied, "You're looking at fifteen of them now."[20] One may doubt that the fifteen were quite open about their convictions, for the canny Diderot, one of their number, became skilled (after some months in prison) at dodging the authorities. But if one had to choose a particular date for the commencement of avowed atheism, it might be 1770, the publication date of Holbach's comprehensive polemic, *Le Système de la nature ou les loix du monde physique et du monde moral*. In England, according to David Berman, a historian of British atheism, the first published avowal dates from 1782.[21]

Building, or overbuilding, on Newton, Holbach argued that the laws of nature compose a system that determines everything, the moral as well as the physical world, mind as well as matter. The deterministic thrust of the treatise is not in the least pessimistic, however, for Holbach believed that man is only unhappy because he is ignorant of nature. The atheist becomes a kind of revolutionary hero who destroys the chimera of religion and theism that impedes progress; man should become instead a worshiper of reason and nature. Here is a rather typical Holbachian effusion: "*O nature! Souveraine de tous les êtres, et vous ses filles adorable, vertu, raison, vérité! Soyez à jamais nos seules divinités; c'est à vous que sont dus l'encens et les hommage de la terre.*"[22] Divinity, incense, homage? In hindsight it is easy to see that Holbach's laws of nature have acquired a religious resonance, like Marx's laws of history, which also welcomed atheism as a force that removed the rubble impeding progress.

Systematic materialists in the eighteenth century were sufficiently scandalous—La Mettrie for example, the author of *L'homme machine*, was forced to flee to Frederick the Great's Prussia—but what disturbed Diderot about a book like *De l'homme* by Helvétius (and probably also about Holbach's treatise, though he was said to have contributed to it) was that it left little room for moral *speculation* and failed to acknowledge the respects in which man, however much like other animals, also differed from them. With his quicksilver intellect, Diderot was emphatic without being dogmatic, about religion or anything else. I discuss him in detail in Chapter Two as the first of my literary atheists because his opposition to God was complex, imbedding an appreciation of the cost of radical social change and of the difficulty of combining a necessitarian philosophy with an interest in moral questions.

One further word about deism before we turn our attention to Kant and the Romantics. The Revolution was of course around the corner when Diderot died in 1784, and, during it, atheism became for a radical wing (most notably for Jacques Hébert and Pierre Chaumette, who were soon to be guillotined) a banner to be flaunted as an open political act. But ironically, the figure known to us as the bloodiest of the revolutionaries, Robespierre, was a deist, who, a few months before his own beheading, proclaimed mandatory worship of a Supreme Being, an act which offended Jacques-André Naigeon, friend and associate of Holbach and Diderot who lived on into the next century.[23] Deism originated in the seventeenth century and faded in the nineteenth. But the two most popular and vigorous works of deistic philosophy, Thomas Paine's *The Rights of Man* and *The Age of Reason*, were both published during the years of the Revolution. Paine was a passionate deist, who in *The Age of Reason* described traditional Christianity, because "it professes to believe in a man rather than in God," as "a species of Atheism—a sort of religious denial of God."[24] Paine's commonsense Reason retained some influence throughout the nineteenth century, particularly for morally earnest nonbelievers who wanted to express their opposition to Christianity and who organized into groups with such names as Freethinkers, Rationalists, Humanists, and Secularists. TomPaine.Common Sense is today a website espousing (with scarcely more sense of irony) anti-establishment opinions. The name in 1837 was still sufficiently vital that Georg Büchner could use it for an important antitheistic role in *Danton's Death*.

The Inward Turn: Kant and the Romantics

In some ways the very embodiment of the Enlightenment, Kant was also a major architect of a new era of thought, as is evident in his reconstruction of the God question. He agreed with Hume that you could not reason about God the way you reason about physical objects. The traditional proofs for divine existence proved nothing, for metaphysical ideas such as God and immortality possessed only an illusory or symbolic reality. We can say that, after Newton made a First Cause unnecessary and after Hume riddled the Design argument, Kant completed the rout of the formal "proofs" by deflating the so-called ontological argument. It held that if God lacked the attribute of existence, he would not be perfect. Kant showed that this is to confuse existence in a logical sense (attribution) with existence in a grammatical sense (predication).

But Kant turned Hume's skeptical method against his agnostic conclusion and made a distinction between theoretical and practical reason, between metaphysics and morality. Experience remained the basis of understanding, but experience, he came to believe, included more than sensation and impression, its content for Hume. Kant asserted memorably that the moral law within us was as undeniable as the starry heavens above. God was a thought, not a being, but that thought was to be identified with "the highest moral principle in me." Good is only realizable, he argued, if its highest form is assumed to exist, and he was willing to call this form God. In effect, he found a new role for the deity, not creator of the universe or loving father but supporter of the moral law within us. For Kant, it was the Protestant individual conscience that governed ethical thinking, an inward turn comparable to his "Copernican revolution" in epistemology based on the premise that "experience contains intellectual structure [and so] is already organised in accordance with the ideas of space, time, substance and causality."[25]

In the thinking of Kant, and of Rousseau as well, the eighteenth-century ideals of reason and nature remained standards of universal application, but the act of interiorizing them had immense consequences, greater than either of these sons of Enlightenment could have anticipated or welcomed. One large consequence, which will bear directly on our understanding of modern atheism, was the emergence of a perceived gap between objective reason on the one hand and subjective imagination or feeling on the other. Kant, comments Richard Rorty, "was appalled at the Romantic attempt to make idiosyncratic poetic imagination, rather than what he called the 'common moral consciousness,' the center of the self."[26] He probably would not have understood the need for the ardent defense in Wordsworth's Preface to the *Lyrical Ballads* of the importance of poetry versus that of science. Or Coleridge's concern that the present age could not read the Bible properly because it "recognizes no medium between *Literal* and *Metaphorical*" meaning.[27] Or, especially, the effort of Schleiermacher to root religious belief in deep and creative personal experience because he assumed (like a true Romantic, like Blake or Emerson) that the best Christians are those whose experience is deep enough to write a Holy Scripture themselves.

Isaiah Berlin has described the epistemological shift from Enlightenment to Romanticism as the greatest turning point in the history of thought. "During the entire span of the central tradition of Western thought," he wrote, "it had been assumed that all general questions [that is, questions ranging from 'what are the best values' to 'does God exist'] were…questions of fact," answerable in the form of universal truth. The skeptic Hume and the atheist Holbach, Berlin pointed out, shared with G. E. Lessing the belief that the moral *goal* was the same for everyone. But when it began to be believed that truth was made rather than found, the notion of a universal standard of truth to be discovered either out there independent of our language about it or in an intrinsic human nature could no longer be maintained. Berlin was well aware of Romanticism's own universalizing tendency, apparent for example in the systematic philosophies of Hegel and Marx. But he believed that its most salutary legacy, partly in spite of itself, was in fostering pluralism, the recognition that individuals and groups have different and to some extent incompatible moral goals and centers. He was concerned to show that we are heirs of both the Enlightenment and Romantic traditions, and implied that some tension between them was not a bad thing.[28]

Richard Rorty provides very helpful amplification of Berlin's main point, and in so doing brings us back to the God question. He says (with a nod to the philosopher Donald Davidson) that, although the world is out there, descriptions of the world are not, and truth can only be understood in terms of those descriptions. Then he adds, crucially, "The suggestion that truth, as well as the world, is out there is a legacy of an age in which the world was seen as the creation of a being that had a language of his own." To capitalize the word truth, Rorty writes, means "treating it as something identical either with God or with the world as God's project." The pluralism that Berlin and Rorty promote makes some people anxious because it seems to imply moral relativism, but Rorty shows very clearly that the whole concept of moral relativism is inextricably connected with that of moral absolutism and that this very antithesis is obstructive and best put aside.[29] I don't think this threatens the meaning of truth in science. Such truth could be understood as that kind of description of the world especially useful for predicting and controlling what happens. And since this mode of thinking is, in E. O. Wilson's words, "increasingly the habit of educated peoples,"[30] it is scarcely deprecated by Rorty's line of argument.

The shift of sensibility marked by Romanticism is important in this study because it decisively alters the meaning of theism and thereby of atheism. Hume and Kant showed that the existence of God is not something that can be proved or disproved. But as Romantic writers from Blake to Feuerbach converted God into a specific achievement of the human imagination, his existence came to be understood as a myth, albeit one that aroused strong feelings. Thus, although the question of whether or not a supernatural God actually exists was now seen by some leading thinkers as unanswerable and futile to pursue, God as an imaginative idea, an opportunity for rhetorical intensity made available by cultural tradition, remained to be reckoned with. Jacques Derrida may have had some such notion in mind (although his philosophy tends to ignore the *will* to rhetoric) when he scolded Karl Marx for his impatient dismissal of the "ghosts of religion": "(Of course they do not exist, so what?)."[31]

One important result of this reorientation of the God question is that the distance between the understanding of more and of less educated populations widens, causing social awkwardness. Down to the present day, the question of God's objective existence continues to be debated and discussed as if Hume and Kant had never written, as if the question were susceptible of a meaningful answer. Walk into the Religion section of any well-stocked bookstore and you will find half a dozen new books arguing on one side of the question or the other. In intellectual circles this debate is mostly ignored (although the old design argument, attached to new scientific speculations, has managed to gain some notoriety). But one cannot, like the positivist A. J. Ayer, simply dismiss "all utterances about the nature of God," because they are nonverifiable, as "nonsensical."[32] This is to deprecate the whole world of expressive language, as used by art, philosophy, and religion, fields that continue to make potent use of them. A trickier question is whether the God invoked by poets and the God invoked by religious believers can be treated in the same way. This study will insist on the assumption that the language of religion, in the post-Enlightenment world, has lost its claim to be advancing a kind of truth superior to or different from that advanced by literature, but religion does enjoy greater social influence, and for this reason the claims made for "higher truth" still sound plausible. This complex fact creates tension between religion and literature.

The theological inward turn as the Romantics promoted it is probably best represented in Feuerbach's *The Essence of Christianity*. Feuerbach has been called "the father of modern atheism,"[33] and one can see why. After him it becomes almost a commonplace among intellectuals to understand theology as a kind of anthropology. But, to most modern readers surely, *The Essence of Christianity* is charged with an idealizing passion that hardly seems atheistic in spirit. It is far more a celebration of the idea of man than an undermining of the idea of God. Although Feuerbach writes (in the 1849 preface) "atheism is the secret of religion," he quickly adds, "the secret of religion...is the divinity of human nature." He claims he would "awaken religion to self-consciousness," but this means "the consciousness of the infinity of the human mind." Man is already God before God became man, so traditional theology becomes unnecessary. Feuerbach can fairly claim that his robust humanism does not even lead to unbelief since it only asks us to accept the human origin of ideas of God, not to deny their validity.[34] He was, we know, influenced by Hegel, who incorporated divinity entirely within the scope of historical process but then idealized *that*, as Spinoza had divinized material substance.

What is dubious about Feuerbach today is not of course the human origin of God-ideas but the assumption that all such ideas are impressive and admirable and that they ennoble man. One wishes that Montaigne could have mounted a reply, reminding us that some ideas of God are silly or worse, and do no credit to the human imagination. We must not underestimate, however, the liberating influence of his book from the time it was first published in 1835. It excited the humanistic enthusiasm of the young Marx (who would later, in his 1845 *Theses on Feuerbach*, claim that it did not go far enough because it only sought to interpret, not to change, the world), and of the young George Eliot, then Marian Evans, who conscientiously translated it. Nor did Nietzsche fail to absorb its lesson that the apotheosizing will of man outlives the "death" of God.

In fact, one of the most interesting features of nineteenth-century thought generally is the way the Romantic tradition internalized the religious vocabulary of the Judeo-Christian tradition, not so much discarding as displacing it. M. H. Abrams and Harold Bloom have studied this practice in Romantic poetry particularly, and Thomas Carlyle in *Sartor Resartus* (1836) codified it as unofficial doctrine, not only in a phrase like "Natural Supernaturalism" (which gave Abrams a title) but in declaring that "LITERATURE" rendered the Godlike visible.[35] Carlyle's work points us toward a "religion of art," which, like the "religion of humanity" maturing a bit earlier, is a distinctive nineteenth-century creation.

Feuerbach was only one of the first to espouse what Auguste Comte, John Stuart Mill, and others actually called, usually in capital letters, a Religion of Humanity. Marx certainly belongs in this tradition too, even though he would hardly have wished to call his idealization of man and of socialism a religion, since religion for him was a pathology that needed to be cleared away. (Many since of course *have* described Marxism as a religion, even "the greatest alternative to Christianity ever formulated.")[36] Comte, using the long historical perspective like Hegel and Marx, argued that a naïve age of theology had been replaced by an age of metaphysics or abstract thought and that this was now being replaced by a "positive" and "scientific" age, in which the focus of religious idealization was the human race itself. His *Introduction to Positive Philosophy* attracted enthusiastic readers, including George Eliot and G. H. Lewes. Mill's essay, "The Utility of Religion," also sees "a Religion of Humanity" as a fitting replacement for supernatural religion, for it "fulfills the essence of religion, a strong and earnest direction of emotions and desires toward an ideal object." (That secularized definition of "religion" is hard to improve upon as an account of the Victorians' displacement of religious faith into an idealization of morality, although equally good is Matthew Arnold's describing religion, in *Culture and Anarchy,* as "the greatest and most important of the efforts by which the human race has manifested its impulse to perfect itself.") W. K. Clifford, Huxley's atheistic colleague and a notable mathematician, also embraced a "Kingdom of Man."[37] Mrs. Humphry Ward wrote a didactic dialogue called "The New Reformation" teaching that, since traditional Christianity has been undermined by the Higher Criticism, we must now put our faith in achieving a higher level of humanity.[38] Swinburne's "Hymn to Man" (which concludes, "Glory to Man in the highest!") also belongs in this tradition, as perhaps does Mazzini's doctrine of universal brotherhood and really the whole humanitarian movement.

The theme of a Religion of Art, the idea of ascribing a transcendent importance to art and artist, arose first among the critics of Germany and was passed on via the Romantics to mid and later Victorians—to Tennyson, Browning, Arnold, Ruskin, Pater, Wilde, Henry James, and W. B. Yeats.

With notable help from Flaubert as well, it influenced also the modernist movement as represented particularly by Joyce, Woolf, Proust, and Musil. The American versions derived from Emerson and from Whitman (who in "Passage to India" identified "the poet" as "the true son of God") tended to idealize Artist more than Art, but both continued to be sacrosanct words into the mid-twentieth century, enjoying perhaps a last hurrah in the New Criticism that flourished from the thirties to the fifties. In Chapter Two, I will study a late form of the religion of art in Wallace Stevens, a qualified form because Stevens knew that "the death of one god is the death of all."

It is important to understand that the artists, if not the essayists, whom we associate with a religion of art were, in the nineteenth century, troubled about shifting the sense of holiness away from traditional faith. Coleridge's "Kubla Khan" knows, especially in its resonant conclusion, that the poet and his creative exuberance are dangerously competitive with what is deemed sacred, and the speaker in Tennyson's "Palace of Art," which is indebted to Coleridge's poem, after daring to call great writers "Gods" and herself a "God holding no form of creed,/ But contemplating all," is stricken and must purge away guilt to regain her palace. Browning deals with the same theme less timidly but with protective irony nonetheless; the speakers in his poems who exalt art are likely to be either moral monsters like the Duke of Ferrara; or pagans like Cleon; or a bishop like Blougram who knows that he ought to subordinate art to faith but is inclined to consider the "artist whose religion is his art" superior to himself; or a great artist like Fra Lippo Lippi who distinguishes the needs served by high art from those satisfied by prescribed religious observance but who also believes that art's "beauty" and "wonder" and "power" are *equally* man's work and God's.

Matthew Arnold has proved to be the most influential spokesman for this secular faith, foreseeing in his essay "The Study of Poetry" a displacement of the power of religion to the power of poetry. But this is really asking the arts, whose very spirit is to interpret *anew* and always *differently*, to function the way sacred texts have functioned, binding a group to a change-resistant tradition. In literary criticism, however, it is probably true to say that the Arnoldian form of a religion of art has lasted longest and died hardest.

It is worth adding a word about a 'religion of science,' which also distinctly emerged in nineteenth-century thought. It is inseparable from a certain kind of positivism like Comte's or dogmatic atheism like Clifford's, Charles Bradlaugh's or Robert Ingersoll's. And, probably because the prestige of science continues to grow, it still enjoys some currency whereas the religion of humanity and the religion of art are now out of date. A recently published book, *How We Believe: The Search for God in an Age of Science* by Michael Shermer, oddly fideistic and skeptical by turns, exemplifies this idealization in its contemporary form. It exalts recent cosmological speculations that deliberately blur "the lines between science, myth, and religion" as "deep and sacred science."[39] *Sacred* science? Evidently a process of de-divinization, as Nietzsche and Rorty have imagined it, is not historically inevitable.

Doubt and Darwinism

"One of the great differences between eighteenth-century and Victorian scepticism," wrote David Daiches in his fine book *God and the Poets*, "is that the former was regarded as a liberation...whereas the latter was always a source of *worry*." His explanation, quite a plausible one, was that "geology presented threats to religious belief that Newtonian science had not presented."[40] Geological evidences of the earth's great age, undermining religious faith in the literal truth of the Bible, were worrying believers well before the publication of *Origin of Species*, and confidence in reason and nature as universal standards, a confidence that had supported the deists, dissolved during the post-Revolutionary era. Only a few among the new generation of rebels, like the young Percy Shelley (and his was a special case, as we shall see), wanted to wear the badge of atheist.

In the emerging Victorian age, the characteristic effort of leading literary figures to preserve Christian morality without subscribing to Christian theology or doctrine was frequently anxious, often resulting in a compromise that may be better described as a conflict. Doubt soon came to play a major role in nineteenth-century literary and philosophical discourse. When the term agnosticism was introduced by Huxley in 1869, it filled a long-standing need, making finer logical discrimination possible, although in practice the self-styled agnostics (Huxley, Leslie Stephen) were sometimes too passionate to abide by its definition. Doubt, the antithesis of faith, had the advantage of conveying uncertainty rather than dogmatic unbelief, and allowed for, indeed encouraged, the expression of conflicting thoughts and feelings. Carlyle and Mill are usually cited as cardinal instances of this conflict in nineteenth-century Britain, but their wrestling with the problem is so set upon a logical solution that it leads them toward impasse or contradiction whereas the poets allow the contrary reports of both "head" and "heart" to be clearly heard.

One can understand why Nietzsche expressed impatience with the hyperlogical Mill's "offensive clarity" and saw Carlyle's "craving for faith" as that of "an atheist seeking to be honoured for *not* being so."[41]

Carlyle was angry both with those who held closely to Christian dogma and those, like Jeremy Bentham, who abandoned or attacked it. He wanted to show Doubt defeated by Faith and not trapped in what *Sartor Resartus* calls a Centre of Indifference, but he could not convince himself that this moral victory could be achieved, and so ended at an impasse. He conveyed a strong and influential sense for the Victorians of the *necessity* of faith (wouldn't a society without confidence in God lose its soul to commerce?) yet he could not discover any but the vaguest basis for believing. He became for many an exemplary martyr to doubt.

Mill valued the ethical example of Jesus but found the doctrines and perhaps even the institutions of Christianity something of a hindrance to a full humanity. In his posthumously published *Three Essays on Religion*, he was intent on bringing theistic hypotheses before the bar of science, trying to base conviction on degree of probability. With scrupulous logic, he shredded a particular theistic argument and then allowed it to stand as no more unproved than proved. For example, on the basis of inductive logic he found the argument from design still strong—but did this mean there is an intelligent will in the universe? Mill referred to "the recent speculation" of Darwin as "not so absurd as it looks," and then tried to have the argument both ways: "This theory if admitted would in no way be inconsistent with Creation. But it must be admitted that it would greatly attenuate the evidence for it." On immortality: there is no evidence in science against it but an absence of evidence in its favor. On miracles: we have no access to them but the testimony of witnesses should be taken seriously. In his extreme judiciousness Mill himself seems to be aware that he has left the matter up in the air, for at the end of these essays he returns with relief to the idea of separating the morality of the Gospels from the whole business of theism.[42]

William James, at the century's end, succeeded better than Carlyle or Mill, and exerted more influence on twentieth-century thinking about religious belief, by starting frankly from "the subjective part" of our experience, and developing the point that the ideals to which our emotions are attached, especially God, "produce effects in this world" and so are themselves to be accounted realities.[43] However, he went just a step beyond this pragmatic psychology to suggest that religious belief is as testable as a scientific hypothesis and is objective in the same way. Especially in the essays collected under the title of *The Will to Believe* he also sought a *logical* resolution of the tension between subjective and objective perspectives.[44]

Consider in contrast how a similar conflict is played out in a small handful of poets and novelists—Shelley, Tennyson, Browning, Melville, and Dostoevsky.

The skeptical aspect of Shelley links eighteenth- and nineteenth-century unbelief, but his kind of Romantic idealism may be described as both theistic and atheistic, all parts of one complex sensibility. His youthful pamphlet, "The Necessity of Atheism," was subversive enough to get him sent down from Oxford, but is not as dogmatic as its title implies. Indebted to Hume, it is a skeptical survey of the evidence, concluding that, since no proof can be adduced for the existence of God, no criminality attaches to disbelief. Today we would describe the pamphlet as conscientiously agnostic. But from the passional, imaginative Shelley we get a different report, combining emphatic repudiation of God and religion (as in the opening of "Queen Mab," baldly declaring "there is no God") and testimony as well of a strong religious sensibility, indicated at once by the poet's note to that declaration: "This must be understood solely to affect a creative [i.e., anthropomorphic] deity; the hypothesis of a pervading spirit coeternal with the universe remains unshaken." Indeed, the spiritual quality in his work was so apparent to his nineteenth-century readers that, for one of them, William Gladstone, he was "the only real religious poet of the age."[45] "Visionary skepticism," Harold Bloom's phrase, and the similar phrase used by Stuart Curran, "skeptical idealism," are apt descriptions of Shelley's paradoxical Romantic stance. The complexity of Victorian writers (of artists more than essayists) is better described by the word conflict.

Perhaps the readiest way to illustrate this kind of complexity, at the risk of laying out too schematic an overview, is to speak of a struggle between heart and head where head is understood as a metaphor for what one tries to believe and heart for what one cannot help believing. Then we might say that such a conflict is more sharply drawn in Tennyson, Browning, Melville, and Dostoevsky than in writers like Carlyle and Mill. Tennyson's "head" cries for Faith, His "heart" for Doubt. In contrast, Browning tries to doubt but his instinct prompts commitment. Comparably, Melville strives to believe but cannot help doubting whereas Dostoevsky strives to doubt but cannot help believing. This concise general description at least has the advantage of indicating readily why the work of all four poets and novelists contains so much *internal drama*.

Tennyson held to a belief in spiritual progress, cultural and personal, which he liked to express in metaphors of evolution. "In Memoriam" looks ahead at its end to a "far off divine event/ Toward which the whole creation moves"; "The Higher Pantheism" to a spiritual perfection beyond nature and ordinary perception; "By An Evolutionist" to a general notion of moral improvement over time, even in the face of age and decay; *Idylls of the King* to the supercession of one good but potentially corrupting custom; "Demeter and Persephone" to the replacement of the pagan by the Christian era. There was in Tennyson's work, as in that of so many Victorians, a sort of obligatory "trope of onwardness."[46] But his sensibility was brooding and nostalgic, and this created an atmosphere of doubt in conflict with his ostensible faith. T. S. Eliot judged "In Memoriam" a religious poem "not because of the quality of its faith, but because of the quality of its doubt."[47] And Tennyson himself acknowledged something like this: "It is too hopeful this poem, more than I am myself."[48] "The Higher Pantheism" betrays its lack of conviction by conceptual vagueness, a feature seized upon by Swinburne in his wickedly funny parody, "The Higher Pantheism in a Nutshell," which concludes: "One who is not, we see, but one whom we see not, is./ Surely this is not that: but that is assuredly this." Formally, the Tennysonian conflict is better expressed in *Idylls* and "Demeter" where the very idea of mounting to something nobler can be persuasively expressed with sadness because it is rendered from the point of view of a speaker who is losing a past that possesses grandeur and glamour.

Doubt is more assertive in Browning, but it energizes, even stimulates Faith. "I show you doubt, to prove that faith exists./ The more of doubt, the stronger faith." Bishop Blougram's apologia is based on his knowledge that "belief/ As unbelief...shakes us by fits," and that, just as a man of faith can fall into doubts, so a man in doubt can be surprised into faith even by worldly intimations of glory (a sunset, someone's death, a chorus from Euripides). For Browning, then, faith is hardly a doctrine but a positive state of mind that will return of itself, especially to the robust heart. The irony that we find in his "Cleon" contrasts strikingly to that in Tennyson's "Demeter and Persephone." Demeter glimpses truly a bright Christian future but broods on the absence of her daughter and the injustice of Zeus; Cleon is mistaken in believing that the new Christianity will not mar his pagan way of life, but is honored nonetheless for rejoicing in it.

Finally let us briefly compare two philosophical novelists far to the West and East of Britain. In Melville we find little sense of a Victorian compromise but instead an energetic doubt in collision with a powerful will to believe, in Dostoevsky a powerful faith in collision with a corrosively acute skepticism.

For the sake of conciseness I launch my remarks from two familiar but crucial passages, the first from one of Hawthorne's notebooks (of 1856), the second from one of Dostoevsky's letters (of 1854):

> I think [he] will never rest until he gets hold of a definite belief. It is strange how he persists...in wandering to and fro over these deserts [i.e., fruitless speculation on "everything that lies beyond human ken"]. He can neither believe, nor be comfortable in his unbelief, and he is too honest and courageous not to try to do one or the other.[49]

> I'll tell you of myself that I have been a child of the age, a child of disbelief and doubt up until now and will be even (I know this) to the grave. What horrible torments this thirst to believe has cost me and continues to cost me, a thirst that is all the stronger in my soul the more negative arguments there are in me. And yet...[I] believe that there is nothing more beautiful...and perfect than Christ, and what's more, I tell myself with jealous love, there cannot be. If it were proved that truth lay outside of Christ, I would prefer to remain with Christ rather than walk with the truth.[50]

It is evident that both Melville and Dostoevsky understood religious doubt as the crux of the conflict they were experiencing. Indeed, I cannot think of any other nineteenth-century writers in whom doubt is so forceful a presence. (In Kierkegaard and Nietzsche doubt was ratcheted up to "dread," used in the one case to launch a radical leap into faith, in the other to explore a potentially creative nihilism.) I shall try to illuminate the doubt-faith conflict in these great writers by touching on the difference between their broadly similar ways of wrestling with it.

Melville hurls into spiritual battle his defiers (like Ahab) or explorers of a spiritual wasteland (like Clarel) or even his very plot (as in *The Confidence Man*) in a vain quest for certainty, assurance, resolution. The proliferation of deific metaphors in *Moby-Dick* does not underline Melville's skepticism but rather his feeling of being trapped by metaphor in his desperate effort to get at the unmediated truth. Nor, as Walter E. Benzanson noted, did he "soften up in his later years as Whitman and Emerson did, but remained unsimple and hard to the end."[51] He continued to seek resolution and continued to fail. This may be illustrated by the great story of his old age, "Billy Budd." Fifty years ago our best critics judged that this tale of an innocent sailor wrongfully condemned but blessing his condemner exemplified its author's late-achieved reconciliation with fate. W. H. Auden gave memorable expression to this view in his poem on Melville, which begins, "At the end he sailed into an extraordinary mildness." In the decades since, however, interpretation has turned to the other extreme, finding radical irony in Billy's benedictory words, "God bless Captain Vere." My own view is that Mellville was *trying* to believe in this reconciliation but could not do so. The story illustrates a conflict wrestled with and left unresolved, yielding, as the final picture of Billy, not the martyr but the condemned sailor "in the darbies," hopelessly imagining his own annihilation among the "oozy weeds" of the ocean floor.

If we consider "The Legend of the Grand Inquisitor" in *The Brothers Karamazov* a sufficiently illustrative instance of the conflict I am concerned with here, it would be difficult to say that Dostoevsky, despite his strong religious views in maturity, was any more successful than Melville in achieving a *resolution* of the doubt-faith conflict, but what an unforgettable *picture* of it he has given us! A silent Christ listens to the powerful indictment of the Grand Inquisitor, and bestows on him an ambiguous kiss. Christ seems to agree with the Inquisitor's indictment that his high example is too hard for frail human beings to follow, that their spiritual need for miracle, mystery, and authority must be mediated by worldly figures, even by priests and kings serving their own political interests. This fiercely skeptical turning against his own faith (expressed through the atheist intellectual, Ivan Karamazov) has lost none of its power a century later, has even acquired some confirmatory evidence from actual history. Yet Dostoevsky was always exposing rationalistic explanations, and should Ivan's be exempted? His explanation itself is strong, yet perhaps the spirit in which it is presented is errant and qualifies the truth of what he says. In that light Christ's kiss is complexly suggestive. It might constitute a blessing on Ivan for being right or express pity for his being wrong—or the gesture may imply that Ivan speaks a kind of truth without knowing it, offering a parable whose real truth is that the rationalistic path to religious truth is misguided. Christ's avoidance of words would then become eloquent. And this implication seems borne out by the fact that Alyosha, listening to his anguished brother, hints (without of course contrary explanations) that he understands not so much what Ivan thinks he said but what he has said in spite of himself. Christ's example, even if seldom followed, would then stand as the counterweight to the Inquisitor's powerful words, as Alyosha's haloed presence at the end of the novel may imply. Yet

Ivan's brilliantly critical intellect is so corrosive that this saving faith is felt both as fragile and precious. Dostoevsky's art arouses in the reader a desire for a grace infinitely gentle and almost out of reach.

Let us now focus the issue of Doubt on Darwin and Darwinism, which altered the whole contour of this debate in the nineteenth century, in large part by bringing science squarely into the picture, where it has remained ever since.

The shock to theism from the publication of *Origin of Species* was as to an extent anticipated by books like Charles Lyell's *Principles of Geology* and D. F. Strauss's *Life of Jesus*, the one making people familiar with the idea of evolutionary time's immense length, the other telling us that Christianity was a mythology, whatever historical truths and ethical wisdom it also contained. But its impact was enormous. As Richard Dawkins put it, Darwin made it possible for the first time to be "an intellectually fulfilled atheist,"[52] one who now possessed a theory that could convincingly explain the intricacy of nature's design without recourse to a supernatural creator.

Moreover, Darwin's theory of natural selection was, in outline at least, easy to understand (compared, say, to the theory of relativity in physics). Its difficulty arose from the *emotional* resistance it generated. Every religious system is anthropocentric, but here was a comprehensive story of life explaining that human beings were only one of nature's experiments, neither the first nor the last. Gillian Beer suggests that this resistance was all the keener in that *Origin of Species* (unlike psychoanalysis, another blow to our pride) does not discuss the human situation or "privilege the present."[53]

It was, then, a wound to human vanity that required responsive action. People felt forced to take sides and, in doing so, to put their theism on the line. One could either discard theism as it had been known, reject the theory altogether, or attempt to infuse it with a quasi-scientific theology, as did Herbert Spencer, George Bernard Shaw, and, in the course of the twentieth century, such figures as Teilhard de Chardin and Holmes Rolston, III.

Newton's theory had involved an explanation for the motion of matter that allowed Newton himself to retain a deity that, though unconcerned with the daily life of man, supervised the laws of physical change. Darwin's theory of biological change made such a compromise more difficult to accept. (The naturalist Philip Gosse did notoriously claim that God had planted the fossil evidence, and similar arguments have been used by Creationists in our day, but as the anthropologist Eugenie Scott cleverly remarked: "an omnipotent God by definition can do anything he wants, including interfering in the universe to make it look exactly like there was no interference!")[54] Darwin himself was so reluctant to give offense to the devout that on the last page of *Origin of Species* he refers to "the laws impressed on matter by the Creator" and offers us a kind of moral uplift: "we may look with some confidence to a secure future of great length [where] all corporeal and mental endowments will tend to progress towards perfection."[55] But it is clear in context that the word "Creator" is meant to be vague, for what Darwin means by "origin" is *always* development over time and *never* why or how life first began. ("We still don't know exactly how natural selection began on Earth," Dawkins reminds us.)[56] In other words, Darwin sedulously avoided metaphysics, shying away even from the word chance, so often associated with his theory, because random mutation was, after all, a material process like any other. The "uplift" must also be carefully understood. Darwin does not promise an indefinite future for the *human* species but only for species themselves, which have often died out while others have survived catastrophes or have come into being. His phrase "progress toward perfection" is an instance of tact carried rather far, for those who survive in the "struggle for existence" are in Darwin's terms only the best adapted, not the best by any moral or aesthetic standards we might apply. In a sense his enemies, like the geologist Adam Sedgwick, who loathed the theory's "unflinching materialism" that repudiates "final causes" (i.e., moral goals in nature),[57] understood the theory better than did friends like Herbert Spencer who turned it into a progressivist social philosophy.

For Spencer, religion and science alike were founded on what he called "unknowableness," giving an air of scientific respectability to religion and of mystery to science. (No wonder J. M. Robertson, the historian of nineteenth-century freethought, considered him the "cleverest of agnostics.")[58] Samuel Butler and Bernard Shaw, more combatively, decided that Darwin had banished mind from the universe, and Shaw's defense was called, with a nod to Henri Bergson, Creative Evolution, according to which biological mutation in human beings was partially a product of the will. His ambitious effort to make a religion out of scientific materials, most fully on display in his *Back to Methuselah*, preface as well as play, is now one of the curiosities of intellectual history, but it testifies to the strength of a desire still very much alive—to unify religion and science.

The case of Huxley, Darwin's bulldog, is instructive in another way because Huxley did understand the anti-teleological implications of Darwin's science and yet could not refrain from exploiting them to attack religion. This would not have mattered if Huxley had been a self-conscious literary imaginer like Mark Twain or Thomas Hardy, writers whose attacks on God retain the "as if" quality of fiction not pretending to be otherwise. But Huxley the "agnostic" sometimes slides unwittingly into what must be called dogmatic atheism.

Ably explaining the logical problem with Spencer's famous phrase "survival of the fittest," Huxley said it was a "fallacy" that because "animals and plants have advanced in perfection of organization by means of the struggle for existence and the consequent 'survival of the fittest,' therefore men, in society, men as ethical beings, must look to the same process to help them towards perfection. I suspect that the fallacy has arisen out of the unfortunate ambiguity of the phrase 'survival of the fittest.' 'Fittest' has the connotation of 'best,' and about best there hangs a moral flavour."[59] Huxley drew, I think, the right conclusion from his clarification: "Let us understand, once and for all, that the ethical progress of society depends, not on imitating the cosmic process, still less in running away from it, but in combating it."[60] Thus far Huxley stays true to the meaning of his agnosticism—simply a not knowing rather than an anguished doubting, a scientist's verdict of no evidence concerning a supernatural moral intelligence. But his irritation with religion overrode this understanding. "The good of Christianity," Huxley asserted warmly, "is largely counteracted by the insistence that disbelief in their astonishing creed is a moral offense. If we could only see, in one view, the torrents of hypocrisy, cruelty, the lies, the slaughter, the violation of every obligation of humanity which has flowed from this source along the course of the history of Christian nations, our worst imaginations of hell would pale beside the vision."[61] This is the language of Mark Twain served up in defense of Charles Darwin.

Agnosticism is so very useful a word in a discriminating study of atheism that we must consider its fate with some concern, must consider in particular the positivistic edge it acquired in the late nineteenth century, which made agnosticism difficult to distinguish from (dogmatic) atheism. W. K. Clifford declared categorically, "It is wrong everywhere and for anyone to believe anything upon insufficient evidence,"[62] a statement that particularly irritated William James, and indeed its insistence on judging religion as if it were science rules out all faith. Huxley himself declared that agnosticism "is not a creed of any kind," but he could not refrain from echoing Clifford and writing of "absolute faith" in the principle of not believing on insufficient evidence.[63] Other Victorians agnostics also used the word to mean a *conviction* of unbelief rather than a scientific scruple about lack of evidence.

Consider the case of the positivist agnostic, Leslie Stephen, who in 1876 published *An Agnostic's Apology*, using the word apology in the sense of *apologia*, doubtless to serve as a riposte to John Henry Newman's fideistic *Apologia pro vita sua*. With a bitter edge that probably had something to do with the fact that he was in youth ordained as a priest and later renounced holy orders, Stephen asserted that to claim ignorance about what cannot be known—"metempirical knowledge" he called it—is "positively a duty." We must be "agnostic," he wrote, "because all philosophers disagree, all debates about matters like free will, divine justice, or the argument from design, are contradictory."[64] Views like Newman's, he implied, cannot be supported by conscience but only by the authority and enforcement of the Church. And the pathos of "My God, my God, why hast thou forsaken me"—the verse from Psalm 22 uttered by Jesus during the crucifixion—is fraudulent because the speaker is divine as well as human, an illogic scorned by Stephen but which even a non-Christian might judge a brilliantly inventive myth.

Let us briefly contrast Stephen's supposed "agnosticism" to the "atheism" of a character created by his famous daughter, a contrast which will help us see how the modulations of good fiction help us make a distinction between "dogmatic" and "literary" atheism:

> As we are a doomed race, chained to a sinking ship (her favourite reading as a girl was Huxley and Tyndall, and they were fond of these nautical metaphors), as the whole thing is a bad joke, let us, at any rate, do our part; mitigate the suffering of our fellow-prisoners (Huxley again); decorate the dungeon with flowers and air-cushions; be as decent as we possibly can. Those ruffians, the Gods, shan't have it all their own way,—her notion being that the Gods, who never lost a chance of hurting, thwarting and spoiling human lives were seriously put out if, all the same, you behaved like a lady....To see your own sister killed by a falling tree...a girl too on the verge of life, the most gifted of them, Clarissa always said, was enough to turn one bitter. Later she wasn't so positive perhaps; she thought there were no Gods, no one was to blame; and so she evolved this atheist's religion of doing good for the sake of goodness.

Virginia Woolf's subtle rendering of Clarissa Dalloway's musings allows for a more complex view of the Gods than does her father's assertive, logic-driven prose. Clarissa moves by degrees from bitterness at those ruffians the Gods to what she calls an "atheist's religion," an attitude close to indifference except that a residue of bitterness remains. Unlike Stephen's essay, Woolf's paragraph gives us intellectual skepticism combined with the emotional experience of rejecting something or someone once desired and now lost. Stephen's "agnosticism" is stiffer and less alert to feelings than is Clarissa's "atheism."

Like a brash Leslie Stephen, Charles Bradlaugh adopted an antitheistic stance on logical grounds, but he insisted on calling his position not agnosticism but atheism, a word he was determined to purge of its offensive connotations. Bradlaugh had been elected President of the London Secular Society in 1860 and, a few years later, became editor of *The National Reformer*, which in his hands became a sort of personal testament in defense of atheism: "[atheism] is in no wise a cold barren negative; it is, on the contrary, a hearty fruitful affirmation of all truth, and involves...the highest humanity." Either God is meaningless because the word conveys no idea, Bradlaugh continues like a logical positivist, or "God is affirmed to represent an existence which is distinct from the existence of which I am a mode," and so must be denied as impossible. He added that there can only be one explanation of the universe and, since it cannot be theism, it must be atheism![65] This is dogmatic atheism with a vengeance. (Huxley and Frederic Harrison, during the scandal of Bradlaugh's attempt to be seated in Parliament without taking the traditional oath, distanced themselves from the provocateur's "arid conceit of Atheism.")[66] Bradlaugh recognized no truth other than his own yet insisted that his was objective.

Consider one more telling instance of unbelief from the twentieth century, that of Bertrand Russell, whose mode of rejecting theism is similar to those we have been considering. Russell was of course a far more sophisticated logician, but, although he wanted to look at religion and divinity fairly, he could not quite do so, as his positivistic bias turned scrupulous doubt into a conviction of unbelief. In "Why I Am Not a Christian" he wrote: "I think all the great religions of the world—Buddhism, Hinduism, Christianity, Islam, and Communism—both untrue and harmful. It is evident as a matter of logic that since they disagree, not more than one of them can be true."[67] More careful than Bradlaugh, he does not say flatly that atheism is the only truth, but he tells us not merely that only one religion can be true but that none can be true. Similarly, in a little essay called "Am I An Atheist or An Agnostic? A Plea for Tolerance in the Face of New Dogmas," he developed an argument that sounds careful but is nevertheless so restricted by logic that it cannot even accept Homer's gods, let alone the Christian God, in terms of poetry. The argument is quite moving in its way, perhaps the end of a line, because it shows that even a highly intelligent positivist in a post-Enlightenment age can carry an argument against the existence of God only so far without building on the inward turn of Kant and the Romantics.

> As a philosopher, if I were speaking to a purely philosophical audience, I should say that I ought to describe myself as an Agnostic, because I do not think that there is a conclusive argument by which one can prove that there is not a God.
>
> On the other hand, if I am to convey the right impression to the ordinary man in the street I think that I ought to say that I am an Atheist, because when I say that I cannot prove that there is not a God, I ought to add equally that I cannot prove that there are the Homeric gods.
>
> None of us would seriously consider the possibility that all the gods of Homer really exist, and yet if you were to set to work to give a logical demonstration that Zeus, Hera, Poseidon, and the rest of them did not exist you would find it an awful job. You could not get such proof.[68]

Russell quite understands that agnosticism is a concept to be appreciated by an educated audience and that a popular audience would understand its diffident skepticism as plain atheism. But he cannot say that the existence of Homeric gods does not present us with the same problem as does the existence of a Christian God because we more readily accept them as products of imagination. His scruples show Russell to be mired, for all his freethinking, in a Christian tradition that had been sophisticated by philosophy and hence seemed to require the kind of logical explanation that amounts to a denial of God.

Uses of Negation in Twentieth-Century God-Talk

Superficially the topic of atheism has lost intellectual steam over the last century, as more people in the West have come to lead lives not so much against as away from God and religion. In American society at least, religion itself remains a strong force, even stronger than we suspected thirty years ago. But the word theology has acquired a musty connotation. Introducing *Critical Terms for Religious Studies*, Mark C. Taylor, for example, cites Ray L. Hart's observation that "Theological Studies [have become] the *bête noire* within Religious Studies"; according to Hart's students, what is wrong with their curriculum is that it still (in 1991) "includes theology."[69] But the vocabulary of *negation* is forceful in much twentieth-century discussion of religious belief. Although less is said about Doubt versus Faith, theology and literature alike have been challenged and sophisticated by concepts like Nothingness, Absence, Silence, and Otherness. One might say that a modernist version of "negative theology" has come into use.

Negative theology itself is not atheism, dogmatic or literary. But the pressure of modern atheism is felt in the oblique and even ironic approaches to theism adopted in the twentieth century both by theologians and by literary artists with a religious bent. I will discuss a variety of such approaches in this segment of the chapter, and end it with remarks on three atheistic philosophies—those of Freud, Sartre, and Derrida—that span and represent the century as a whole.

When the Christian and Platonic traditions began to intersect and philosophic modes of thinking about God developed, it became clear that it was difficult to talk about the nature of God in positive terms. This difficulty initiated a tradition of negative or "apophatic" theology (also called the *via negativa*, although that phrase sometimes denotes a spiritual way or practice rather than a theology as such), which sought to describe the nature of God by saying what he is *not*. Plotinus (2nd-3rd century) wrote, "We say what He is not, but what He is we do not say."[70] Pseudo-Dionysius (also called Dionysius the Areopagite or just Dionysius, 5th-6th century) affirmed in *The Divine Names* that one could only posit negative statements about God.[71] Meister Eckhart (13th–14th century) declared that the divine nature has no name, and pursued this idea by introducing an ingenious and lasting distinction between *Gott*, about whom one can more or less speak, and *Gottheit*, about which one cannot.[72] Leading medieval theologians like Augustine and Aquinas also described the nature of God by way of negation—it was infinite, immutable, incorruptible, unnamable, and so forth—but as a rule they sought to analogize or make more intelligible the difference between divine and human whereas the others tried to widen and mystify it. As the names cited suggest, negative theology is akin to mysticism, an instructive kinship as long as we think of mystical writing not as a literal claim of inexpressibility (a contradiction) but as a verbally adept way of saying the unsayable. It is no wonder that the paradoxes of mystics like Dionysius and Eckhart are admired by a philosopher as fascinated by unsayability as Derrida.[73]

In the modern tradition stemming from Kant, who thought that theology ensnared philosophy in the illusion of believing that God is the sort of object that can be characterized in terms of "being," the problem shifts. Because anthropomorphism and therefore "being" is under suspicion, the problem for innovative theologians in the last century or so has been to talk about God without resorting to what Heidegger called "ontotheology." And Heidegger, influenced by Nietzsche, put negation squarely at the center of modern theological discourse.

He appealed to the literary imagination of his day when he wrote in *Being and Time* of human beings thrown out into a historical, time-bound world where they must struggle for spiritual authenticity. His key word *Dasein*, an ordinary German word meaning existence, was broken into its components, *da* (there) and *sein* (being), to suggest that a struggle for authentic existence would lead us to a "there" beyond "here," and he would soon go on to press hard a distinction between "being" in the sense of a thing that exists as an object and "Being" in the sense of something more mysterious that needed to be disclosed. "The truth of Being," in Heidegger's view, has been long concealed from metaphysics, which "thinks of Being only...as [existential] beings."[74] To disclose Being required us to think deeply about a fundamental question—"why is there any being at all and not rather Nothing."[75] It was necessary to encounter the reality of Nothing, so to speak, before we could begin to experience the truth of Dasein.

Heidegger came to shun humanism as much as traditional theism, hoping to evoke a lost spiritual home that man needed to recover, a state preceding any philosophic distinction between mind and world. As Sartre's expositor Hazel Barnes observed, Heidegger's Dasein was suffused with "an air of the numinous,"[76] which is certainly borne out by his reply to Sartre, the celebrated "Letter on Humanism," describing Dasein as "high" and "holy" and labeling as "blasphemy" the thought that man can be the master of Being rather than its shepherd. The word "humanism," he implied, confused the issue.[77] One can see why his biographer Rüdiger Safranski, while calling Heidegger an "atheist," always places the word within quotation marks.[78]

Imaginative theologians of the twentieth century have devised various tactics to avoid associating God with being in an existential sense of the word. Paul Tillich identified divinity with what each of us understands as "depth" or "ultimate concern," a maneuver that makes it virtually impossible to be an atheist but risks merging theism with humanism. Scorning such compromise, Karl Barth, like his predecessor Kierkegaard, thought of God as utterly beyond any relation with man; thus any language mere human beings invent must fall short of describing Him. Jean-Luc Marion in the pointedly titled *God without Being (Dieu sans l'être)* found Tillich's idea of God as the ground of everything "idolatrous" because it retains traces of the empirical, hence of ontotheology. It is an "idol" that stops and satisfies the gaze rather than an "icon" that points beyond itself to the unthinkable and unutterable. Emmanuel Levinas, in books called *Totality and Infinity* and *Otherwise than Being: Beyond Essence*, thought of Infinity as working wholly from within, like a Kantian ethical imperative. Influenced by the Jewish tradition, he shifts the emphasis from loving God to loving the Torah, and finds a commanding "call to responsibility" in the idea of what is good rather than what is true. Jacques Derrida, recognizing but resisting the fact that the unsayability of deconstruction's *différance* resembles that of negative theology, argued that, in negative theology, God's essentiality is still an *ulterior* presence whereas for deconstruction divinity can *never* present itself. And so, claimed Derrida, with a touch of one-upmanship, "I quite rightly pass for an atheist."[79]

All this, of course, is very abstract, but the intent is clear enough—to save theology by somehow freeing the concept of God from any anthropomorphic taint. It is hardly surprising that positivist philosophers, wanting to show that all utterances about God are meaningless, have found such sophisticated theologizing irritating. An anthology called *Critiques of God*, first published in 1976, is no less than a testament of rationalistic protest against placing the concept of God out of range of the assaults of logic. In it, Ernest Nagel allowed for only two meanings of theism: the traditional one, which is inadequate because of lack of evidence about the existence of God; and the one that equates God with "a symbolic rendering of human ideals," which not only evades the metaphysical issue but is also a sense of the word theism "that most believers...would disavow." Sidney Hook chided Barth for violating human reason by describing God as "altogether Other"; Hook contended that this "destroys the possibility of any solid ground for faith or revelation," ground that only reason can provide. Michael Scriven scoffed at the fancy theology that claims "all religious language is symbolic and not to be taken literally"; "this move," he said, "throws out the baby of belief with the bath water of mythology; it is too sophisticated for its own good." All of these positivist critics base their attack on the assumption that any statement about God must be strictly logical—on which grounds it can be shot down. They judge such statements as if they were propositions. They appear to want to *defend* "the baby of belief," but what they really manage to do is score off the absurdity of symbolic and expressive language, "the bath water of mythology." But if they cannot link theology with poetic truth, their position becomes oddly similar to that of literalminded believers. In any case they leave modern theology without a leg to stand on: it is either hopelessly naïve or too sophisticated for its own good.[80]

My own concern in this survey is twofold. First, to suggest (as above) that an updated negative theology, suiting the temper of an age anxious to separate divinity from the concept of "being," is a kind of severe poetry, i.e., imaginative meaning made out of concepts rather than sensuous language. And, second, to prepare the way for showing that, in the twentieth century, literary imagining concerned with God has made use of similar strategies.

I have selected a little handful of storytellers whose approach to God is ironic in its use of negation but whom we rightly associate with the major *normative* religious traditions in the West: Graham Greene and Flannery O'Connor representing the Catholic tradition; Iris Murdoch and John Updike the Protestant; and Franz Kafka the Jewish.

Moral paradoxes that reverse worldly notions of worth and success were of course a prominent feature of Christ's utterances and have been consolidated into Christian doctrine as dramatized in the fiction of Graham Greene. A ready example is the epigraph to *The Heart of the Matter*, drawn from Charles Péguy, which implies that the sinner like the saint has a privileged understanding of Christianity. This underlines the story's main point about its protagonist Major Scobie, who is a sinner on several counts (he admits to loving his mistress more than God, considers God a failure, and knowingly as a Catholic commits suicide), yet unknowingly is also a saint. Our realization of this is not based only on his compassionate motives, because this novel, like all of Greene's, stays close to Catholic doctrine in judging that, without God's grace and love, human attachments are corrupt and human nature itself is sinful. It also derives from Greene's bold handling of the idea that it is not man who has failed God but God who has failed man.

Greene is making resourceful use of Christianity's inventive turn on its Jewish legacy, the imagining of God not only as caring for and judging man but actually, through Christ, becoming man, sharing the suffering of man and taking on the burden of his sins. That is, the "failure" of God is linked with his humanity. This idea is nicely worked out in one of Greene's best later novels, *The Honorary Consul*. A group of would-be revolutionaries are facing death after an incompetent and failed kidnapping plot. An outsider who has been drawn into it by way of his human attachments declares, in a crucial piece of dialogue, that the world is so horrible it could not possibly be compatible with the idea of God. Léon Rivas, an ex-priest, defends God on the surprising grounds that our evil is his too, and he asks rhetorically, "How could I love God if He were not like me?" Although Rivas has taken a wife, embraced violence, and in fact been excommunicated by the Church, he puts his faith in believing that God, like human society, will evolve painfully after long struggle. This in itself may not be Greene's faith, but it points to his normative belief that Christ is both God and man so that to bring God down to the human level is also to raise man up to the divine. In a last broken sentence before dying, Major Scobie had written, "Dear God, I love...." Greene had used a similar trick earlier, in *Brighton Rock,* and he meant to suggest in both cases that a man who has lost his faith in God has nonetheless managed to express it at the moment of death. The apparent condescension to God on the part of Scobie and Rivas (Greene's original turn) is finally a tribute to God or, more exactly, a bringing together of God and man, however unknowingly on man's part.

The harsher imagination of Flannery O'Connor will have nothing to do with bringing God closer to man, which helps to explain why she typically makes use of Protestant fundamentalism to convey what we can recognize as an essentially Catholic vision. Her work is not concerned with divine justice but only with an alien transcendence that the reader is allowed to perceive as an ironic form of grace. The peculiarly negative vehicles of O'Connor's positive faith (e.g., Hazel Motes in "Wise Blood," the Misfit in "A Good Man is Hard to Find," the bible salesman in "Good Country People") do not attract our pity as do Greene's protagonists. Because their involuntary and stubborn attachment to the Jesus Christ they deny is combined with crudeness or violence, their stories are shaded toward the comic grotesque rather than toward pathos and tragedy. On the face of it they are anti-Christs, marked out as prophetic instruments against their will and against any conventional appeal to our sentiment.

Hazel wants above all to get rid of the figure of Jesus in the back of his mind but his efforts are in vain. He considers Jesus a trick, mocks anyone who would claim to be redeemed by him, asserts he doesn't "believe in anything," and sets himself up with persistence as the preacher of a new church, the "Church Without Christ": "I'm going to preach there was no Fall because there was nothing to fall from, and no redemption because there was no fall, and no Judgment because there wasn't the first two. Nothing matters but that Jesus was a liar." This is an admirably comic version of negative theology, an involuntary affirmation of faith by way of negating its elements.

The Misfit in "A Good Man is Hard to Find" has escaped from the penitentiary into the woods where a family on vacation are stuck in their car, and explains calmly to the naïve but terrified grandmother, as her family is led away and audibly shot to death, that "Jesus thown [*sic*] everything off balance." Much more aware of his punishment than of his sin, he must augment his meanness to restore the balance, since the morally desirable alternative of a conversion experience is beyond his range: "'If [Jesus] did what he said, then it's nothing for you to do but thow everything away and follow Him, and if He didn't, then it's nothing for you to do but enjoy the few minutes you got left the best way you can—by killing somebody or burning down his house or doing some other meanness to him. No pleasure but meanness,' he said, and his voice had become almost a snarl." We notice, however, that, in the way he is finally touched on the shoulder by the dying grandmother, his eyes made "red-rimmed and pale and defenseless-looking," that he has become an unwitting vehicle of divine grace.

The smooth talking Bible salesman in "Good Country People" takes pleasure in deceiving not only the naïve Mrs. Hopewell but particularly and shockingly her intellectual and atheist daughter whose wooden leg he has her remove in the barnloft and then will not return. He brushes off her accusation of Christian hypocrisy: "I hope you don't think I believe in that crap!...I may sell Bibles but I know which end is up." And then he delivers the *coup de grâce*: "You just a while ago said you didn't believe in nothing...you ain't so smart, I been believing in nothing ever since I was born!" He believes in nothing whereas she doesn't believe in anything. It would be hard to register more neatly than this the difference between nihilism as a passionate perversion of faith and nihilism as an intellectual position. Although Flannery O'Connor described herself as "an author congenitally innocent of theory,"[81] this stands her in good stead as a storyteller, allowing her to feel her way toward a position that an analytic writer would probably pose more logically and less suggestively. Her characters believe in the rooted sinfulness of the world but are also touched by a divine grace they hate and deny. O'Connor implies that the modern world—exemplified by rural Georgia in the mid-twentieth century—cannot offer any unironic or exalted image of her own Christian faith, and so she exploits the contrast between two kinds of negativity, a passive and an active atheism, a secular indifference and a rage fueled by a frustrated desire to believe. Her anti-Christs wear their damnation like a badge of faith.

What Greene and O'Connor have most in common as Catholic novelists using negation to spark their vision are, first, a conviction of the sinfulness of man and his resistance to belief, and, second, a strategy for intimating transcendence that involves leading their moral vehicles *away* from God.

Iris Murdoch and John Updike are similarly representative as Protestant novelists of our time. Each is an original writer within a recognizable religious tradition yet each makes bold use of negation and irony in representing the search for God.

Murdoch's literary imagination was engaged early on by Sartre's existential atheism: "It had long been known," she explained in a monograph, "that God was dead and that man was self-created. Sartre produced a fresh and apt picture of this self-chosen being,"[82] a picture, we may add, with a theatrical flair, useful for a novelist. But Murdoch soon developed, both in her novels and in her philosophical writings, a critique of Sartre's position, based on the claim that his existentialism ignored moral questions arising from the complexities of human interaction, questions that could and should be illuminated by a "sovereign" (that is, metaphysically grounded) idea of Good. One cannot, she consistently assumes, simply return to the Christian God that was. What lies ahead, rather, is each individual's strenuous spiritual task to approach the Good, an ideal based on Plato's "good beyond being," sometimes said to be the first of the apophatic theologies. The quest of her striving characters is impeded not by a rooted sinfulness but by illusion and muddled vision, at bottom by vanity and egotism. This egotism is very stubborn, however, and Murdoch's novels are obsessed by the impediments that *self* creates. The characters most honored are those who have achieved, with difficulty and only approximately, a negation of self in their relations to others. The purity of their attention to otherness, their extreme tolerance in the face of the formless, contingent world, makes them appear unremarkable, undistinguished, unassertive, almost invisible, seemingly uninteresting. Alternatively there is the possibility of self-transcendence through art or love, but these excitements are temporary because egoism and illusion are so likely to reassert themselves. Hence *dis*illusionment in her fictions can be a profoundly religious experience, and falling *out* of love can be represented as a spiritual enlightenment. Murdoch liked to represent the human experience of the divine as an experience of chastisement (sometimes symbolized by the beating of Marsyas by Apollo), a stripping away of moral error, an "unselfing." Her numerous novels, especially in the latter half of her career, can look messy and overcrowded, but once you get accustomed to their pervasive ironies, to the endless ways in which imitations of Good are shown to be perversions of Good, you see what an original religious imaginer she is—yet a writer within a tradition of individual spiritual questing that may fairly be called Protestant.[83]

With John Updike I focus on one novel, *Roger's Version*, whose epigraphs are drawn from Kierkegaard and Barth. A middle-aged professor of theology, formerly a preacher, Roger is confronted by a young physicist who wants the cosmos to make sense, and tries to use his sophisticated science to support his belief in a providential God. Rather like the philosopher Richard Swinburne, he has convinced himself on grounds of probability theory that there are just too many mathematical coincidences, and therefore believes that God is breaking through, unable to hide any more. Roger demurs, silently quoting from Barth's *The Problem of Ethics*: "There is no way from us to God—not even a *via negativa*—not even a *via dialectica* nor *paradoxa*. The god who stood at the end of some human way—even of this way—would not be God." The grand intensity of such negation of the human makes him feel clean and revitalized. But where can one find anything corresponding to the purity of this vision in the world one knows? Driving along in an ordinary American city, Roger is struck by the absence of majesty all around, by the paltriness, in his society, of sin. No answer can be found either in physics (the young man's theory is demolished gently by a mature physicist) or in Christian preaching, devastatingly summed up by Roger who remembers how he did it: "Raise doubts, then do the reassurances. People have no idea what they're hearing, they just want a certain kind of verbal music. The major, the minor, and back to the major, then Bless you and keep you, and out the door to the luncheon party."

But Roger finds a kind of answer to his question in heightened sexual sin, a triply illicit bedding with his niece: "We lay together on a hard floor of the spirit, partners in incest, adultery, and child abuse. We wanted to be rid of each other, to destroy the evidence, yet perversely clung, lovers, miles below the ceiling, our comfort being that we had no further to fall. Lying there with Verna, gazing upward, I saw how much majesty resides in our continuing to love and honor God even as He inflicts blows upon us—as much as resides in the silence He maintains so that we may enjoy and explore our human freedom. This was *my* proof of his existence. I saw…the immense distance measuring our abasement. So great a fall proves great heights. Sweet certainty invaded me. 'Bless you' was all I could say." One could object here that Updike is facile in his assumption that transcendence is implied by sexual abasement, more fascinated by the idea of God's otherness than disturbed by human weakness. (I do not disagree with James Wood who finds Updike in this novel too comfortable and complacent about so difficult idea as the unbridgeable distance between God and man, and basically unable to represent religious anguish.)[84] Yet the novel illustrates rather memorably the individual soul's pursuit of transcendence by negative means.

Franz Kafka, despite his exceptional originality, is often thought of as an essentially Jewish writer, and perhaps this little account of the negativity of his religious vision can help to suggest why. In Kafka's universe paradise is never lost but hovers just out of reach. God is not punishing us for eating from the tree of knowledge but forbidding us to eat from the tree of life and thereby escape consciousness of our human situation, a consciousness that vainly imagines an innocent past or redeemed future. There is no prelapsarian time because birth itself is a fall into this awareness. The story called "A Report to the Academy" tells us that evolution from ape to human is really devolution into this awareness, for the ape's memories only begin from the time when he is taken over by humans and placed inside a cage where he feels forced into becoming human. Nor, at the end, can death be imagined as a release, for, as "The Hunter Gracchus" tells us, our ship of death may lose its way and condemn us to perpetual homelessness. When death occurs, as in *The Trial*, it is utterly without significance or pathos and so achieves no closure. Kafka disliked the ending of "The Metamorphosis" because it did seem to imply that Gregor's death was redemptive, giving his family a new lease on life. Redemption is never to be anticipated in Kafka's world.

Freedom in this world is an illusion. As one of Kafka's parables puts it, "all things possible do happen, only what happens is possible." It sounds Spinozistic, but God in Kafka's world is characterized not by the perfect congruence of law and freedom but by the complete absence of freedom. For my purpose the crucial Kafkan parable is "The Coming of the Messiah," which ends: "The Messiah will come only when he is no longer necessary; he will come only on the day after his arrival; he will come, not on the last day, but on the very last." The parable establishes a link to the main idea of normative Jewish theology, that the Messiah has not yet come but will come at some future time. But the Kafkan future is not continuous with our temporal experience—it is a time after time. The parable implies that divine salvation does exist but also that it does not exist for *us*. Erich Heller describes Kafka's religious stance as "negative transcendence" because truth and human existence are forever divided and irreconcilable.[85] What is positive in Kafka's theology concerns only God, for whom there is "plenty of hope…no end of hope," but man's destiny is "to accomplish the negative," a condition of hopelessness.[86]

In Kafka's world the unbridgeable distance between human and divine is at best a subject for ironic humor. His wit is reminiscent of Heine's jokes at the expense of God and religion or of the joke about the poor man who takes a job at the gate outside the shtetl to wait for the Messiah lest He pass by unnoticed. Asked after some time how he likes his job, he replies, "Well, it doesn't pay much, but I think it's steady work." This is not denial of or protest against God's existence, not atheism dogmatic or literary, but it is thinking about God ironically, one major element (I believe) of the Jewish tradition.

Rounding out this survey of twentieth-century uses of negation in writing about God (and deferring until Chapter Two a consideration of two important writers, Stevens and Beckett), I will comment finally in this chapter on three major philosophers—Freud, Sartre, and Derrida—who have a place in this survey because of their great impact on the literary imagination of their age. They have created what may be called "powerful mythologies," to borrow Wittgenstein's phrase describing the work of Freud,[87] mythologies that are usually labeled psychoanalysis, existentialism, and deconstruction. What I hope to show in relatively brief compass is how their atheism, far from being an incidental feature of their thought, is central to it and central to its influence.

Whenever in a discussion of modern atheism the name of Freud comes up, as it often does, *The Future of an Illusion* or a passage in *Civilization and Its Discontents* is usually cited to illustrate his dismissive view of God and religion. In the latter he describes the image of God in the minds of many as a "careful Providence...in the figure of an enormously exalted father...who can be softened by their prayers and placated by the signs of their remorse." He goes on to characterize this picture as "so patently infantile, so foreign to reality, that to anyone with a friendly attitude to humanity it is painful to think that the great majority of mortals will never be able to rise above this view of life."[88] The dismissive tone gives a misleading impression of the tremendous importance of the subject to Freud's thought as a whole. Freud's self-characterization as a "godless Jew" certainly holds, and his more-in-sorrow-than-in-anger stance is typical enough of his thought, but his psychoanalysis is emphatically concerned to understand the importance of the child's image of the exalted father, and his therapy focuses on teaching us to gain some freedom from our infantile fears of this figure.[89]

One of its sharpest insights is that these fears are difficult to become conscious of and control precisely because we are so reluctant to surrender the infantile need for protection to which they are linked. So the need to believe ourselves loved by a divine figure holds many adults in varying degrees of thralldom. Religion inevitably plays a major role in this atheistic philosophy. Freud studied its origins, meditated on its power and effectiveness, and sought to place it among the other most notable products of civilization. He understood very well that religion has given a lot of people a lot of support and that, without it, the incidence of mental illness would be far greater than it is, although of course he deplored the circumstances responsible for this dependence. His position, if not his tone, was not so different from that of Marx, who understood (in his commentary on Hegel's *Theory of Right*) that exploited peoples, given their material conditions, require religious illusions, although our demand should be to change the conditions that make those illusions necessary.

The originality of Freud's adversarial stance toward religion lies in his bold questioning of its commanding morality, specifically its derivation from a God-given inner voice. He demonstrated that conscience is a very malleable agency and that our moral sense derives rather from our individual childhood histories. Thus his psychoanalysis veers sharply away from Enlightenment faith in an essential human nature and away particularly from the Kantian faith in the voice of conscience as the law of God.

Freud profoundly influenced moral philosophy by showing that an individual's virtues and vices, strengths and weaknesses, must be understood according to the vicissitudes of individual history. The fluctuating moral level of one's behavior can only be understood from the specific attachments and developments in that history. They cannot be derived from universal constructs like Good and Evil. Even though we generally agree on what constitutes morally superior behavior, we learn from Freud that *the* moral sense does not exist, and that no *book* of virtues will have much practical effect. The Ten Commandments, one of many attempts to make universal moral rules, have from the beginning been widely and flagrantly flouted. We behave as well we do for more complex and personal reasons, not because we try to obey moral laws but because our self-esteem is adequate to the occasion, and that happens when we feel, hardly consciously, that we have achieved some independence from the specific bondages of our individual histories.

Richard Rorty makes this point especially well. For him, Freud is "the moralist who helped de-divinize the self by tracking conscience home to its origin in the contingencies of our upbringing," and who "suggests that we condemn ourselves for failure to break free of that past rather than for failure to live up to universal standards." Rorty seems to me exactly right. And if this seems like moral relativism, Rorty wisely recommends the usefulness of discarding the whole antithesis of absolute and relative and (taking cognizance of Isaiah Berlin's "Two Concepts of Liberty") beginning to think of persons and groups as different, self-creating moral centers, endlessly negotiating their mutual arrangements.[90]

Ironically, Freudianism at mid-century was becoming itself a kind of religion, "autonomous man" being held up as a normative ideal, the vehicle for an impossibly broad self-liberation. Freud himself always tried to dampen such expectations. He said psychoanalysis was not a *Weltanschauung*, could not cure the discontents of civilized man, could not offer "consolation," which is "at bottom...what they are all demanding."[91] He even said that his therapeutic procedure was, strictly speaking, endless. Thus, when therapeutic results proved to be slow, uncertain, and expensive, the excitement gradually waned.

There were, of course, other reasons as well for the decline of Freud's popularity, ranging from the rapid growth of pharmacological psychiatry and neuroscience to the radical subversions of his methods and ideas by the intellectually influential French Freudians. This isn't to say that psychoanalysis has turned out to be a fraud, as some have claimed. Not only does it persist as a useful therapy to some with more modest expectations but, as its scientific claims have lost authority, it has been taken up in a major way by the human sciences as a reservoir of psychological insight. One cannot pick up a brochure from a major university press without coming across a title that includes the name of Freud or the word psychoanalysis. Like a literary or philosophical classic, he has continued to be, and will continue to be, reread and rethought. Like Plato, Kant, and Wittgenstein, he has expanded our conception of mind permanently, a fact demonstrated in convincing detail by the philosopher and psychoanalyst, Jonathan Lear, in his *Open Minded: Working Out the Logic of the Soul*.[92]

Sartre's existentialism caught the Western imagination in the wake of World War II, a moment marked by the 1945 lecture called "Existentialism is a Humanism," its reputation backed up by the striking novel *Nausea* and the ambitious treatise *Being and Nothingness*. Iris Murdoch heard a lecture by him in that year and described its charismatic effect on the audience as that of a rock-star's, an experience duplicated for her only when she heard a lecture by Jacques Derrida thirty-five years later.[93] Existentialism is a humanism because it heroicizes man's complete independence of God. Man is only what he makes of himself, and existentialism itself is only an attempt to draw the full conclusions from a consistently atheistic position.[94]

The moral ideal on which all this pivots is what Sartre calls "freedom," not the measured autonomy sought by Freudian therapy (and derided by Jacques Lacan) but something more uncompromising—totally self-responsible choice. He stigmatized as *mauvaise foi* the attempt to excuse our actions by an appeal to any determining cause whatever, whether metaphysical (here a withering glance at Christianity) or psychological (there a withering glance at psychoanalysis)—"bad faith" meaning in this context something like rationalization, i.e., screens for reasons that are accessible to consciousness yet are not acknowledged by us. They are the products, then, of a cowardice for which we must be held responsible. Thus Sartre is not so much quarreling with the personal and caring God of the Judeo-Christian tradition, as for the most part are my literary atheists in Chapter Two, but with the philosopher's God, a First Cause that determines the existence of Man and thereby compromises human freedom. Freedom is total for Sartre, for better and worse. If Graham Ward is right that theology cannot accept the idea of human autonomy, then clearly a Sartrean cannot tolerate theology.[95]

The mutual exclusiveness of Man and God in Sartre's work is an idea that ought to be formulated in slightly more philosophical language because it gains force when understood as a rebellion against a particular tradition. In the scholastic theology that Sartre absorbed in his French education, God's existence, unlike man's, is the same as his essence; there is nothing in the least contingent or unnecessary about it existence whereas human existence (as the hero of *Nausea* memorably perceives) is radically contingent. "This is what absurdity deeply means," comments Arthur Danto: "not silly or meaningless or inconsequential, but contingent."[96] Alasdair MacIntyre puts it a little differently since for him meaning is equated with God's existence: "[Sartre's God] embodies an impossible ideal of self-sufficiency, a meaningfulness against which we measure human life and find it contingent and meaningless....God is what man uselessly and hopelessly aspires to be."[97]

Sartre's atheism is thus more mundane, less "religious," than Heidegger's. The nothingness that surrounds consciousness in Sartre is more an inevitable result of reflection than a primordial matrix, and the *angoisse* and sense of *délaissement* induced by confronting it lack the pathos of the Heideggerian vocabulary from which they derive. For this reason Sartre's atheism is also more rousing. It asks us to do without a contradictory concept like God, to have the courage to choose and act, knowing that our human situation is defined entirely by what we do.

Existentialism proved an exciting idea to the post-War generation because it asked dramatically for a break from the past—from the sense of our debt to the past—and it seemed all the more heroic because it not only said life was ours to make but also that the responsibility this entailed was burdensome. It is not surprising that Heidegger believed Sartre's lecture, "Existentialism is a Humanism," to be a betrayal of his own philosophy, and that he promptly responded to it in his "Letter on Humanism." Although Sartre had aligned himself with Heidegger as an "atheist existentialist," as distinct from the "Christian existentialism" of Karl Jaspers and Gabriel Marcel, it is clear that his atheism was more unequivocal, and was presented with much more of what Iris Murdoch nicely called "humanist bounce."[98] It is no wonder that his devoted expositor, Hazel Barnes, found herself irritated by Heidegger's elusive spirituality and no wonder that a contemporary theological philosopher who follows Heidegger, Don Cupitt, finds himself irritated in turn by Sartre's "lack of spirituality."[99]

The so-called death-of-God theologies (which enjoyed some prestige from about 1955 to 1970)[100] found Sartre's dialectical energy particularly stimulating—this was the kind of atheism that Christians like the American novelist Walker Percy welcomed because it seemed to clear the ground in a great sweep and thus make room for transcendence, the longing for which was assumed to lie waiting in the empty human soul.

During the 1960s and 1970s Sartre's reputation fell sharply. To some extent this was due to his reckless, uncompromising commitment to Soviet Communism. Also, Paris was abuzz with new, *anti-humanistic* theories, deriving from the linguistics of Ferdinand de Saussure and the anthropology of Claude Lévi-Strauss. These bore successively the labels of structuralism, post-structuralism, and deconstruction. In the latter decades of the century, they were largely consolidated under the broad heading of postmodernism.

The most representative philosophic atheist of the postmodern period has been Jacques Derrida, who wondered if even Heidegger, the avowed enemy of humanism, had "returned to it as if by magnetic attraction" when he spoke of man as "the shepherd of being."[101] Derrida's own assault on humanism carried to an extreme the idea that language was too metaphoric a medium to reflect truth, an error he dubbed "logocentrism." He sought through the procedures of "deconstruction" to subvert the tradition by which speech was placed above writing and the author placed above the reader, a tradition that supported writerly authority and hence stability of meaning. If we remove this hierarchy, we are left, in the words of one commentator, "with language as an infinitely free play of metaphor whose meaning is always indeterminate, always sliding from one seemingly stable place to another, without any fixed point of origin from which we can take our bearings or any final point of resolution."[102] Meaning was thus not only endlessly uncertain but also endlessly deferred, an idea Derrida tried to capture in his coinage *différance*, combining the French words for differ and defer. The popularity of deconstruction in the 1970s and 1980s had something to do with the very boldness of putting meaning itself into so much question, but its radical skepticism, in the practice of literary criticism at any rate, became rather boring by arriving so predictably at a verdict of indeterminacy.

Then, particularly under the challenge of Michel Foucault and a renewed interest in history and ideology, Derrida roused himself to develop the political and religious implications of his own thinking, articulating them in a number of publications—"How to Avoid Speaking: Denials," *Circumfession, The Gift of Death, Specters of Marx,* and *Politics of Friendship,* among others. Could he wrest from his radical skepticism anything religious, perhaps what his devoted exegete, John Caputo, called "religion without religion," perhaps something resembling a negative theology?

The basic paradox of negative theology is how to speak of a transcendence that is unspeakable. Derrida recognized, according to Caputo, that this difficulty was analogous to his own, how to "name *différance*, that word or concept that is neither word nor concept."[103] He had earlier, in *Speech and Phenomena,* insisted that his coinage did not constitute a negative theology because the unnamable space it opened up could not be filled in by an ineffable God. But perhaps the mystical thrust of negative theology could undo the metaphysics inherent in positive theology, for in positive theology the concept of God is the stable guarantor of meaning whereas negative theology puts the proper name into question and thus blurs the distinction between concept and the ever-sliding sign. This is the thesis subtly argued by Kevin Hart, whose book *The Trespass of the Sign* reminds us that "deconstruction's target is metaphysics, not theology as such," and that therefore its link to atheism is "not inevitable."[104]

In fact, however, deconstruction's "conversation with Christian theology," as Hart puts it, or even with Jewish theology, is tenuous. When in the 1980s Derrida returned deliberately to the subject of religion, he tried to find a way around, not through, negative theology, arguing that its negations are haunted by the presence of God whereas deconstruction taught absolute heterogeneity (*tout autre*) derived from no category of being, absent or present. He declared with great assurance, "The promise of which I shall speak will always have escaped the demand of presence."[105] *Specters of Marx* went on to call this promise "the experience of the impossible."[106]

Derrida defined himself as both a man on the left politically and also in some sense religious, admitting to an "absolutely private language in which I speak of God all the time."[107] One might wonder whether so private and elusive a political and religious commitment amounts to anything, but he forges ahead in *Specters of Marx*, laying new stress on the Marxist (and Jewish) legacy of messianic yearning. Rejecting the crude logocentrism of Marx, based on the commitment to a specific ideology, Derrida goes on to discover in messianism one idea, which he calls justice, that cannot be deconstructed: "What remains irreducible to any deconstruction…is perhaps a certain experience of the emancipatory promise; it is perhaps even the formality of a structural messianism, a messianism without religion, even a messianism without messianism, an idea of justice—which we distinguish from law or right or even from human rights."[108]

With similar boldness in *Politics of Friendship* he defends the ideal of democracy but a democracy always to come. At the end of many meandering pages, the book concludes: "For democracy remains to come…it will remain indefinitely perfectible…never present…a non-presentable concept."[109] How democracy and justice so defined can serve as a call to responsibility (as, with a nod toward Levinas, he apparently wishes them to) is something of a mystery. But by devising an idiosyncratic version of the Jewish and Marxist messianic traditions, Derrida works out a sort of religious atheism. Perhaps this turn in his thinking should be written off as what Mark Lilla calls "chutzpah."[110] It certainly illustrates the difficulty, even for a literary philosopher, of trying to say the unsayable in a persuasive way.

Samuel Beckett, faced with a similar problem but not constrained by the logical demands of discursive form, could express his own relation to negative theology more convincingly. And perhaps that is why Derrida's tribute to Beckett is an uneasy one—"an author to whom I feel very close; but also too close."[111]

NOTES

1. Lucien Febvre, *The Problem of Unbelief in the Sixteenth Century: The Religion of Rabelais*, trans. Beatrice Gottlieb (Cambridge: Harvard Univerity Press, 1982).
2. See David Wootton, "New Histories of Atheism," in Michael Hunter and David Wootton, eds., *Atheism from the Reformation to the Enlightenment* (Oxford: Clarendon Press, 1992), 13–52.
3. The first English use of the word has been traced to Sir John Cheke, Regius Professor of Greek at Cambridge. The evidence involving Marlowe and Raleigh is fully discussed in Michael Hunter, "The Problem of Atheism in Early Modern England," *Transactions of the Royal Historical Society*, fifth series, No. 35 (London, 1985), 135–57. Hunter mentions also many other uses of the word up to the time of the Civil War. Nashe's phrase and other instances of the term's applicability are cited in Karen Armstrong, *A History of God* (New York: Ballantine Books, 1991), 288. For another roundup, see Michael J. Buckley, S.J., *At the Origins of Modern Atheism* (New Haven: Yale University Press, 1987), 9. See also James Turner, *Without God, Without Creed: The Origins of Unbelief in America* (Baltimore: Johns Hopkins Univeristy Press, 1985), 26.
4. Carlo Ginzburg, *The Cheese and the Worms: The Cosmos of a Sixteenth Century Miller*, trans. John and Anne Tedeschi (Baltimore: Johns Hopkins University Press, 1980).
5. See Tullio Gregory, "Pierre Charron's 'Scandalous Book,'" in Hunter and Wootton, *Atheism from the Reformation*, 99. The "scandalous book" was titled *De la sagesse*.
6. Buckley, *Origins of Modern Atheism*, 357. Kors, *Atheism in France 1650–1729: The Orthodox Sources of Disbelief* (Princeton: Princeton University Press, 1990), xiii. See also David Berman, *A History of Atheism in Britain: Hobbes to Russell* (London: Croom Helm, 1988).
7. Quoted in James Wood, *The Broken Estate: Essays on Literature and Belief* (New York: Random House, 1999), 242.
8. René Descartes, *The Philosophical Writings of Descartes*, vol. 1, trans. John Cottingham, Robert Stoothoff, Dugald Murdoch (London: Cambridge University Press, 1985), 210.
9. David Berman, "Disclaimers as Offence Mechanisms in Charles Blunt and John Tolland," in Hunter and Wootton, eds., *Atheism from the Reformation*, 255–72. See also in this volume, Richard Tuck, "The 'Christian Atheism' of Thomas Hobbes," 111–30.
10. Jim Holt, "Infinitesimally Yours," *New York Review of Books*, 20 May 1999, 64.
11. Dorinda Outram, *The Enlightenment* (London: Cambridge University Press, 1995), 40.
12. Peter Gay, ed., *Voltaire's Philosophical Dictionary*, 2 vols. (New York: Basic Books, 1962): 2:473, 1:95–105.
13. Quoted in Buckley, *Origins of Modern Atheism*, 272.
14. David Hume, *Writings on Religion*, ed. Antony Flew (La Salle, IL: Open Court, 1995), 283.
15. Richard H. Popkin, "Scepticism in the Enlightenment," in *Scepticism in the Enlightenment*, ed. Richard H. Popkin (Dordrecht/Boston/London: Kluwer Academic Publishers, 1997), 6.
16. Hume, *Writings on Religion*, 291.
17. Hume, *Writings on Religion*, 17.

18 Letter to Voltaire, 11 June 1749, in *Correspondance de Diderot 1713–1757* (Paris: Éditions de Minuet, 1955), 78.
19 Buckley, *Origins of Modern Atheism*, 27.
20 The fullest version of this widely cited anecdote appears in Ernest Campbell Mossner, *The Life of David Hume*, 2nd ed. (Oxford: Clarendon Press, 1980), 483.
21 David Berman, *History of Atheism in Britain*, 3.
22 Paul Henri Thiry, baron d'Holbach, *Système de la nature ou des lois du monde physique et morale*, vol. II (Hildesheim: Georg Olms, 1966), 420.
23 See Alan Charles Kors, "The Atheism of Holbach and Naigeon," in Hunter and Wootton, eds., *Atheism from the Reformation*, 213–30.
24 Michael Foot and Isaac Kramnick, eds., *The Thomas Paine Reader*, (London: Penguin, 1987), 424.
25 Roger Scruton, *Kant* (Oxford: Oxford University Press, 1982), 28.
26 Richard Rorty, *Contingency, Irony, and Solidarity* (Cambridge: Cambridge University Press, 1990), 30.
27 Samuel Taylor Coleridge, *The Statesman's Manual* (1816), in Coleridge, *The Major Works*, ed. H. J. Jackson (Oxford: Oxford University Press, 1985), 661.
28 Isaiah Berlin, *The Sense of Reality: Studies in Ideas and Their History*, ed. Henry Hardy (New York: Farrar, Straus & Giroux, 1996), 170–77.
29 Rorty, *Contingency*: 5, 4.
30 E. O. Wilson, *Consilience: The Unity of Knowledge* (New York: Vintage, 1998), 49.
31 Quoted in John D. Caputo, *The Prayers and Tears of Jacques Derrida: Religion without Religion* (Bloomington: Indiana University Press, 1997), 119.
32 Alfred Jules Ayer, *Language, Truth and Logic* (New York: Dover Publications, 1952), 115.
33 Marcel Neusch, *The Sources of Modern Atheism*, trans. Matthew J. O'Connell (New York: Paulist Press, 1982), 52.
34 Ludwig Feuerbach, *The Essence of Christianity*, trans. Marian Evans (New York: 1885): 6–7, 20, 77–78.
35 Thomas Carlyle, *Sartor Resartus*, eds. Kerry McSweeney and Peter Sabor (Oxford: Oxford University Press, 1987): 169, 191.
36 A. N. Wilson, *God's Funeral* (New York: Norton, 1999), 92.
37 Quoted in Wilson, *God's Funeral*, 197.
38 Mrs. Humphry Ward, "The New Reformation: A Dialogue," in Thomas Henry Huxley, *Christianity and Agnosticism: A Controversy, consisting of papers by Henry Wace, D. D., Prof. Thomas H. Huxley, the Bishop of Peterborough, W. H. Mallock, Mrs. Humphry Ward* (New York, 1889), 284–312.
39 Michael Shermer, *How We Believe: The Search for God in an Age of Science* (New York: W. H. Freeman, 1999), 29.
40 David Daiches, *God and the Poets* (Oxford: Clarendon Press, 1984), 112.
41 Friedrich Nietzsche, *Twilight of the Idols*, trans. Duncan Large (Oxford: Oxford University Press, 1998): 43, 49.
42 John Stuart Mill, *Collected Works: Essays on Ethics, Religion, and Society*, ed. F. G. L. Priestley (Toronto: Toronto University Press, 1969): 449, 450, 462, 484.

43 William James, "Conclusions" and "Postscript," in *The Varieties of Religious Experience* (London: Longmans, Green, 1928).
44 In a letter of 1904, James regretted the use seven years earlier of his phrase "the will to believe," wishing he had written instead "the right to believe." See Louis Menand, *The Metaphysical Club: A Story of Ideas in America* (Farrar, Straus & Giroux, 2001), 490–91.
45 Quoted in J. M. Robertson, *A History of Freethought in the Nineteenth Century* (London, 1929), 94.
46 The quoted phrase is used and developed in H. Porter Abbott, *Beckett Writing Beckett: The Author in the Autograph* (Ithaca: Cornell University Press, 1996), 32–42.
47 Quoted in Robert W. Hill, Jr., ed., *Tennyson's Poetry*. (New York: Norton, 1971), 619.
48 Quoted in Hill, ed., *Tennyson's Poetry*, 628.
49 Quoted in Malcolm Cowley, ed., *The Portable Hawthorne*, (New York: Penguin, 1976), 651.
50 Quoted in David Lowe and Ronald Meyer, eds., *Dostoevsky's Letters*, vol. 1 (Ann Arbor, MI: Ardis Publishers, 1988), 194–95.
51 Walter E. Bezanson, Introduction, *Herman Melville's 'Clarel: A Poem and a Pilgrimage to the Holy Land'* (New York: Hendricks House, 1960), ix.
52 Richard Dawkins, *The Blind Watchmaker: Why the Evidence of Evolution Reveals a Universe without Design* (New York: Norton, 1996), 6.
53 Gillian Beer, *Darwin's Plots: Evolutionary Narrative in Darwin, George Eliot and Nineteenth-Century Fiction* (London: Routledge and Kegan Paul, 1983), 13.
54 Quoted in Shermer, *How We Believe*, 115.
55 Charles Darwin, *The Origin of Species*, in Philip Appleman, ed., *Darwin*. 2nd ed. (New York: Norton, 1979), 130–31.
56 Dawkins, *Blind Watchmaker*, 165.
57 Quoted in Appleman, ed., *Darwin*, 222.
58 See Robertson, *History of Freethought*, 213–18.
59 Thomas Henry Huxley, *Evolution and Ethics*, in Appleman, ed., *Darwin*, 326.
60 Appleman, ed., *Darwin*, 328.
61 Thomas Henry Huxley, "Agnosticism," in *Christianity and Agnosticism*, 39.
62 Quoted in Wilson, *God's Funeral*, 196–97.
63 Huxley, "Agnosticism: A Rejoinder," in *Agnosticism and Christianity*, 115.
64 Leslie Stephen, *An Agnostic's Apology and Other Essays* (New York: 1893), 2ff. In 1873 Stephen had published *Essays on Freethinking and Plainspeaking*.
65 Charles Bradlaugh, *Humanity's Gain from Unbelief and other Essays* (London, 1929): 25, 57.
66 Quoted in Walter L. Arnstein, *The Bradlaugh Case: A Study of Late Victorian Opinion and Politics* (New York: Oxford University Press, 1965), 158.
67 Bertrand Russell, *Why I Am Not a Christian and other Essays* (New York: Simon and Schuster, 1957), v.
68 Bertrand Russell, "Am I An Atheist or an Agnostic?" in *Collected Essays 1943–1949* (New York: Arno Press, 1972), 47–49.
69 Mark C. Taylor, ed., *Critical Terms for Religious Studies* (Chicago: University of Chicago Press, 1998), 12–13.

70 Quoted in Shira Wolosky, *The Negative Way of Language in Eliot, Beckett, and Celan* (Stanford: Stanford University Press, 1995), 104.
71 Armstrong, *History of God*, 248. For more illustrations of "negative theology" see Taylor, ed., *Critical Terms for Religious Studies*, 147–48.
72 Michael Sugrue, "Lecture Twelve: Meister Eckhart from Whom God Hid Nothing," *The Great Courses on Tape: The Bible and Western Culture, Part I* (Springfield, VA: The Teaching Company, 1998), 51.
73 Dionysius is quoted in John D. Caputo, *Prayers and Tears of Jacques Derrida: Religion without Religion*, xxiv. Eckhart is quoted in Jacques Derrida, "How to Avoid Speaking: Denials," trans. Ken Frieden, *Languages of the Unsayable: The Play of Negativity in Literature and Literary Theory,* eds. Sanford Budick and Wolfgang Iser (Stanford: Stanford University Press, 1987), 52.
74 Martin Heidegger, "The Way Back Into the Ground of Metaphysics," in Kaufmann, ed., *Existentialism from Dostoevsky to Sartre*, revised and expanded (New York: New American Library, 1975), 268.
75 The question is raised at the end of "The Way Back Into the Ground of Metaphysics" (*Existentialism*, 278) and featured in *Introduction to Metaphysics*, trans. Ralph Manheim (New Haven: Yale University Press, 1997).
76 Hazel E. Barnes, *An Existentialist Ethics* (New York: Knopf, 1967), 401.
77 Martin Heidegger, "Letter on Humanism," in *Philosophy in the Twentieth Century: An Anthology*, vol. 3, eds. William Barrett and Henry D. Aiken, trans. Edgar Lohner (New York: Random House, 1962), 288–91.
78 Rüdiger Safranski, *Martin Heidegger* (Cambridge: Harvard University Press, 1998).
79 The information in this paragraph has been distilled from a variety of primary and secondary sources, but see particularly: Graham Ward, ed., *Theology and Contemporary Critical Theory* (New York: St. Martin's Press, 1996); Graham Ward, ed., *The Postmodern God: A Theological Reader* (Oxford: Blackwell, 1997); Taylor, *Critical Terms for Religious Study*; *The Levinas Reader*, ed. Seán Hand (Oxford: Blackwell, 1989); Safranski, *Martin Heidegger*; Barnes, *An Existentialist Ethics*; Jean-Luc Marion, *God without Being*, trans. Thomas Carlson (Chicago: University of Chicago Press, 1982); Regina M. Schwartz, "Teaching a Sacred Text as Literature, Teaching Literature as a Sacred Text," *Profession* (New York: PMLA, 1998): 186–198; Derrida, "How to Avoid Speaking"; and John Caputo, *Prayers and Tears of Jacques Derrida*. Derrida's "I quite rightly pass for an atheist" is quoted in Caputo, xviii.
80 Peter Angeles, ed., *Critiques of God* (Amherst, NY: Prometheus Books, 1997). See particularly the following essays: Ernest Nagel, "Philosophical Concepts of Atheism," 6ff.; Sidney Hook, "Modern Knowledge and the Concept of God," 29ff.; and Michael Scriven, "God and Reason," 97ff.
81 O'Connor, prefatory note to "Wise Blood," in *3 by Flannery O'Connor* (New York: New American Library, 1962).
82 Iris Murdoch, *Sartre: Romantic Rationalist* (New York: Viking, 1987), 9.
83 For an elaboration of these ideas, see my *Iris Murdoch's Fables of Unselfing* (Columbia, MO: University of Missouri Press, 1995).
84 Wood, *Broken Estate*, 192–99.

85 Erich Heller, "The World of Franz Kafka," in *Franz Kafka: Twentieth Century Views: A Collection of Critical Essays*, ed. Ronald D. Gray (Englewood Cliffs, NJ: Prentice-Hall, 1963), 110–12.
86 The phrases in quotation marks are drawn from Harold Bloom, *Ruin the Sacred Truth: Poetry and Belief from the Bible to the Present* (Cambridge: Harvard University Press, 1989), 167.
87 Wittgenstein, *Aesthetics, Psychology and Religious Belief*, 52.
88 Sigmund Freud, *Civilization and Its Discontents*, trans. James Strachey (New York: Norton, 1962), 21.
89 Regina M. Schwartz, in an interesting essay titled "Freud's God," sees the importance of religion in his work quite differently. Focusing especially on *Moses and Monotheism*, she claims that psychoanalysis, far from liberating us from the "mass neurosis" of religion, is derived from religion. This is to put the emphasis on Freud's speculations into pre-history (which she chooses to call the postmodernist rather than modernist Freud). But if our concern is his influence as a modern atheist, what is relevant is precisely his understanding of religion as a mass neurosis from which psychoanalysis offers some measure of freedom. Schwartz's essay appears in Philip Blond, ed., *Post-Secular Philosophy: Between Philosophy and Theology* (London: Routledge, 1998), 281–304.
90 Rorty, *Contingency*: 30, 33, 44–47.
91 Freud, *Civilization and Its Discontents*, 92.
92 Jonathan Lear, *Open Minded: Working Out the Logic of the Soul* (Cambridge: Harvard University Press, 1998).
93 Iris Murdoch, *Sartre: Romantic Rationalist*, 10.
94 Sartre's lecture is reprinted in Kaufmann, *Existentialism*, 287–312.
95 Graham Ward, *Theology and Contemporary Critical Theory*, xlii.
96 Arthur C. Danto, *Jean-Paul Sartre* (New York: Viking, 1975), 12.
97 Alasdair C. MacIntyre, "Existentialism," in *Sartre: A Collection of Critical Essays*, ed. Mary Warnock (Garden City, NY: Anchor, 1971), 28.
98 Iris Murdoch, *Existentialists and Mystics: Writings on Philosophy and Literature*, ed. Peter Conradi (London: Chatto & Windus, 1997), 115.
99 Hazel Barnes, *An Existentialist Ethics*, 401ff. Don Cupitt, *The Religion of Being* (London: SCM Press, 1998), 138.
100 Three representative examples are: Gabriel Vahanian, *The Death of God: the culture of our post-Christian era* (New York: Braziller, 1961); Thomas J. J. Altizer and William Hamilton, eds., *Radical Theology and the Death of God* (New York and London: 1966); Richard L. Rubenstein, *After Auschwitz, Radical Theology and Contemporary Judaism* (Indianapolis, 1966).
101 Derrida, "How to Avoid Speaking," in *Languages of the Unsayable*, 55.
102 Mark Lilla, "The Politics of Jacques Derrida," in *New York Review of Books*, 25 June 1998, 38.
103 Caputo, *Prayers and Tears of Jacques Derrida*, 2.
104 Kevin Hart, *The Trespass of the Sign* (London: Cambridge University Press, 1989): xi, 43, and *passim*.
105 Derrida, "How to Avoid Speaking," in *Languages of the Unsayable*, 15.

106 Derrida, *Specters of Marx*, trans. Peggy Kamuf (New York: Routledge, 1994), 35.
107 Caputo, *Prayers and Tears of Jacques Derrida,* xviii.
108 *Specters of Marx*: 59, 73.
109 Jacques Derrida, *Politics of Friendship*, trans. George Collins (London: Verso, 1997), 306.
110 Lilla, "Politics of Jacques Derrida," 40. Lilla's acute assessment of Derrida's political and religious views is expanded in *The Reckless Mind: Intellectuals in Politics* (New York: New York Review Books, 2001), 164–90.
111 Jacques Derrida, "This Strange Institution Called Literature: An Interview with Jacques Derrida," in Derek Attridge, ed., *Acts of Literature* (New York: Routledge, 1992), 60.

CHAPTER TWO
Seven Literary Atheists

HAMM: Let us pray to God.... *(Attitudes of prayer. Silence. Abandoning his attitude. Discouraged.)* Well?
CLOV (*abandoning his attitude*): What a hope!...
NAGG:...(*Pause. Abandoning his attitude.*) Nothing doing!
HAMM: The bastard! He doesn't exist!

Samuel Beckett, *Endgame*

The survey method adopted in Chapter One was intended to provide a broad overview of modern atheism but did not allow for a nuanced view of particular writers or convey the imaginative complexity of a particular body of writing, which are basic to my understanding of literary atheism. In this chapter, therefore, I will focus on only seven writers, developing the implications of each one's thought in some detail. I hope also that the sequence of Denis Diderot, Georg Büchner, Friedrich Nietzsche, Mark Twain, Thomas Hardy, Wallace Stevens, and Samuel Beckett will constitute a supplementary survey that uses representative cases to illustrate major shifts of emphasis from the mid-eighteenth to the mid-twentieth century. Diderot and Büchner exemplify respectively pre- and post-Revolutionary literary atheism, the one more intellectually speculative and the other more emotionally desperate. Nietzsche undertakes a psycho-historical analysis of theology and meets the challenge both to religion and art resulting from the new prestige of science. Twain and Hardy illustrate in different ways the bitter literary atheism of a post-Darwinian age, the one by way of extravagant satire, the other by way of brooding on the lack of fitness between man and the cosmos. Stevens speaks for an age in which religious doubt is less worrisome but the need to believe remains. And Beckett's post-War probe of nothingness rejects consolation yet creates out of the very lack of hope an art of seemingly endless invention. A study of these writers will more than adequately explain why I am deliberately connecting the subjects of atheism and literature.

I must clarify a little further the purpose of this chapter by distinguishing literary atheism from two other somewhat similar stances with which it might be confused. The more important of these is that of the original poet of the modern era who rejects traditional theism but for whom some idea of God is important. Such writers (one could instance Shelley, Hölderlin, Yeats, Rilke, Lawrence, Hart Crane, and Norman Mailer, among many others) devise their own god, which we properly identify by prefixing the name of its creator in the possessive case.

A second exception should be made of those writers who *are* atheistic but so assertively that they are in effect propagandists, lacking the complexity of the literary atheist. Perhaps they are best called "antitheists," a term Algernon Swinburne often used to describe his own position. The group would include, along with Swinburne, such writers as Sade, Prosper Mérimée, and James Thomson. They love to hate God and religion, and they may be outrageous, amusing or even eloquent without becoming, as atheists, very interesting. Swinburne is perhaps the most complex of these, but his neopagan attacks on Christianity, as in the lushly sonorous "Garden of Proserpine" that turns Christian hopes of immortality and resurrection exactly upside down, are marred by a certain complacent satisfaction. The same is true of such a quotable phrase as "the Supreme Evil, God," from "Atalanta in Calydon." Being a skilled poet, Swinburne is not quite a propagandist—he is giving us picture more than argument, and is a notable stylist—but a certain monotony does characterize his antitheistic efforts.

The Pre-Revolutionary Atheism of Denis Diderot

The belief that only natural causes operated in the material world, we observed in Chapter One, was the defining issue of the first phase of modern atheism extending from Descartes to Diderot. Diderot certainly shared this belief, but he was also too much the speculator and moralist to be content with a merely skeptical line of thought. He wanted to explain *why* matter moved and *why* human beings, since they were part of the material world, found themselves so concerned with virtue and moral choice.

Diderot's commitment to materialism and thereby to atheism emerged by quick stages in three works composed in his mid-thirties, from 1746 to 1749, although an inclination to *play* with ideas is already noticeable in them. *Philosophical Thoughts* (*Pensées philosophiques*) was influenced by the Earl of Shaftesbury's deistic *Inquiry Concerning Virtue and Merit* that Diderot, at first impressed by the idea that moral sentiment depended on belief in God, had translated and introduced a year earlier, but he carried the inquiry beyond deism in a challenge to Pascal's fideistic *Pensées*. Although the work mixes deistic and skeptical views, the latter have a sharper edge, as in the tart exposure of a so-called miracle (LIII) or in this epigrammatic flourish: "The thought that there is no God has never frightened anyone but rather the thought that there might be one, of the kind that people describe" (IX). We catch this tone again in a section concerned with the existence of God (XIII), where Diderot observes that "skepticism is the first step toward truth."[1] The less interesting piece that followed, *The Skeptic's Stroll*, surmises that the atheist's position may be right although the deist's is more likely, thus officially honoring the deist while inclining to the atheist. And the third and more important piece, *Letter on the Blind, For the Use of Those Who See*, shows us a blind mathematician whose inability to appreciate the argument from design—and by extension any kind of theism—is a lesson for those who see, teaching that they cannot know any more than the blind about the deity. Reminding his interlocutor that an Indian believes the globe remains suspended in the air because it is borne on the back of an elephant, who rests on a tortoise, etc., he enjoins him to "confess your ignorance right away, and spare me the elephant and the tortoise."[2]

The authorities burned *Philosophical Thoughts* (although a copy was printed and became rather popular), searched Diderot's lodging and carried off "The Skeptic's Stroll," warning the author not to write anything else against religion. But Diderot went ahead with the bolder *Letter on the Blind*, and sent a copy to Voltaire, France's leading man of letters at mid-century but known to be, despite his anti-clericalism and distaste for theology, a deist. In fact Voltaire was somewhat disturbed by it, replying that "it is quite impertinent to guess what [God] is, or why he has made the world, but it seems to me very bold to deny that he exists." Diderot's reply to this bends over backward to be tactful ("I believe in God, although I live very well with atheists") without surrendering its main point, the unimportance of believing in God. "It is very important," he wittily remarks, "not to confuse hemlock with parsley, but not important at all to believe or not to believe in God."[3]

Not long after the publication of *Letter on the Blind*, Diderot was seized and put into prison for a few months, an experience that made him more prudent and canny, but not more compromising, in the service of truth. He submitted his work to the authorities when he could, withheld much of it from publication in his lifetime, and threw himself into the huge and extended enterprise of the *Encyclopedia*, which, though an object of suspicion and subject to several kinds of censorship, was also a source of pride to France and enjoyed the support of some people of influence. At times Diderot clothed what he wrote in deadpan irony in order to deceive naïve readers while getting his subversive point across to more knowing ones, as in this passage from *The Interpretation of Nature*: "Religion spares us many errors and much labour. If it had not enlightened us on the origin of the world, how many different hypotheses should we have been tempted to take for the secret of nature."[4]

Diderot's nimbleness, then, was stimulated by circumstances, but was also characteristic, and led him to bring to the speculative essay a striking dialogic art. From the beginning, even in works not formally in dialogue, his habit was to oppose one opinion to another, and this underwent remarkable development in such mature works as *Rameau's Nephew* and *D'Alembert's Dream*. In the first of these, it isn't just a question of balancing *Moi* against *Lui* in vigorous debate. Yes, *Moi* represents a side of Diderot, the bourgeois man of good sense and good will, but the characteristic mobility of the writer's mind is mostly represented by *Lui*, the nephew, who takes over and dizzies us with telling subversions of conventional moral assumptions, rather like Shaw's Don Juan in debate with a sensible, bourgeois Devil. In the second, Diderot and D'Alembert debate materialism one evening, and the more conservative D'Alembert in his sleep then carries Diderot's thoughts even farther, which, overheard, are interpreted for our benefit by a Diderot stand-in to a mystified lady. In both cases, the writer is less interested in driving at firm conclusions than in the pleasure of speculation itself.

Diderot liked to call himself "the philosopher," meaning by philosophy the endlessly fascinating art of inquiry, neither the systematic skepticism of Hume on the one hand nor the dogmatic materialism of La Mettrie, Holbach, or Helvétius on the other. His model inquirer was Montaigne, whose grand art is that he "never tries to prove (*prouver*) but is always experimenting (*prouvant*)."[5] Diderot may be called a rambunctious Montaigne, full of strong opinions but always wary of dogmatism. His postscript to *The Interpretation of Nature* sums up his stance with admirable concision: "Never forget that *nature* is not *God*; that a *man* is not a *machine*; that a *hypothesis* is not a *fact*." Both deists and overly enthusiastic materialists like Holbach were apt to confuse nature and God; La Mettrie and Helvétius to confuse man with a machine; and perhaps eighteenth-century science to confuse hypothesis with fact. Unlike the dogmatic atheist, Diderot would allow room for a play of perspective, and thus for a potential humanism to emerge even out of determinism. Herbert Josephs was on target in commenting that Diderot was fascinated above all by the "searching mind itself."[6]

The "ism" that Diderot was most committed to was materialism, and his most thorough studies of its implications are *The Interpretation of Nature* (1753) and *D'Alembert's Dream* (1769). But—drawing on Descartes, Bacon, and Newton, and carrying their thinking a step or two farther—he made a serious effort to show that matter was not merely inert. *Ame* was not to be imagined as either separate from *corps* or behind it but inseparable from it. Diderot worked out what has been called a dynamic materialism, and John Hope Mason provides in this connection helpful background to indicate that mid-eighteenth century European speculation was moving away from a mechanical view of nature based on astronomy and physics and moving toward a dynamic view based on biology, physiology, and chemistry.[7] Diderot was alert to these developments, to the new idea that nature was not stable or fixed but always evolving. His science is of course now antiquated, but we are nonetheless astonished to see how far he was able to go in understanding change, development, growth, even evolution, without any knowledge of Darwin or genetics. For him, there could be no essential distinction between men and animals if the basic fact of life was change and development, although such a doctrine was highly offensive to the Church. Nor did he make a fundamental distinction between organic and inorganic matter, exercising a good deal of ingenuity in showing how they interact. To be sure, as a serious moralist he was thus obliging himself down the line to explain what *was* distinctive in man, but his dynamic materialism in itself retained appeal for some even into the nineteenth century, like Karl Marx who also wanted to account for the dynamic nature of nature without recourse to a supreme intelligence.

Since Diderot was at bottom not what we would call a scientist but a moralist concerned with virtue and happiness, the greatest challenge he faced as a speculator starting from the premise of atheistic materialism was that it became difficult to account for the moral dimension of man. How could one explain morality if there is no freedom of will and hence no moral choice, if behavior is ruled by material processes beyond our conscious control? And if Diderot was a determinist (though this word did not come into use until the nineteenth century), in what sense can he also be called a humanist? One book about him is divided into two parts, the first about his materialism and the second about his humanism.[8] This seems too schematic, but how may we put both "isms" into the same frame? Aram Vartanian labels Diderot a "dualist in spite of himself."[9] This is suggestive, but dualism also implies a separation, so perhaps the way his supple intellect moves between different points of view is better captured by a label like perspectivism that allows for a degree of flexibility.

Diderot first seriously engaged the problem of fitting together material and moral man in the so-called "Letter to Landois," pursued it in *Refutation of a Work Entitled 'On Man' by Helvétius,* and, by implication rather than direct argument, rounded out his view in the novel *Jacques the Fatalist and His Master.* This sequence will now be my concern, before a summing up.

Landois was an earnest but untalented writer who, having contributed a few articles to the *Encyclopedia,* then wrote an angry letter to Diderot in 1756 about slow payment, lack of comment on his work, and the malignant way in which he was treated by the world in general. According to P. N. Furbank, whose excellent pages on the subject I draw upon, the Landois letter, though it has not survived, probably made jibes at the hypocrisy of "virtue."[10] Recognizing an occasion for a clarifying statement of principle, Diderot wrote an important rejoinder, which may never have been sent but was published by his friend Grimm and is known as the "Letter to Landois." It explained that virtue is not opposed to the passions (the traditional view) but only helps us choose among them. Everything we do we do for our own sake, but this is obscured by the fact that we have conflicting desires (perhaps an anticipation of some theorizing in modern evolutionary psychology about multiple mental "modules" as an explanation of why human behavior is not always adaptive in the Darwinian sense). We do not choose what we desire, we cannot want to want, and so the "act of choice is a banal little event," as he pointed out in the article on Will in the *Encyclopedia.* But we think we have free will because we are aware of willing.

As early as *Philosophical Thoughts* Diderot had defended both "virtue" and "the passions," but hadn't coordinated them. Here he does so, and so I will amplify Furbank's description and analysis by noting that the "Letter" interestingly anticipates two important later thinkers. One is Kant who remarked in the *Critique of Practical Freedom* that it is possible to regard the same event as being, in one aspect, merely an effect of nature and, in another aspect, the result of freedom. The other is the contemporary biologist E. O. Wilson who writes, in his influential book *Consilience,* that, although freedom of the will is an illusion, we believe in it because of our conscious effort (given our partial ignorance of the determining causes) in choosing.

But Wilson's view, be it noted, is not quite perspectival in my sense of the word. It comes at the problem only from the scientific point of view, never entering, as the literary man does, into the subjective world of the chooser. Diderot would have understood what Wilson calls the "unity of knowledge" more flexibly, ready as he always was to move between a scientific and a humanistic point of view. As he commented neatly in "Elements of Physiology," "man is both a book and the reader of that book." Shuttling between these perspectives was basic to his thinking. Addressing the same problem, Kant later described it as "the antinomy of freedom," and Nietzsche, that consummate perspectivist, similarly distinguished between freedom spontaneously experienced and the intellect's knowledge that everything is causally determined. Sharpening Nietzsche's phrasing to the point of paradox, one of his biographers puts it this way: "we live from freedom, but when we try to analyze it, it cannot be grasped."[11]

Diderot returned to the issue of free will when he had to explain what was unsatisfactory about the reductive determinism of Helvétius's treatise *De L'Homme*, which he read and re-read during the 1770s, not because of its intrinsic merit but because of the direct way it challenged him to articulate a broader view of the nature of man. For Helvétius, all human behavior was the result of sensation and environment. It was a purely quantitative theory of self-interest that anticipates in some respects Bentham's calculus of pleasure and pain, and Diderot's response, as Arthur M. Wilson suggests, to some extent resembles John Stuart Mill's response to Bentham.[12] Diderot did not want to dispute the issue of determinism as such and thereby abandon the materialist hypothesis, but he took a more complex view of human nature. Helvétius left out too much. Men act as well as react, judge as well as feel, find pleasure in doing and thinking as well as in sensing. For Helvétius people are interchangeable counters, as if (said Diderot nicely) he has never observed children. For Diderot, people were not only different from one another but their minds were plastic, modifiable by education. This seems to compromise his determinism, but I think it is a only a way of saying people are agents as well as objects, are readers of the book as well as the book itself. Arthur M. Wilson says that "the effect of Helvétius's ideas upon Diderot was to strengthen and deepen Diderot's humanism,"[13] which is certainly true, but let us add that his humanism and materialism are best understood as differing perspectives that sometimes clash, in which case they can be coordinated only with irony. Which brings us to *Jacques the Fatalist and His Master*.

Quoting some of the first page or two will provide a basis for pertinent commentary:

> How did they meet? By chance like everyone else. What were there their names? What's that got to do with you? Where were they coming from? From the nearest place. Where were they going to? Does anyone ever really know where they are going to? What were they saying? The master wasn't saying anything and Jacques was saying that his Captain used to say that everything which happens on this earth [*ici-bas*], both good and bad, is written up above [*là haut*]....
> *The Master*. And you stopped the bullet with your name on it.
> *Jacques*. You've guessed it. Shot in the knee. And God knows the good and bad fortunes brought about by that shot....
> So you can see, Reader, that I am well away, and that it's entirely within my power to make you wait a year, or two, or even three years for the story of Jacques' loves, by separating him from his master and exposing each of them to whatever perils I liked.[14]

Vartanian observes that "Jacques *acts* on the assumption of freedom, but theorizes on the assumption of necessity."[15] That discrepancy does indeed lead us directly to what is puzzling in the book, but the statement doesn't go far enough, for the narrator handles the reader much the way Jacques handles his ostensible master (whom he is destined to overturn in the narrative), and one could say of the narrator that, *like* Jacques, he acts on the assumption of freedom and theorizes on the assumption of *chance*. Necessity and Chance are linked in the conceptual underpinning of this Sterne-influenced mock-novel as metaphysical forces that rule our lives from *above*, and are not consistent with the materialistic premises of Diderot's thought. It is sometimes said that this novel mocks the Spinozistic universe, and this is partly true, but one needs to add that, in Spinoza's scheme, freedom is not something opposed to necessity but is fused with it. Diderot, in contrast, wants to dramatize the ironic tension between freedom and necessity (or chance), between the belief that we are able to choose versus the belief that choice is already determined.

The notion of fatalism in the novel is too often associated with determinism, an awkward association since Diderot didn't have the latter word, and an inaccurate one as well. To be a fatalist is to believe that all our actions are compelled by forces beyond our power and thus to make a mockery of freedom, as Jacques in his pronouncements does, but to be a determinist (even *avant la lettre*) is to believe merely, as Diderot did, that every event has a material cause. Such a belief does not mock our ability to act on the assumption of freedom, even if that assumption is, from the materialist's point of view, an illusion (or what the cognitive scientist Steven Pinker calls an "idealization"). The "Letter to Landois" sought to demonstrate logically that morality was not opposed to the involuntary passions. The *Refutation of Helvétius* argued that the complex human being thinks and acts as well as merely sensing and being acted upon. And *Jacques the Fatalist* turns away from philosophical arguing to literary showing, to exploit with nimble wit the irony and comedy of the two perspectives clashing—and clashing four times over: within Jacques, within the narrator, in the relation between Jacques and his master, in the relation between narrator and reader.

For the 1772 New Year celebration at Holbach's house, Diderot composed satiric verse, as he had on the two previous anniversaries, for the private pleasure of his friends. On this occasion his elaborate piece (entitled *Les Eleuthéromanes*, "Maniacs for freedom") adopted a classic verse form that licensed anger, probably because Louis XV had just angered a number of libertarians by stripping *Parlement* of its authority and thus taking a serious step toward tyranny. One inflammatory distich in Diderot's festive ode ("And for want of a rope his hands will knot/ The guts of the priest to strangle kings") had the misfortune of being published in 1795, after his death, and, according to Furbank (to whom I am indebted for an account of this incident), "it was seized on with outraged zest by the enemies of the Revolution, and for many years afterwards it would earn Diderot a reputation as an arch Jacobin."[16]

I make a point of this because, while Diderot was certainly libertarian and egalitarian in his political sympathies and became more so toward the end of his life, he was not a radical revolutionary, and this fact contributes to the complexity of his overall stance. Impulsive as he was, he also had a realistic sense of what could be done and even what prudently should be done in view of the superior power of state and church. This is clearly evident in two of his shorter dialogic works, "Conversation of a Father with his Children" and "Conversation with a Christian Lady." In the first, "Denis" waxes justifiably indignant at a manifestly unjust law which ought to be disobeyed, but the last word is given to his kindly father who is pleased that someone is around who thinks as his son does but also relieved that there are not many such around, potential subverters of government. In the second, the figure standing in for Diderot demonstrates to a charming titled lady that her reliance on religion is purely conventional, and not at all a necessary support for the morality of her behavior, but when she finally turns to ask whether *he* would tell the truth about his irreligion before magistrates or would receive last rites near death, he says he would compromise his principles, an untroubled hypocrite. The tone throughout their conversation is gallant and gracious, a little testament to the highly civilized discourse possible in the days of the *ancien régime*.

It is remarkable that the pre-Revolutionary atheism of Diderot, even allowing for his uniqueness, should be relatively free of doubt and anguish, compared to the agonized religious doubting that we find throughout the nineteenth century. Various reasons for this difference have been offered, and I want to touch on two of them. One is that most of the *philosophes* were able to believe in progress, aware of dramatic gains already made and sensing that the very oppressiveness of the Monarchy and the Church made their power vulnerable to further modification. (The horrors of the Revolution and its aftermath they could, of course, not foresee.) The other is that they were ignorant not only of the failure of the Revolution but also of "the inward turn" that drove the deity out of the heavens only to reinstate him within the human mind where he was more difficult to dislodge. Diderot, for all his sophistication, was free of the sort of self-consciousness that would beset, among many others, Büchner, Nietzsche, Twain, and Hardy.

The Post-Revolutionary Atheism of Georg Büchner

Büchner too embraced an atheistic materialism and wrestled with the deterministic moral philosophy that it entailed, a position made more difficult by the fact that, unlike Diderot, he *was* also a passionate revolutionary. He was keenly disappointed by the collapse of the French Revolution's ideals, and tried hard in his short, intense life to organize a Society for the Rights of Man, but, when he abandoned his efforts to overthrow the Hessian regime and fled to Strasbourg to escape imprisonment, his outlook came to be pervaded by a sense of historical necessity and of man's helplessness in the face of it. The Enlightenment commitment to reason and the acknowledgment of a Supreme Being that he found in Voltaire are repudiated throughout his small *oeuvre*,[17] whose anguished general theme is, "if God existed, he could not endure the senseless suffering to which man is subject."[18]

On the basis of his study of the French Revolution, Büchner strongly opposed the idealist view of history that he found in Hegel and Fichte. If he had lived longer, he probably would have opposed Marx's utopianism as well, although sharing his sympathy with the oppressed. While working on *Danton's Death* he wrote in a letter: "[Studying the Revolution] I feel as though I had been annihilated by the dreadful fatalism of history. I find a terrible uniformity in human nature, an inexorable force, conferred upon all and none, in human circumstances. The individual: mere foam on the wave, greatness pure chance, the mastery of genius a puppet play, a ridiculous struggle against an iron law to acknowledge which is the highest good, to defeat impossible."[19]

This suggests the antiheroic nature of the work being composed, but its author is too bitter for resignation. The letter goes on to find the word "must" that appears to govern both human history and human psychology a "damned word." Büchner's first work, a pamphlet called "The Hessian Messenger" (although toned down considerably by his collaborator, Ludwig Weidig), sounds like a mixture of biblical jeremiad, Zola's *J'accuse,* and the screeds of the young Shelley directed at the reactionaries of England. Doubtless his great play is set in the midst of the Revolution so that some of this ardor could still be appropriately expressed, although it is ardor dampened by a sense of failure deriving from the lack of present political opportunity. His subsequent works, Victor Price comments, showed that "his political convictions were undercut by a sense of the pointlessness of life."[20]

Büchner was a serious scientist as well as a writer, working in medicine and biology, and he represented his characters with clinical precision and objectivity, but, in doing so, he could not suppress a cry of pain. This contradiction helps to account for the extraordinary tension that critics find in his work and for the adjectives they regularly use to describe it—powerful, relentless, inexorable, passionate, personal, bitter, and the like.

The description of *Danton's Death* as "antiheroic" is certainly apt, and has been well developed by Herbert Lindenberger, who subtitles his chapter on the play "Antirhetoric and Dramatic Form," and by Victor Brombert, who discusses it in a book titled *In Praise of Antiheroes*.[21] Danton himself is of course the central antihero, a character who, as Lindenberger puts it, keeps defining throughout the play the idea that life is "essentially a series of games which we play to pass our time away and to remind us as rarely as possible of the great emptiness that stares at us from behind the surfaces of things." Lindenberger is particularly perceptive in contrasting Danton's natural tone and lively sense of metaphor to Robespierre's cliché-ridden deadness of language and tendency to use abstractions like Vice and Virtue.[22] But we should notice that, if not a hero of action, Danton is in fact a hero of insight.

There is little progressive movement in the play, but Danton, though doomed (as the title implies), begins with a margin of hope and gradually achieves, as he approaches death, a full realization of "the iron law" of history. He is someone who can acknowledge this law, and is the only character allowed a glimpse of the future, of the condemnation of Robespierre himself and of the dictatorship to follow. Finally, he realizes that even death will not bring him peace: "If the greatest peace of all is God, doesn't it follow that nothingness is God? But I'm an atheist. That damned argument: something cannot become nothing, there's the misery."

We will return to this curious and interesting "countertheology" presently, but first it is important to show that the character called Thomas Paine is also a hero of insight, linked to Danton not only in terms of patriotism (Danton says to him: "What you did for the good of your country I tried to do for mine") but also as an epicurean. He explains, in terms of this philosophy, how the actions of people can be imagined as both determined by their natures and yet in some sense heroic as well. Lindenberger sees that Paine "expounds views not much different from Danton's own," but I think mistakes his role somewhat when he goes on to say that, "though generally a sympathetic character in the one scene in which he appears, [Paine] expresses views as a dogmatist, passionately and earnestly [whereas] Danton is beyond that."[23] Precisely because Danton cannot expatiate on his views without becoming less convincing as the drama's central character, Büchner needs a figure like Paine to fill in the conceptual underpinning. Nor is Paine quite a dogmatist. Rather, he *has his own way* of being authentically antirhetorical. His first few speeches (delivered to Chaumette, nicknamed Anaxagoras because he claims to be an atheist) are indeed catechistic in form and dogmatic in tone, leading the critic Ronald Hauser to infer that he has built "a catechetic haven for himself,"[24] but we soon discover that Paine is himself *mocking* the pedantry of theological speculation in order to demonstrate that falling back on reason doesn't work, for you cannot "explain an imperfect effect proceeding from a perfect cause." Voltaire did so only because "he didn't dare break with gods any more than with kings." Once this intent made clear to us, Paine speaks passionately:

> Why go through that rigmarole [i.e., the ingenuities of theological argument] just to make ourselves out the sons of God? I prefer a lesser father; at least I can't reproach him with educating me beneath my station, in a pigsty or in the galleys. Do away with imperfection; that's the only way you'll prove the existence of God. Spinoza tried it. We can deny evil but not pain. Only reason can prove God. The senses reject

Him. Take note, Anaxagoras, Why do I suffer? That is the rock of my atheism. The least twinge of pain, should it convulse a single atom, splits creation from top to bottom.

It is of little importance that the historical Paine was himself a deist, not an atheist. Büchner is getting at something original and impressive here. Theodicies like *Paradise Lost* and Pope's *An Essay on Man* understood pain and suffering as part of the evil of life that could be justified eventually by Christian faith in a providential will. Büchner, on the other hand, pointedly distinguishes pain (*Schmerz*) and suffering (*Leid*) from evil (*Böse*). For Evil can be explained away, as it was by Spinoza, who ascribed it to inadequate understanding. But if we are bound by our bodies, then pain and suffering can never be justified, and they cry out that the world we inhabit is forever imperfect. Even the cynical Laflotte in *Danton's Death*, ready to betray the prisoners, endorses in an aside the Paine-Danton-Büchner view: "pain is the only sin and suffering the only vice." A political solution to the problem of pain is implied, but it is too utopian to be more than another cry of pain: do away with imperfection, and then we can call ourselves children of God.

How is so intensely moral a position compatible with a deterministic philosophy that, like Diderot's, belittles freedom of the will? A further speech of Paine's addresses this question: "First you prove God from morality and then morality from God! What's the point of your morality? I don't know whether there's anything good or bad *per se*. I don't have to change my way of life on that account. I act according to my nature. What suits it is good for me, and I do it. What's contrary to it is bad for me, and I don't do it." That is to say, Büchner, like Diderot and to some extent like Schopenhauer (without direct influence in either case), shows that choice is merely the superficial aspect of desire itself, the foam on the wave. There is no resort to a dualism of mind and body, though Büchner protests the contradictory human situation and Diderot speculates on it with lively irony.

In the play it is of course Danton, the natural man, the epicurean, who embodies and expresses a deterministic position with most dramatic authority, confronting Robespierre, the disciple of Rousseau and apostle of Virtue, known as the Incorruptible. Throughout the play Robespierre talks of virtue and vice, one crushing the other, apart from actual people and their feelings. Here is the key exchange between him and Danton, an exchange that significantly connects Christ with Epicureanism, a way of linking Christ with the admirable but altogether human antiheroism of Danton:

ROBESPIERRE: You deny the existence of virtue?
DANTON: And of vice. There are only Epicureans, coarse ones and fine ones. Christ was the finest. That's the only difference between men that I've been able to discover. Everyone acts according to his nature—in other words he does what does him good.

Christ as exemplary Epicurean obeys as he must the law of *his* nature, and Danton identifies himself with this idea of Christ. So, up to a point anyway, does Robespierre, who in a possibly sympathetic soliloquy speaks of "the Son of Man...crucified in all of us [as we] writhe in bloody sweat in the Garden of Gethsemane." It's hard to know whether the stress here falls on the speaker's pomposity or on the idea that Robespierre too, like Danton and the Epicurean Christ, must obey the law of his nature, for in other works by Büchner there are are also troubled characters associated with Christ—Woyzeck for one and also Lenz who at one point in his anguish tries (but fails) to raise a child from the dead.

The play is set in the spring of 1794 when the Terror reigned. Danton had helped to bring about the present situation but is now disillusioned, even fatalistic about what will come, though also, in odd spurts, ironic, thoughtful, and indignant. When the play finally found its audience fifty years after Büchner's death (thanks to the Naturalistic movement in German drama led by Gerhard Hauptmann), what took most getting used to was not only that the collage-like arrangement of scenes did not seem to constitute a plot with a rising and falling action but also that the protagonist Danton seemed too passive. But clearly Danton is meant in the play not merely to be destined for death but to think about death. Diderot had said the question "*why anything exists* is the most embarrassing that philosophy could ever have asked itself," and suggested puckishly that "only revelation can answer it."[25] Büchner's materialism, expressed in Danton's meditation quoted earlier, comes at the question from the other end—how can something, the created world, turn into nothing? And if it cannot, if there is no nothingness, then the created world is a wound, a perpetual hopelessness, and so may be called a perpetual severance from God. Indeed, the intensity of Büchner's pity seems to spring from the perception that human beings are forever deprived of God. Maurice Benn commented perceptively: "If [men] were creatures of God there would be hope for them; but they appear to [Büchner] like lost children, without a father and without hope—and it is precisely this hopelessness that inflames his pity."[26] Danton embodies this pity. He is the character who broods most on decomposition and decay, on the subversion of any political hope for man by the very meaninglessness of the universe.

Danton is passive without being a static characterization. He speaks of boredom without being boring. The charm of the natural man, touched by a sense of futility, is expressed in his relations with women and with friends, and in several scenes he mounts a dignified protest against Robespierre and all he represents. But Robespierre too is allowed for a moment to despair, a bit like Claudius in the prayer scene of *Hamlet*. After speaking rigidly of vice and virtue to Danton, we find him alone on stage asking himself a series of hard questions and even wondering (like Danton and Paine) if he *wills* his own acts: "Are not our actions dream actions, only more sharply defined, more complete?...Whether thought becomes action, whether the body carries it out, is mere chance."

The hard objectivity with which all of the characters are presented does not come across as coldness because, while there is little conventional sentiment bestowed on individuals, there is much pity generated for the human situation itself. Büchner discovers his characters in extreme states and situations, often near or in a state of madness. While the major characters of *Danton's Death* manage, with some effort, to maintain a hold on sanity, Danton's friend Camille Desmoulins is driven very near to madness when condemned to death, and his wife Lucille is driven *over* the edge. Danton's wife Julie, contrary to the historical record (she remarried and outlived even Büchner), commits suicide in one brief but strong scene. Woyzeck's half-madness is memorable (thanks in part no doubt to Alban Berg's opera), and J. M. R. Lenz (the Storm and Stress poet with whom Büchner clearly identifies) draws back from his madness only at the end, after much anguish. In a letter Büchner concisely explained this aspect of his art, saying, "my laughter is not at *how* a human being is but rather at the fact *that* he is a human being; about which he can do nothing; and at the same time I laugh at myself because I must share in his fate."[27]

Because Büchner's atheism is not rooted in skeptical speculation but in horror that the world is so, it is volatile and even in some sense religious. He experiences the impotence of God with extraordinary keenness. In Michael Hamburger's words: "Wherever atheism occurs in his work...it is as revolt, experienced with an intensity that can be described as religious."[28] I don't think this makes him a believer, but it does confront us with his very remarkable deathbed utterance that has been construed by some as a statement of faith: "We do not suffer too much pain, indeed we suffer too little, for through our pain we are brought nearer to God."²⁹ This seems to contradict the protest that runs through his work against pain and suffering; it seems to let pity slide into resignation. Perhaps deathbed words at odds with the drift of one's published work should not be emphasized, but in fact these words touch on a truth imbedded in the author's vision. For to say that pain is the rock of one's atheism is also to imply that it is in the most extreme state that one is most aware of the terrible absence of God. Another way of stating the point, a way that helps to justify the image of *approaching* God, is that Büchner is identifying his own extraordinary pity with the unrealized and *unrealizable* pity of God. On his author's behalf surely, Lenz spoke these words, which were found blasphemous by his pastor-friend: "If I were almighty, if I were that, I could not endure this suffering; I would save Man from it, save him. All I ask is rest, rest, just a little rest."

Beyond Religion: Friedrich Nietzsche

The books known to have influenced Nietzsche in his youth included materialist and anti-theological classics like *Force and Matter* by Ludwig Büchner (Georg's brother), *History of Materialism* by F. A. Lange, Feuerbach's *Essence of Christianity,* and D. F. Strauss's *Life of Jesus Critically Examined*—books that he read against a background of the Higher Criticism and emerging Darwinist science.³⁰ He soon turned from the study of theology (his father had been a Lutheran pastor) to classical philology and then to philosophy. We know that what attracted him most in Schopenhauer, his chief precursor in the work he was to undertake, was not only the assumption of atheism, which supported his own materialist bias, but also the psychological interest in the will, which would lead him to probe extensively into the *motives* of religious belief. Like Freud after him, Nietzsche achieved some of his keenest insights in asking not *what* people believe but *why*. Yet his own temper was enthusiastic as well as critical, positive as well as skeptical. Although he was too independent to accept the beliefs of others, especially the untenable beliefs cherished by the religion he knew that there were universal moral truths and that all moral agents were the same, he himself was seeking something not against but *beyond* religion, something he found in the volatile spirit of creativity itself.

The principal agent that jolted Nietzsche into the kind of oppositional stance we regard as characteristic of him was, I think, Darwin. He had to express his profound agreement obliquely because his heroic cast of mind protested against thinking of individuals, especially exceptional ones, in terms of mass behavior. For Darwin, progress was measured by the success of species rather than individuals whereas for Nietzsche "the feeling of being STRONGER, quite aside from its usefulness in the struggle [with others], is the real progress: it is from this feeling that the will to struggle first arises."[31] But it was the premise of man-beast kinship on which he pivoted to explain this will to struggle, so brilliantly conveyed in the opening pages of "History in the Service and Disservice of Life." True, he in effect acknowledges there, human beings are also animals, but the beasts live "unhistorically" whereas human beings grow to maturity under an ever-increasing burden of the past, a past that would crush their spirit unless they could to some extent forget or repress it. "Without forgetting, it is utterly impossible to live at all." Spurred by Darwin, Nietzsche is arguing for a dynamic understanding of the human past and against what he saw as the "modern" tendency to see history only as benign process and accumulated knowledge. (Hence the title of the book in which his essay was published, Unmodern [*Unzeitgemässe*] Observations.) History serves as well as disserves life, but there must be a *counterthrust* as well, "the strength to develop uniquely from within to transform and assimilate the past."[32]

This dynamically oppositional cast of mind afforded Nietzsche fresh insight into the way religions maintain their grounding. They wish to believe that the morality they embrace is absolute, derived from a metaphysical God. And because many believers scarcely understood that they were thus making a false objectification of morality, Nietzsche exposed their thinking with penetrating irony. Under the heading of "God's honesty," he writes: "Would he not be a cruel god if he possessed the truth and could behold mankind miserably tormenting itself over the truth?—But perhaps he is a god of goodness notwithstanding—and merely *could* not express himself more clearly! Did he perhaps lack the intelligence to do so? Or the eloquence?"[33] The mockery becomes increasingly mordant, almost Beckettian, for it is *our* lack of honesty and not God's that is in question.

One of the most original aspects of Nietzsche's thinking is the genealogical method he developed to analyze the process by which morality came to be divinized. He did not ask whether a theistic idea was true or false but how it originated and gained its power. Thus he was not concerned, as former atheists had been, with mere refutation: "In former times, one sought to prove that there is no God—today one indicates how the belief that there is a God could *arise* and how this belief acquired its might and importance: a counter-proof that there is no God thereby becomes superfluous. When in former times one had 'refuted the proofs of the existence of God' put forward, there always remained the doubt whether better proofs might not be adduced than those just refuted: in those days atheists did not know how to make a clean sweep."[34]

Kant and Schopenhauer had already done much to question the metaphysical basis of Christian morality, but they hadn't gone far enough, hadn't made a "clean sweep." After removing this support in the *Critique of Pure Reason*, Kant turned around in the *Critique of Practical Reason* and seemed to re-enthrone, by way of the categorical imperative, the old postulates of God, freedom of the will, and immortality. That so immensely sophisticated a thinker as Kant could do this impressed Nietzsche, as it showed how tenacious was the human need to universalize morality. Despite his emphasis on the will, Schopenhauer too gave us little insight into the origin of moral ideas because he was mesmerized by the power of aesthetic contemplation to release us from the will's base compulsions, and so endorsed the Christian idealization of self-denial, self-sacrifice, and compassion.[35] Nietzsche made a similar point about George Eliot and the English in general, who are "rid of the Christian God and are now all the more convinced that they have to hold on to Christian morality."[36]

He was calling into question our tendency to protect moral truth from analysis rather than such truth itself. But this can be easily misunderstood because of the forcefulness of his assault on *the* truth. A striking statement such as "There is no such thing as moral phenomena, but only a moral interpretation of phenomena" sounds like the veriest relativism.[37] But we must be careful here. Yes, what seems to us the truth about the world is produced by interpretation; as Arthur Danto puts it, the world of Nietzsche "has no structure...and takes whatever form we give it."[38] But the reason why we should not confuse interpretation with fact, why we should not locate truth in the world external to our minds, is that doing so leads us to create single, overarching explanations and prevents us from understanding that moral truth is necessarily grounded in the strength of individual judgment, in *perspective*, "that fundamental condition of all life," according to the preface to *Beyond Good and Evil*. A less startling and therefore more persuasive way of expressing this idea is found in the *Notebooks of the Early 1870s*: "All knowledge originates from separation, delimitation, and restriction; there is no absolute knowledge of the whole."

The pertinent difference between Nietzschean perspectivism and what is called relativism is ably explained by Robert C. Solomon. Interpretations, Solomon writes, are not abstractly isolated "from any context in which they might be evaluated.... There is *always* such a context, and it is defined in part by the character and circumstances of the person who holds the interpretation." But insightful interpretation generally includes more factual evidence, and that is why it is likely to collide with other interpretations rather than simply to go its own way, one of an infinite number. As Solomon makes clear, Nietzsche's main argument here is directed against the habit of religious believers to assert that there is a moral point of view *in itself*.[39]

From his early, important essay, "On Truth and Lie in an Extra-Moral Sense," Nietzsche suggested that what we call truths are metaphors that we have forgotten are metaphors, and thus "lies" or "errors." But we cannot, of course, discard them. The difficult wisdom to be learned is that "truth is the kind of error without which a certain species of life could not live."[40] Fields of knowledge that generate warmer emotion, like religion and the arts, are at greater risk here, but science is not exempt, as shown by its own tendency (as Nietzsche knew it) to theologize. To speak for example of the laws or purposes of nature is to imply the existence of some sort of supreme intelligence. Nietzsche wanted us to understand that, while Darwin's science had unsettled religion, it could not do the work of religion, for he knew that scientists mythologized according to their emotional need as well as seeking objective truth. Science is at its best, he believed (and most modern scientists would agree), when its aims are more modest, when it does not try to address the big questions addressed by religion, philosophy, and the arts.

Nietzsche's basic respect for science has been underestimated, partly because his preoccupation with the will to power blurred his (and our) thinking on the matter. He tells us that science, with its greater reserve, is in a better position than religion and the arts to understand itself as only one among other interpretive practices, not uniquely privileged. In one important and neglected section of *Human, All Too Human* brought to our attention by Rüdiger Safranski, Nietzsche writes of the scientific outlook, because of its detachment and commitment to objectivity, as enabling us to better understand the *relation* between perspectives. From that vantage we see how the the "cool regulator" of the intellect is opposed to the "hot power source" of the emotions. In this passage, he is arguing that neither intellect nor emotion should dominate or suppress the other. In fact, "a higher culture must give man a double-brain, two brain chambers, as it were, one to experience science, and one to experience nonscience."[41] Safranski comments that, had this double-brain idea (called by *his* translator "the bicameral system of culture") not vanished from the late work, "Nietzsche might well have spared himself some of his mad visions of grand politics and the will to power."[42]

Because religion, more than other discourses, tended to dogmatize about morality, "atheism" was a particularly liberating idea. Atheism meant in general the philosopher's freedom to question everything. "The man of faith, the 'believer' of every sort is necessarily a dependent man,"[43] but for the creative man, intellectual dependence is hardly tolerable. As Zarathustra put it, "what could one create if gods existed?"[44] Indeed, "a complete and definitive victory of atheism might deliver mankind altogether from its feeling of indebtedness" and thus constitute "a second innocence."[45]

"Definitive victory" expresses Nietzsche's philosophic aim in its utopian aspect, evoking the possibility of a dissolution of existing values. But such dissolution poses also the prospect of "weightlessness," "the void," "nihilism." In a utopian mood, Nietzsche like Zarathustra pictures "the higher man" as a free-floating self-creator, laughing and elevated at once. In *The Gay Science* this picture is called "our cheerfulness" and ascribed to the bracing prospect of an "open sea" and a "new dawn" wherein "all weight is to be determined anew."[46] Nihilism was potentially a creative matrix, allowing for a rethinking of fundamentals. *The Will to Power* begins by asking "What does nihilism mean?" and answers, "*That the highest values devaluate themselves* [because] 'why' finds no answer."[47] In his multi-volume study of his predecessor, Heidegger singles out this passage to demonstrate that Nietzsche is not looking at nihilism discouragedly from without but thinking of it as a reversal from within that is meant to generate a creative countermove.[48]

Given this much contextualization of the terms atheism and nihilism in Nietzsche's philosophy, let us turn to "God is dead," the notorious cry in the parable of the madman from *The Gay Science* (#125).

Because the Christian God is a cultural rather than supernatural phenomenon, to say that he is dead is to suggest that a certain theistic idea (God the Father, God the Judge, God who died in pity for men) has lost its significance in the modern age. But Nietzsche hardly wished to live in a morally insignificant age and was therefore concerned that others, unprepared for the challenge to replace the "death" of God out of their own self-making, belittled the event's importance. The parable is full of ironic implications, and I will spell out three of them here.

Those hearing the madman "did not believe in God" and so "laugh" at his cry as if he were raving. They think they have discarded the metaphysics of religious faith but are retaining it through their faith in the moral coherence of their world. They fear that the destruction of such coherence would "wipe away the entire horizon," and thereby induce a sense of weightlessness, of "straying...through an infinite nothing." To say with Nietzsche that god is dead, writes Richard Rorty, is to say that human beings "serve no higher purposes,"[49] but the listeners are not prepared to live in so undefined a world. They understandably fear "an infinite nothing," because "if you gaze for long into an abyss, the abyss gazes back into you."[50]

The second implication has three aspects. The parable is given to us by by a madman because, first, only a madman can break the grip of custom and so prepare the way for a new understanding; second, someone possessed of the knowledge that God is dead is maddened by it (he *has* looked into the abyss); and, third, being "mad" or clowning is a way of recognizing the fact that others are not ready for one's knowledge. It takes time to "vanquish a shadow" and go beyond religion altogether. The madman is an anti-Christ or even a new Christ, knowing that for the tidings he brings "my time is not yet."

The third implication of the parable that I think worth clarifying here is that it presents ideas as events. It says that "we ourselves" or "they themselves" have already done the murderous deed yet also that "the event is on the way." Although it is illogical to talk about an event as both behind and before us, it makes sense if one is talking about the movement of ideas, especially about the unconscious or underlying tendency in such movement. When people at last understand their condition, they will have need of a new bible, like *Thus Spoke Zarathustra* about to be written. For the need to believe outlives the death of God. People do not wish life to be void of purpose.

One can see why Karl Jaspers wrote that Nietzsche "found in atheism not simply a loss but rather the greatest opportunity."[51] In fact, what has unsettled Nietzsche's readers more than his atheism is the appearance in his work of moral relativism, a topic to which we now return. It makes little sense to call Nietzsche a moral relativist since his own pages are full of strong assertions, which, for all their ironies, are evidently asking to be taken seriously. But if "convictions are prisons" (as he puts it in *Ecce Homo*), what then about his own convictions? Alexander Nehamas resolves the paradox by explaining that, while Nietzsche knows that his truths are views, he knows also that for him they are truths. The implied model here is the literary text, about which the sophisticated interpreter would say neither that one view is absolute nor that it is no better than any other, for one view can be stronger and more persuasive than another. To understand this "most literary of philosophers," Nehamas writes, we must see that his "aestheticism is the other side of his perspectivism." And he demonstrates skillfully how his variety of styles supports this idea, for varying styles *show* perspectives without undermining their force by *saying* they are perspectives.[52]

Challenging Nehamas, Peter Berkowitz in *Nietzsche: The Ethics of an Immoralist* insists that a moralist's views must be understood as *either* universally binding *or* false, and that, because Nietzsche "takes definite sides on questions of morality," his "perspectivism is not, as Nehamas characterizes it, opposed to dogmatism, but rather is a contemporary form of dogmatism."[53] This is falsely to suppose that the forcefulness of his language proves that Nietzsche makes no distinction between the artist's ardor that takes sides on moral questions and the philosopher's more discriminating and detached judgment. Berkowitz's challenge illustrates well the particular difficulty that a literary philosopher—one whose philosophy includes an uncommon interest in the strong subjectivity of artist and moralist—presents to an either-or moralist, who is in this case the real dogmatist.

Nehamas observes that "it is hard to avoid the suspicion that Nietzsche had little of positive value to say."[54] *The Will to Power* talks of meaninglessness as a "transitional stage," but stage to what? His goals are vague, inevitably, given his resistance to teleological thinking. Yet of course his positive tone is unmistakable. He idealized as energetically as he questioned. He unstintingly admired the nobility of ancient Greek culture; found exemplary status in Wagner and Schopenhauer before his break with the one and disagreements with the other; never ceased to admire the Olympian Goethe, whom he later called Dionysian after that word acquired new meaning for him; and about Emerson's work, cherished from youth, he wrote, "I have never in a book felt myself so much at home....I dare not praise it, it is so close to me."[55] Moreover, words like "joy," "affirmation," "life-enhancing," "health," and "strength" pervade his work and intensify his rhetoric. Carl Jung remarked that Nietzsche was too positive a spirit to be an atheist,[56] and this is certainly true if you understand atheism as merely a form of denial. But repudiation of God was for him the necessary prelude to the bracing and open-ended work of self-creation. I will therefore round out my picture of Nietzsche as literary atheist by commenting in turn on his three most notable slogans—*Ubermensch*, Will to Power, and Eternal Return—to show how each clarifies his effort to think beyond religion without creating a new religion.

Nietzsche liked to distinguish "noble" and "base" types of human being and culture. The one is "complete, wholly successful, happy, powerful, triumphant"; the other is "more good-natured, cleverer, more comfortable, more mediocre...more Christian."[57] But such wording by itself can be misleading if used to define the *Ubermensch*, for in *Zarathustra*, where the "overman" is most fully articulated, the most distinctive attributes are not stability or serenity but an endless becoming and strenuous self-overcoming. The *Ubermensch* thrives on opposition, digests pain, absorbs suffering. It was Nietzsche, after all, who more than anyone taught us (in *The Birth of Tragedy*) that the complete and successful art of ancient Greece was infused by a strong Dionysian element—"how much did this people have to suffer to be able to become so beautiful!"[58] The *Ubermensch*, then, is perhaps best seen as a prophetic figure, not a person who has already overcome the all-too-human self but one ever in the process of doing so. The English translation closest in spirit to this idea, though awkward, is "the beyond man," used by George J. Stack. For the single quality that best defines the type is exuberance. It signifies creative energy rather than fixed form, a process rather than a realization, a potential man (both anti-Christ and anti-nihilist) who would emerge at some future time.

The "Will to Power," not worked out definitively before Nietzsche's collapse but too important to be ignored, also denotes a kind of instinctual energy. It is best understood in relation to Schopenhauer"s Will, which it seeks to revise.[59] The latter is conceived too simply as mere instinct or drive, without a dynamic sense of what stimulates it or what it opposes. There is no point in writing as Schopenhauer does about the unfreedom of the will. People speak of the unfreedom of their will as an excuse to blame others for their suffering, and speak of its freedom as an excuse to blame themselves and endure masochistically a Christian conscience. The real point, more cruel perhaps (because assuredly not democratic), is that wills are not free or unfree but strong and weak. To speak like Schopenhauer of self-preservation or like Darwin of the struggle for existence implies that the will is merely natural rather than a will to superiority, a will to be other than nature. If one thinks of it in connection with art, as Nietzsche usually does, then surely Stendhal understood it better than Kant or Schopenhauer when he wrote of art stimulating rather than quieting the mind. In short, the Will to Power is not a natural given but a creatively active displacement of divine agency.

The Eternal Return, introduced in *The Gay Science* and developed in *Zarathustra* and thereafter, is a still more complex concept, and in truth not quite coherent. It is perhaps best explicated by detouring through Nietzsche's analysis of the "ascetic ideal."

The story of the Christian conscience goes something like this. Once upon a time there were the noble Greeks, whose legacy was, alas, pushed aside by ignoble Christianity and its later complement, democracy. The gods of their polytheistic religion did not judge or pity human beings, and through their acts kept bad conscience at a distance. Thus the Greeks were beyond *ressentiment*, the mainspring of "the slave rebellion in morals" initiated by Judeo-Christianity. In the case of Epicurus, for example, pain was a source of strength whereas for Christians it became a source of fear.

Like others after him who have speculated on the decline of the West, Nietzsche does not know exactly whom to blame for this degradation. Perhaps the rabble got the upper hand and led us into Christianity. Perhaps the trouble began with the salvationist morality taught by Jesus and Paul, for sometimes Nietzsche contrasts the naïve consciousness of power and self-delight in the Old Testament with the fussier and more sectarian spirit of the New. But he also thought of the whole Bible as a miserable affair among Jews: "Sin as it is experienced wherever Christianity now holds sway or has held sway, is a Jewish feeling and a Jewish invention."[60] "The Jew" (i.e., Jesus, although *The Anti-Christ* will put the onus on Paul) was the baleful originator, teaching goodness and pity rather than power, creating a sinful conscience. Nietzsche was not anti-Semitic in the sense that the Wagners were, although in earlier works he did echo some of their opinions.[61] In some ways he is an anti-anti-Semite. (See, for a strong example, the section on the "good European" [#475] in *Human, All Too Human*.) But he did exploit an anti-Semitic vocabulary in his attacks on Christianity. In effect he blamed Christianity on the Jews. His view is in parallel opposition to that of Freud, who in *Moses and Monotheism* sought to explain the anti-Semitism exploding around him as revenge against Christianity for the curbing of instinctual freedom.

Nietzsche is working with a very broad brush here, but the psychological nub of his argument is sharp-edged. As the old insouciant freedom of the instincts was restricted and disciplined by a new doctrine of moral accountability, people began to blame themselves for their suffering. They began to feel sin and guilt, which turned the kind of suffering that an Epicurus had robustly *absorbed* into a torment. That is, suffering led to more suffering by way of conscience, an analysis not very different from Freud's of the origin of the superego. Moreover, a god of love and pity intensely close to us and concerned with our sin reinforced this misery. Pity ("self-pity's kin" when there is a "too too human god," according to Wallace Stevens in "Esthétique du Mal") thus weds us to "the ascetic ideal." Only a strong spirit like Zarathustra's can cry out, "Pity is obtrusive [and] offends our sense of shame."[62] But modern democracy is the heir of Christianity and has taken over this enervating morality of goodness.

Nietzsche's personal stake in this attack on the ascetic ideal is somewhat puzzling—and it is fair to wonder about it because *Beyond Good and Evil* begins by advising us to consider what is personally at stake in any philosopher's thought. There is little evidence of lasting grievance directed at his Lutheran background. References to his father, who died when Nietzsche was not yet five years old, are friendly, and, although he may have unconsciously transferred some resentment against the father's early death to that father's religion, he seems to have had no particular quarrel with practicing Christians (like his loyal friend, Franz Overbeck) or with the Church itself, from which he broke for reasons quite understandable in terms of the needs of a highly original mind for intellectual independence. But the principal fact about Nietzsche's later productive years, along with his extraordinary creativity, was the suffering he endured, caused by persistent illness and the restrictions it imposed. His was largely an ascetic life, though of course a life that cannot be understood apart from the fanatical and triumphant devotion to writing.

This suffering must have seemed meaningless and arbitrary, until he discovered a way to explain it. The Christian tradition of morality that he had absorbed explained suffering by blaming the sufferer, asking that blame be internalized as a sense of sin. This Nietzsche bravely refused to do, calling such theology that of a "hangman-god." But he did eventually find the meaning of his life in pain itself. Zarathustra, for example, pointedly contrasts "My hangman-god" to "My unknown god! My *pain!* My last—happiness!"[63] Nietzsche must have sensed that the ascetic ideal was not so different from his own, for he now spoke of it as an attempt to wrest meaning out of life, seeing that *it* could provide an escape from nihilism. Thus (as the Third Essay of *Genealogy* begins and ends), "man would rather will *nothingness* than *not* will at all." Which brings us back to the Eternal Return.

This strange doctrine holds that everything that happens has already happened and will be exactly repeated ad infinitum. It apparently makes a cosmological claim, but most critics have not been impressed by this, perhaps because the psychological equivalent ('nothing in my life could have been otherwise') sounds more like what is really meant. Nietzsche imagined the Eternal Return, despite or because of the fact that it first induced nausea in him, as "the highest affirmation attainable." *Ecce Homo* states and expands on this idea: "My formula for greatness in a human being is *amor fati*, that one wants nothing to be other than it is, not in the future, not in the past, not in all eternity."[64] The challenge, then, was not simply to endure but to love fate. W. B. Yeats, in his poem "The Gyres," caught the spirit of the Latin phrase in his free translation, "tragic joy." It is not learning how to accept oneself but "how to become what one is," the subtitle of *Ecce Homo*. Yeats's "tragic joy" is suggestive because it links Nietzsche's last book with his first, self-making with tragedy.

In 1872 Nietzsche had associated Dionysus with pain and suffering that turned into joy via the aesthetic experience: "it is only in aesthetic terms that the world is eternally justified." But in 1886, writing an "Attempt at a Self-Criticism" prefacing the reissued *Birth of Tragedy*, he draws back from this formulation, telling us that the earlier statement "made the world at every moment the *attained* salvation of God."[65] In 1872 Nietzsche wanted to aestheticize the universe and thus thought of the artist as an aspect of God: "the genius in the act of creation merges with the primal architect of the cosmos." But in 1886 he wanted to attempt the much more difficult task of aestheticizing himself. Thus divinity became an aspect of artistic genius rather than the other way around. Dionysus is now not just the energy to be transformed into beauty but another name for the artist, which is to say for himself. In 1872 he had agreed with Schopenhauer that tragedy captured the paradox of existence. But in his later work he saw himself as that tragedy, transforming the pain of his existence into ultimate meaning. He would become his own religious redeemer, and attempt to justify himself, as God (to the believer) justifies the world. In the essay "We Classicists" Nietzsche had written: "My religion, if I must use a word of that sort, lies in the task of producing the genius....Religion is *love beyond ourselves*. The work of art is *the perfect image of such self-transcending love*."[66] By the end of his career he realized that the ultimate work of art to be produced was himself.

There could never be a community of Nietzscheans, a movement, a religion. In calling himself the Antichrist or implying (when he used the name

Dionysus) that he was a type of Christ, in titling the autobiographical *Ecce Homo* with an allusion to Christ, Nietzsche must have known he was identifying himself finally with Christianity. But he also knew he could never redeem anyone but himself, that his truest disciples, like Zarathustra's, would not follow him but would find their own way.

Nehamas wryly calls Nietzsche "the first of the last of the metaphysicians."[67] One thinks of various twentieth-century figures influenced by him who have tried to be last of the last. There is Heidegger, trying to elude what Derrida would call a metaphysics of presence by reconfiguring the concept of being. There is Foucault, whose own genealogical method owes so much to Nietzsche, teaching the diffusion of authorial agency. And of course there is Derrida, trying through deconstruction to explain the master's emphasis on perpetual change in terms of endlessly deferred meaning. Perhaps there will never be a last metaphysician, since one's presuppositions about the ulterior relations of ideas have a way of being exposed by later philosophy. But Nietzsche certainly pointed the way. He liked to use a plural pronoun in speaking of the exemplary person—we philosophers, we opposite men, we new men, we modern men, we free spirits, our cheerfulness. This is a *dream* of community since such a person is always single and always changing, emerging, becoming. In the last analysis, Nietzsche's idealizations are always "beyond"—beyond formulation, beyond rule, beyond good and evil, beyond religion.

Mark Twain's Countertheology

Mark Twain was too enraged by the deity he knew—the product of what his *Autobiography* calls "my trained Presbyterian conscience"[68]—to speculate coolly on his existence. God had to be exposed or opposed, not with philosophic argument but with a language tart and vivid enough to drive home his cruelty, injustice, and absurdity. The "damned human race" was theologically damned because God determined both man's character and his behavior. But the attack on God can be made as well through *man* and *his* damnable ways. In practice, an indictment of one usually slides into an indictment of the other:

> [The Bible] begins with an inexcusable treachery, and that is the keynote of the entire biography. [Ignorant Adam could not have been expected to understand the

> prohibition, yet] his posterity, individual by individual, has been unceasingly hunted and harried with afflictions in punishment of the juvenile misdemeanor which is grandiloquently called Adam's sin. And during all that vast lapse of time, there has been no lack of rabbins and popes and bishops and priests and parsons and lay slaves eager to applaud this infamy, maintain the unassailable justice and righteousness of it, and praise its Author.[69]
>
> [God] has almost bankrupted his native ingenuities in inventing pains and miseries and humiliations and heartbreaks wherewith to embitter the brief lives of Adam's descendants....Then...the gifted Christian blandly calls him Our Father!...He equips the Creator with every trait that goes to the making of a fiend, and then arrives at the conclusion that a fiend and a father are the same thing![70]

Twain understands well enough that deities are man-made. But, unlike Feuerbach and Nietzsche, he chooses to blur rather than sharpen the distinction between theology and psychology, and thus to insist on the image of an anthropomorphic divine fiend, never mind the lack of logical finesse. No wonder his minister friend, Joseph Twichell, complained that he was "too orthodox on the Doctrine of Total Human Depravity."[71] Or that William Dean Howells told his friend he had "remained a creature of the Presbyterian God who did make you."[72]

From the 1870s, Twain's theology was influenced by his reading of Paine's deistic *The Age of Reason* and by his exposure to nineteenth-century scientific thinking about time and space, disease, and the Bible. Some of his critics have suggested that these influences sophisticated his theology, but this isn't exactly the case. He seized on the critique of the Bible that he found in Paine and the Higher Criticism to intensify his quarrel with the Bible's God rather than to ease his need to mount it. Twain did not wish to seek a compromise between "primitive" and "abstract" theologies because his narrative art required for its ironic effects their collision and clash.

Thus a theology of general Providence, featuring a Creator working by remote, impersonal law, did not replace the old hated theology of special Providence with its Protestant emphasis on a caring and loving Father, because the artist saw the advantage of having them play against and across one another. When a deistic God of immutable law is invoked, this soon turns into the old anthropomorphic fiend. A passage that begins, "Let us now consider the real God, the genuine God...whose remotenesses are visited by comets only," turns after a page or two into this: "We know that the real God...made all the creatures, from the microbe and the brontosaur down to man and the monkey, and that He knew what would happen to each and every one of them from the beginning of time to the end of it. In the case of each creature, big or little, He made it an unchanging law that that creature should suffer wanton and unnecessary pains and miseries every day of its life."[73] The deist God, then, is fodder for irony. At times even the language of deism is parodied, as in *Letters from the Earth* where God is said to create now a predator and now a victim, each in turn declared blameless because it is obeying "a law of nature": and "the law of nature is the law of God."

The diatribe "What Is Man?" attempts to combine an updated determinism with the old fundamentalism rather than to exploit the incongruity between these viewpoints, and loses much of its rhetorical effectiveness thereby. Humor was essential to Twain's art. In an important letter of 1865 to his brother Orion, the young writer understood he had "a calling to literature of a low order," which, he admitted, is "nothing to be proud of" but "my strongest suit."[74] He was right about this, yet right also when he wrote in the *Autobiography*: "I have always preached...if the humor came of its own accord I have allowed it in."[75] It is the varying combinations of preaching and humor that define his narrative art and account for its characteristics. Twain's brand of antitheism is therefore less dogmatic than, say, that of Charles Bradlaugh, who also liked to write screeds against the Bible and Christian doctrine but who piled up his indictment in a hard analytic style that, while forceful, has no real bite. His satirical humor is more complicit with his own underlying emotions and hence more telling in its effect on us. Bradlaugh is fighting a political battle only while Twain is also wrestling with something in himself, and the result (to adapt a phrase of Yeats) is in the one case rhetoric, in the other art.

What is Twain preaching? A pretty good short answer is "Man's cruel and unjust banishment from Eden." It was offered by the late Stanley Brodwin, who in a series of essays developed the fruitful idea of Mark Twain's "countertheology."[76] The basis of this countertheology Brodwin found to be a revisionary myth of the biblical Adam, an Everyman who is innocent because before the Fall he had no Moral Sense and so could not sin, yet was punished *with* a Moral Sense prompting him to exalt himself as the "delight" of the very God that torments his conscience. This myth illuminates much of the *oeuvre* (not only the later fables) because Twain's early and middle fictions feature a gradually more desperate Adamic figure who finally turns into an irreverent and articulate exposer and opposer of God called "Satan."

Brodwin establishes the key moral elements of the myth, grouping them under three headings: Providence, Lies, and Moral Reform. Providence (the special Providence of the Calvinist tradition rather than the general Providence of the deists) is above all treacherous because it offers salvation and personal love—immense "sarcasms" in view of God's cruelties, beginning with the unjust banishment of Adam but including all the ills that flesh is heir to. By "Lies" Brodwin understands Twain to mean the timidity and conceit that motivate man to exalt this God and commit horrendous cruelties in His name. Since Providence and Lies—i.e., the indictment of God and of Man—are complementary concepts, Moral Reform seems to make an odd third item in the list, but it is in fact crucial. Twain's brand of Protestantism promoted not only the doctrine of human depravity but also—its flip side, as it were—entrepreneurial initiative, and this must have been much augmented by the nineteenth-century American faith in energy, progress, and prosperity that shaped the writer even as he deplored its excesses. Twain's earlier Adamic figures seek to evade reform because they distrust "sivilization"; his later ones (Hank Morgan, Roxana, Joan of Arc) must try to alter history and must fail. The impossibility of reform is central to Twain's vision of man, but we may be puzzled by the bitterness of this conviction unless we see it as the disillusioned result of a thirst *for* reform.

The biblical Adam was a favorite image from early on, and acquired ever more significance as the narrative art turned gradually away from realism toward fable. As early as 1853 (at the age of seventeen) Twain styled himself "a son of Adam" in a squib for his brother's *Hannibal Journal*, and the personal identification remained. In a letter of 1887, in reply to an evocation of childhood days, he said he felt like "a banished Adam" "revisiting a half-forgotten Paradise."[77] During the 1870s, after some dabbling with Noah and Methuselah stories, he wrote "Adam's Expulsion" (1877), the first of many attempts to feature Adam as the chief character of a sketch. Most of these sketches were composed between 1893 and 1905, and carried such titles as "Adam's Diary," "Eve's Diary," "Eve Speaks," "Adam's Soliloquy," "Papers of the Adam Family," and "That Day in Eden" (in which the pathos the First Family's situation is expressed by Satan)—not to mention various references to Adam in the novels and travel books, in Pudd'nhead Wilson's *Calendar* and in Satan-centered pieces like *Letters from the Earth*. Narrativizing Adam allowed for whimsical humor by way of anachronisms, but the basic idea of God's injustice is not lost sight of. The best strokes are the sardonic ones. Wilson notes in his *Calendar*: "Adam was but human—that explains it all. He did not want the apple for the apple's sake, he wanted it only because it was forbidden. The mistake was in not forbidding the serpent; then he would have eaten the serpent."[78] Satan comments: "[Adam and Eve] think ill of death—they will change their mind."[79]

The development of the Adamic figure in Twain's art reaches one climax in *Huckleberry Finn*. The narrators of *Innocents Abroad* and *Roughing It* alternate uncertainly between the joy of fresh discovery and dismay at what is discovered. But, after exposing corruptions of the Reconstructionist era in *The Gilded Age*, Twain developed—in *Tom Sawyer*, *Life on the Mississippi* and especially *Huckleberry Finn*—a more complex tension between a natural man and the fallen world in which that figure must live. Tom and Huck live *in* a world of harrying prohibitions and dishonest theology but they are not quite *of* it; they preserve their unfallen condition "down here below" (to use Huck's own phrasing), by instinctive irreverence, disguise, cunning evasion, and even by lies against lies. It is not easy for them to preserve their freedom from civilized values because these values have to some extent been internalized. A prime example is Huck's decision to lie, in spite of conscience, concerning Jim. He has sufficient natural wisdom to resist the crippling Moral Sense, and, since he is going to hell anyway, has no need to reform. He and Jim may be called pre-Christian or even pre-pagan, as in their charming speculation on whether the stars just happened or were made by the moon. That the Adamic is not a simple idea for Twain is made clear by the fact that vicious Pap represents another version of it. He is the natural man as unregenerate and filthy ("like Adam," comments Huck disgustedly, "he was just all mud"). But he has the credentials: he has no use for Providence, never lies to himself (however repellent his opinions), and will never reform. After discovering how far Pap has exploited his hospitality and benevolent resolve "to make a man of him," "the new judge…felt kind of sore. He said he reckoned a body could reform the old man with a shotgun, maybe, but he didn't know no other way."[80]

Although there is no false romance in the Mississippi River trilogy, in the largest efforts of the following decade—*A Connecticut Yankee in King Arthur's Court*, *Pudd'nhead Wilson,* and *Joan of Arc*—Twain seems to hurl himself against romance itself as if to assert that it is no longer enough for civilization to be merely resisted by an Adamic consciousness: it must also be reformed. None of these books is very successful (although *Pudd'nhead Wilson*, despite its contrivances, is readable), but all are interestingly conflicted in conception. Twain is both impatient with societies that fear to reform and aware that any society (including his own) will resist reform. These books are worth brief comment because they help to account for the turn in the last decades to a fabular art in which a stubbornly oppressive theology is countered by original deployments of Adam and Satan.

In the burlesque plot of *A Connecticut Yankee*, Hank Morgan is thrown magically back into the world of medieval chivalry and attempts, as the ever resourceful "Boss," to blow it all up, replacing it entirely with democracy, freedom from religion, and all the boons of nineteenth-century progress. He goes very far before being stopped by a Church Interdict and Merlin's accompanying machinations, but perhaps he is stopped even more by losing confidence in his right to mount the total violence required to root out the foundations of a cowardly society. Twain wrote in *Life on the Mississippi* that the Civil War was started by the South's love of Sir Walter Scott, and certainly the false romance of chivalry is one of his targets in this book, but that hardly explains the earnestness and thoroughness of Hank's enterprise, or its failure. Brodwin asks the right question about the author's motives: "Why go into the past to form a democratic Utopia—and then destroy it—if that Utopia exists, however imperfectly, in the present?"[81] What stops the Boss is not made altogether clear in this novel "at war with itself," in Bernard De Voto's words,[82] but I think it is significant, as James D. Williams points out, that Twain's revisions work in the direction of making Hank gradually less of an ignoramus, more sophisticated and aware.[83] I infer from this that Hank is meant to realize the impossibility of reform because deep-rooted resistances will always remain. The philosopher Alfred North Whitehead reflected on the general problem raised by this experiment. "It may be impossible," he wrote, "to conceive a reorganization of society adequate for the removal of some admitted evil without destroying the social organization of the civilization which depends on it."[84] Twain himself must have realized that radical reform was as impossible in the nineteenth century as in the sixth. Total destruction is no solution, yet how else to uproot the theology that supports the damned human race? Progress becomes a meaningless process, and so what else can Twain do with Hank Morgan but bring him back to the present, let him give his testimony to M.T., and die?

A somewhat similar dialectic of despair underlies *Pudd'nhead Wilson*. The slave Roxana seeks to reform the manifest injustice of the treatment of blacks in her society by switching babies in the cradle and allowing her "Tom" to live as a white man. But she must fail because she cannot reform the total structure of injustice, which derives not from being black but from being black in a white society—that is, from living in a society "built upon the myth that blacks are different."[85] Superficially, justice is finally served in the novel, when, in a grand courtroom finale, Wilson cleverly proves Tom guilty of a crime, but the underlying injustice is not touched, as Twain makes clear with a final and sharply ironic flourish:

> Everybody granted that if 'Tom' were white and free it would be unquestionably right to punish him—it would be no loss to anybody; but to shut up a valuable slave for life—that was another matter.
> As soon as the Governor understood the case, he pardoned Tom at once, and the creditors sold him down the river.[86]

Wilson's role in the book seems odd, in fact, because he is hardly involved in the action until the end, but, largely through his *Calendar* (used by Twain as chapter-epigraphs), he serves as sardonic commentator on the whole action, and what he comments on is the incorrigibility of the American society he knows. His final entry in the *Calendar* sums it up: "It was wonderful to find America, but it would have been more wonderful to miss it."

The humorlessly hagiographic Joan of Arc book is less complex but no less desperate. Twain develops from the records the noblest human image he can put into words and pits it against the combined power of Church and State, with a foregone conclusion. The narrator refers at one point to "God's good gift of laughter" but it is nowhere in evidence, and it appears that Twain himself was losing faith in its efficacy. In one of *The Mysterious Stranger* manuscripts written about the same time, Satan teaches: "Against the assault of Laughter nothing can stand"—and the assault he has in mind is directed against Catholic and Presbyterian orthodoxy. But the same passage adds dismayingly that the human race lacks the sense and courage to "ever use it at all."[87]

History, ransacked by Twain, yielded a litany of barbarities, nor was any nation exempt. The St. Bartholomew Day massacre, for example, in sixteenth-century France, was "unquestionably the finest thing of the kind ever devised."[88] Twain's pained conscience did, however, go out to the underdog—to the Negro because of lynchings and the Jew because of pogroms and certainly to "animals" to whom in our conceit we consider ourselves superior. Words like "brutal" and "bestial" describing human behavior always elicit from the satirist an ironic response, who delights in showing that "inhuman" behavior is simply the most characteristically "human" behavior of all. One piece about the so-called "highest animal" is called "The Lowest Animal."

From the mid-1890s until his death in 1910, the root idea of Twain's various (and often unfinished) ventures is that both God and Man are insane. What then is left for the moralist/humorist to do? He chose to spin off the Adamic myth by building up the figure of Satan, an unfallen but knowing Adam who could comment on this insanity with some detachment, hence with irony as well as preacherly denunciation.

Twain's fascination with Satan, as with Adam, was of long standing. In the *Autobiography* he told us he had "always felt friendly toward Satan."[89] There is a trail of similar remarks throughout the middle period, ranging from Tom Sawyer's hoping to see "one blessed sinful face" at a revival meeting to the disclaiming of all prejudice, even against Satan, in "As Concerning the Jews." In late Twain, such remarks develop into sketches (with titles like "Satan's Diary," "Sold to Satan," "Letters to Satan," "A Humane Word from Satan") or are worked up into longer narratives like *Letters from the Earth* and *The Mysterious Stranger*. Moreover, several stories that rather boldly venture into preternatural territory—"The Man that Corrupted Hadleyburg," "Captain Stormfield's Visit to Heaven" (especially that part of it known as Sandy's narrative), "The Great Dark"—are clearly linked to the Satan figure without mentioning him. As William M. Gibson put it, "the Satanic stranger, who visits the earth and pities and judges men, dominated his imagination and guided his pen in those years, trailing dozens of lesser characters in his angelic wake."[90]

In *Letters from the Earth*, Satan is imagined as reporting back home to St. Michael and St. Gabriel on how the Human Race experiment is coming along. He finds the earth a strange, appalling place: "The people are all insane, the other animals are all insane, the earth is insane, nature itself is insane." Yet "Man is a marvelous curiosity." Several features of Man seem to him especially curious. Man's constant compliments to God are unconscious "sarcasms," "uttered without a smile." His Heaven is dishonest containing nothing he really values like sexual intercourse. His God does indeed have his eye on the poor since "nine-tenths of his disease-inventions" are bestowed on them. And his God's New Testament, which brought Hell, is even worse than the Old, which brought Life and Death, for "the Deity perceived that death was a mistake; a mistake in that it was insufficient; insufficient in that, while it was an admirable agent for the inflicting of misery on the survivor, it allowed the dead person himself to escape from all further persecution in the blessed refuge of the grave."[91] Satan has much more to say on the malice of

God, for Satan's pen was indeed "warmed in hell," as Twain told Howells he wished his own to be.[92]

The manuscripts of *The Mysterious Stranger*, written between 1897 and 1908, yield no definitive single version, but there are important constants. In all of them "Satan" is a figure from another world who imparts dark truth to an adolescent boy. Satan (called "Philip Traum" and "44" in the two fullest manuscripts) is sometimes said to be Twain's dream self, and the boy is clearly enough an alter ego. Throughout, Satan is scornful of the human record, pedagogical, exuberantly creative, and consolatory. These roles do not coordinate very well (if scornful, why pedagogical, or exuberant, or consoling?), but they do indicate that Twain wanted him to contain and thus replace all aspects of the Christian Godhead: the Father as Judge, as Lawgiver, as Creator, and (through the Son) as loving Redeemer.

The most interesting and most novel roles are the joyous creator of miracles and the subdued consoler. We must, I think, associate Satan's pleasure in performing, in putting on a good show, with Twain's own delight—despite all his misanthropy—in his prolific narrative art. The dream self (in one story, "The Great Dark," a figure like Satan is called the "Superintendent of Dreams") is free of conscience and the flesh, in a sense free of death by virtue of his endless creativity. However, the consolation Satan offers us through the boy is to accept death by lessening its significance. He teaches that people would be no better off if their individual fates were altered because no sane man can be happy in the world as it is. And he closes with one much more dramatic revelation, a vision of the world as it really is—a dream in which *nothing* is real: "There is no God, no universe, no human race, no earthly life, no heaven, no hell. It is all a Dream, a grotesque and foolish dream. Nothing exists but You. And you are but a *Thought*—a vagrant Thought, a useless Thought, a homeless Thought, wandering forlorn among the empty eternities!" "He vanished," concludes the narrator, "and left me appalled; for I knew, and realized, that all he had said was true." Twain meant this famous ending to be in some sense consoling, for, shortly after his wife's death, he wrote to Twichell that such an idea "reconciles everything, makes everything lucid and understandable." But it also comes across as frightening, and the boy is understandably "appalled."[93]

This moving and disturbing ending of *The Mysterious Stranger* expresses the farthest reach of Mark Twain's countertheology. Here for the first and last time he declares plainly, through an exemplary speaker, "there is no God." Yet this statement is inseparable from another that tells us, there is no *world*. Not wholly unlike Captain Ahab and Moby Dick, Twain and the deity end as they began, bound together.

In the Wake of Darwin: Thomas Hardy

Hardy was by no means a systematic thinker. Rather, he was a poet-novelist, a sensibility, who imaginatively filtered ideas that attracted him to express a particular experience and world view. This is a point he made repeatedly, as if to correct readers who were looking for a "philosophy." In one prefatory essay he describes his writings as "unadjusted impressions" having "little cohesion"[94]; in another he asserted that "Positive views on the Whence and the Wherefore of things have never been advanced by this pen as a consistent philosophy"[95]; and in yet another he advised that "no harmonious philosophy is attempted in these pages—or in any bygone pages of mine."[96] If one is asking, then, by what writing his own is most deeply influenced, the best answer would probably be certain visions akin to his own—Shelley's eros that must fail of its own excess, Swinburne's pagan subversion of Christianity, and especially the Bible's Yahweh, a presence neither quite personal nor quite transcendent, as God later became in Christian theology, but whose will is incommensurate with that of his people. Hardy called this presence Immanent Will, Law, Cause, Unconsciousness, and a dozen other quasi-anthropomorphic names, adjusting his idea of God to the deterministic notions of origins and destinies that he derived both from the irrationalism of Schopenhauer (and von Hartmann) and the rationalism of the positivists and Darwinists.

However, during the 1860s and 1870s, the formative period of his development as a writer, Hardy's vision was also influenced by such systematic thinkers as Huxley, Spencer, Mill, Comte, and Stephen, along with Darwin and Schopenhauer, and a good way to understand his kind of atheism is to ask how his resistance to theism differs from that of these questioners. Because his poems and novels emphasize the bafflement of human understanding and desire by an unknowable cosmic will, his stance is sometimes described as agnostic—and indeed he sometimes called himself an agnostic, a "harmless agnostic" mistaken for a "clamorous atheist."[97] But the theme of cosmic unknowability in *his* work can be distinguished from the comparable concept that he found in his reading. For Huxley, Spencer, Mill, and Stephen, doubt or unbelief was to be supported with logical argument. Huxley stressed the place of scientific method, Spencer the processes driving evolution, Mill the undecidability on logical grounds of claims for theism, Stephen the intellectually insulting impositions of religion. But Hardy wrote frankly from his emotions—a gamut of emotions ranging from nostalgia to bitterness— about the withdrawal of God, a withdrawal that has been fairly described as that of "a great Love-object."[98] His personifications of divine knowledge and power confront man with hostility, indifference, uncertainty, and sardonic humor. They express the darker moods of an imaginative artist, the stance of a literary rather than philosophic agnostic or atheist.

Dictated to his second wife by Hardy himself, *The Life of Thomas Hardy* quotes him as saying, "I have been looking for God 50 years, and I think that if he had existed, I should have discovered him."[99] Hardy makes it clear that the only God he has in mind here is the anthropomorphic one that arouses his distrust, for "It is so easy nowadays to call any force above or under the sky by the name of 'God'—and so pass as orthodox cheaply."[100] Accordingly, he found the concluding solace of Tennyson's *In Memoriam* "too easily won from too little evidence;" derided Browning's verse as "comfortably unaware" of what Shelley called "Victorious Wrong" and Sophocles "the vast injustice of the gods"; ridiculed Arnold's partial defense of religious dogma as "hair-splitting."[101] Hardy allowed himself to hope at times for amelioration, but his "overworld" (as *The Dynasts* calls it) remained largely unsupportive of human hopes and aspirations.

Yet there was considerable emotional ambivalence in his view of the Christian religious tradition that fed his young imagination. At times it is invoked with tenderness—when it is associated with childhood or the past or Christmas, as in the charming early novel, *Under the Greenwood Tree*, or in the well-known poem, "The Oxen." In the *Life*, Hardy went so far as to say (somewhat tongue in cheek but not without a certain measure of sincerity): "although invidious critics had cast slurs upon him as [Agnostic, Atheist, or pessimist] they had never thought of calling him what they might have called him much more plausibly—'churchy'—not in any intellectual sense, but insofar as instincts and emotions ruled."[102] In one poem, "God's Funeral," the speaker regrets he cannot buoy the faith of those who mourn God's death, admitting, "what was mourned for, I, too, long had prized." Another, "The Impercipient," a poem that pictures the speaker sitting unresponsively in church, suggests mixed although negatively shaded feelings toward religious tradition. The comic "Respectable Burgher" responds to the Higher Criticism's demythologizing of the Bible neither with satisfaction nor frank dismay but with something like ironic bemusement, and a similar ambivalence marks "Drinking Song" whose rollicking devil-may-care refrains describe Darwin's idea that we are one with creeping things as one of those great thoughts that *diminishes* the world. Hardy's unbelief, tinged with the residue of belief, sometimes admits nostalgia but also fights against it, taking on a bitter edge as a result.

About the novels, critics have remarked that Hardy often honors a pagan life-acceptance and discovers an "ache" in the hearts of characters exposed to enlightened, modern ideas. Christian morality in his two strongest novels, *Tess of the D'Urbervilles* and *Jude the Obscure*, is presented as relentlessly oppressive, especially in regard to sex and marriage. Moreover, their two protagonists, after sloughing off some early passivity, become powerful critics of this morality. One remembers Tess as unwed mother coming across painted inscriptions like THY, DAMNATION, SLUMBERETH, NOT and telling the artisan, "I think they are horrible...crushing! Killing!" Jude similarly turns on his adored Sue, after she so painfully reverts:

> "We must conform!" she said mournfully. "All the ancient wrath of the Power above us has been vented upon us.... It is no use fighting against God!"
> "It is only against man and senseless circumstance," said Jude.

A number of poems, while *telling* us that God is no more than a blind and inhuman force, nevertheless personify this very force and thus in an odd way bring the personal God Hardy repudiates back from the grave in order to give him another kick. The various deific epithets are more or less unflattering—"purblind Doomsters," "Vast Imbecility," "Great Face behind," "Immanent Will," "Spinner of Years"—but even indifference and hostility are human responses. Hardy's God, though hardly comforting, is speaking to us. In fact, a number of poems, ("Nature's Questioning," "The Mother Mourns," "God-Forgotten," "By the Earth's Corpse," "A Dream Question," "A Plaint to Man"), depict God or his proxy Nature as not unmindful of, but as unable or unwilling to relieve, human suffering. When conscientiousness prompts him to introduce a meliorist sentiment, his deity becomes curiously abstract. The Spirit of the Years describes it as "A Will that wills above the will of each,/ Yet but the will of all conjunctively."[103]

Hardy's art always needs to anthropomorphize God to some extent in order to give us some concrete sense of what is adversarial to man and thus to account for the pain inherent in the human situation. In "Hap" the purblind doomsters are not really neutral as the word "hap" implies, but mischievously malicious. The Spinner of Years in "The Convergence of the Twain" evidently relishes arranging the Titanic's collision with the iceberg. The "God" of "Channel Firing" reveals several emotions toward the awakened dead: dismay at man's ongoing folly, pleasure in the prospect of a punishing Judgment Day, pity for man's need of rest (this in parenthesis), and a final indifference to the whole show. In other poems the God figure doesn't remember the creation or claims he didn't expect men to become so conscious and hence critical of his acts, or is represented by his proxies ("Nature's Questioning," "The Sulbalterns") whose very bewilderment and ignorance mark the vast distance between man's spiritual desire and its object.

That Hardy is earnest about all this despite the playful ironies is shown by his persistent effort to take a meliorist rather than pessimist line.[104] In some poems he suggests that the Unconscious Will of the Universe is growing aware of Itself, developing a providential purpose. The idea is given emphasis in the final Chorus of his most ambitious poem, *The Dynasts*:

> But—a stirring thrills the air
> Like to sounds of joyance there
>> That the rages
>> Of the ages
> Shall be cancelled, and deliverance offered from the darts that were,
> Consciousness the Will informing, till It fashion all things fair![105]

Other especially earnest meliorist sentiments are found in poems titled "The Sleep-Worker" and "Agnosto Theo" ("To an Unknown God"). The latter envisions a "Willer masked and dumb" that will grow percipient and mend the human scene so that we may discern "wrong/ Dying as of self-slaughter; whereat I/ Would raise my voice in song."

But, although it can sometimes achieve eloquence, the meliorist sentiment often seems forced against the grain of the writer's temperament. To counter the charge of pessimism, Hardy liked to quote his own line from "In Tenebris II"—"[I]f way to the Better there be, it exacts a full look at the Worst"—but such a sensible view of the matter doesn't really explain why we judge his pessimism to be *characteristic*. In the "General Preface to the Wessex Edition of 1912," Hardy *did* adequately account for his bias, tellling us that "differing natures find their tongue in the presence of differing spectacles. Some natures become vocal at tragedy, some are made vocal by comedy, and it seems to me that to whichever of these aspects of life a writer's instinct for expression more readily responds, to that he should allow it to respond." We must, I think, agree with Martin Seymour-Smith that Hardy's "notions of meliorism are reluctant and confused defences against attacks on him," which, however, testify to his "instinctive decency."[106]

A more interesting question than the source of Hardy's pessimism is why, given the degree to which the writer arranges misfortune for the sentient beings imaged in his poems and novels, they are so seldom puppets. The answer is surely his extraordinary empathy with suffering, both powerful and intimate. The "aged thrush, frail, gaunt and small" that sings joyfully in so incongruous a landscape is empowered by Hardy's own will and does not seem frail at all. The same is true of "the last chrysanthemum," a poignant image of belatedness and isolation but also one of endurance and tenacity. A Blinded Bird seems readymade for sentimental treatment, but Hardy's poem using that phrase as a title ends defiantly: "Who is divine? This bird." Shelley's Skylark, whose descendant was sighted in Rome, is after all just a poor mortal bird—but to have (even indirectly) inspired such a poem, what a bird! It is true that Hardy tends to dwarf the numerous notables that populate his epic-drama, *The Dynasts*, although Kenneth Millard has shown that it is possible to make significant discriminations among them (the English less dwarfed than the French), but the familiar brooding pity for humanity and the mordant irony concerning man's relation to the Overworld are still evident in what Millard himself takes to be the work's central dialogue, that between the Spirit of the Pities on the one hand and the Spirits Sinister and Ironic on the other.[107]

Hardy's pessimism on examination does not really surrender to despair any more than it allows us to surmount it. Margaret Mahar brings out this idea subtly in her commentary on Hardy's fine and famous poem, "During Wind and Rain." The "Ah, no" refrain seems at first simply to cancel out each happy seasonal image, mocking a lilting rhythm with a harsh final line and suggesting the futility of all human endeavor. But the overall logic is not so simple. Mahar contrasts it to that of Shelley's "Ode to the West Wind" from which Hardy's poem derives. To Shelley's final question ('If Winter comes, can Spring be far behind?') "During Wind and Rain" answers, writes Mahar: "both behind and ahead. Hardy affirms the cyclical state of things as they are, and that affirmation is neither quite acquiescence nor a springboard to transcendence." "In his typical lyrics," she generalizes, "past and present [both, in this poem, are represented in the present tense] face each other, and the explanation for the change lies in the…space between." She means that no explanation in terms of cause and effect can be offered, for Hardy thinks of the present not as fulfilling the past but as repeating it.[108]

Is there a similar logic at work in the novels despite the fact that long narrative obviously depends much more on linearity and progressive effects? I think there is. Plot in the great novels, *Tess of the D'Urbervilles* and *Jude the Obscure,* does not so much unfold as accrete, giving us more a sequence of moments than a beginning, middle and end. Irving Howe observed with particular reference to *Jude* that what we remember of the novel are its moments rather than the sequence of events.[109] Only in *The Mayor of Casterbridge* does the tragic conclusion really follow from the character of the protagonist, and *The Mayor* is consequently more perfect artistically than either *Tess* or *Jude.*

Plot in Hardy's novels may be said to function as the agent of the rapacious Immanent Will, exploiting coincidence or whatever other dramatic device comes to hand in order to secure the protagonist's destruction. Hardy's addition of "finished his sport with Tess" to Aeschylus's august phrase "President of the Immortals" is only the most notorious evidence of this will to destruction. So the most interesting question to raise here is why, in the two major novels, character remains so powerfully present.

Hardy's imagination, we have said, was at least as much invested in the sentient sufferer as in picturing the insufficiently sentient opposing force, and in the case of Tess the result is uncanny. Her sensuous presence on the page, as D. H. Lawrence among others perceived,[110] is not just strong but palpable. (The character of Jude is somewhat less immediate on the page, and his story less sensuous, probably because, as Gillian Beer surmises, he sees himself as the precursor of a new order, casting our attention forward, whereas in Tess "the passion for particularity…individuality, and plenitude" remains dominant.)[111] For the sake of his "tragedy" Hardy must make her sufficiently passive to be vulnerable to the combination of man-made morality and senseless circumstance—in short to the plot that is mounted against her. But Tess herself is flawed as an individual only insofar as she embodies her family history. Nor does her character change fundamentally: she is always sensitive to suffering and injustice, and is allowed gradually to be more active in protest against them. Thus to the questions raised by the narrator in the seduction scene—"why so often the coarse appropriates the finer thus, the wrong man the woman, the wrong woman the man"—the only true answer is 'because that's the way things are,' not 'because that's the way these particular characters are motivated to behave.' In the case of Angel Clare (and still more brilliantly in the case of Sue Bridehead) Hardy does anticipate Freud in dramatizing a return of the repressed as an individual as well as cultural phenomenon. But Tess and Jude are brilliant in a different way. They are courageously resistant to an unjust fate. Neither of them is brought round to acquiescence. Jude's valedictory "Let the day perish wherein I was born" echoes Job in the midst rather than at the end of his ordeal, and Tess at Stonehenge is an image of sacrifice rather than pathos. Unlike Henchard and most tragic protagonists, neither is marked by hubris or chastened in the course of the story.

Jude is rather unconvincingly assigned character flaws—susceptibility to drink (like Henchard) and to women. But the sensitive boy hurt by the cruelty of nature ("mercy towards one set of creatures was cruelty towards another") and of man (nobody came with the promised Latin and Greek grammars "because nobody does") is basically the same as the courageous adult who would defy the injustice of human arrangements and of circumstances. In commenting himself on the novel, Hardy can scarcely be said to have even intended to blame Jude's character (apart from heredity) in his fate: "[the novel] is concerned first with the labours of a poor student to get a University degree, and secondly with the tragic issues of two bad marriages, owing in the main to a doom or curse of hereditary temperament peculiar to the family of the parties." Sue's story, like Angel Clare's, could be construed as tragedy, but Jude's like Tess's is something else.

But these are Hardy's most exceptional fictional creations, and it is important to appreciate the fact that his sympathies are not drawn primarily to heroic images. Pain and suffering are, after all, universal. Elizabeth-Jane in *The Mayor of Casterbridge* does not leave the same kind of indelible impression upon us as does Tess or Jude or her supposed father, Michael Henchard, but there is not a more quintessential prose passage in his work—more intimate, honest, and unsentimental—than the one (in Chapter XXV) in which she expresses her disappointment on learning that Donald Farfrae, the one person she thought might be her own, has transferred his affection to the very woman who is now befriending her:

> She had learnt the lesson of renunciation, and was as familiar with the wreck of each day's wishes as with the diurnal setting of the sun. If her earthly career had taught her few book philosophies it had at least as well practiced her in this. Yet her experience had consisted less in a series of pure disappointments than in a series of substitutions. Continually it had happened that what she desired had not been

granted her, and that what had been granted her she had not desired. So she viewed with an approach to equanimity the now cancelled days when Donald had been her undeclared lover, and wondered what unwished-for thing Heaven might send her in place of him.

We should remember that Elizabeth-Jane is destined in her story to reclaim her Donald after all, so what is at issue here is not so much the appropriateness of this passage in the narrative as its truth to Hardy's overall sense of life.

For Hardy as for other Victorian poets, God was dying or disappearing, a not yet completed process. For Wallace Stevens a generation later, the disappearance of God is an accomplished fact, and for Samuel Beckett, a generation after that, his permanent absence is a source of mordant humor. But Hardy was born early enough to be more than a little impressed by the necessitarian theories, rationalist and irrationalist, that he found in Darwin and Schopenhauer. He wished to show human beings not at ease with the unconscious will of the world. To put it another way, his imagination was stirred both by the tyranny of this blind force and by the pitiableness and courage of the sufferer.

Hardy's repeated defense against the charge of pessimism had something to do with his just perception that many of his readers felt his work was depriving them of some religious comfort they needed to live their lives. We have since become able to see this same pessimism more positively, as an admission of spiritual pain that bravely refuses to be allayed in traditional ways. He rejected the Christian God because he believed that the pain of existence was irremediable pain, and he was attracted to the views of Darwinists and of Schopenhauer because they were harsh enough to leave him, as he wished, unconsoled.

A few years ago, George Levine published an interesting and moving essay called "Darwin and Pain: Why Science Made Shakespeare Nauseating." His intricate argument establishes that Darwin's intense experience of "the sufferings of millions of the lower animals throughout almost endless time," augmented by the meaningless and unconsolable loss of his beloved daughter, made the poetry he had loved (*Paradise Lost* is specified along with Shakespeare) repellent to him because poetry lied either by making nature sympathetic or loss redemptive. However, good science is itself deeply imaginative, and what Darwin embraced and found bracing in the theory of natural selection was precisely its challenge to the need for human consolation. Thus, argues Levine, Darwin was seeking through science the kind of poetry and religion he *could* like.[112] To this I would add that Hardy was seeking *through poetry*, the kind of science and religion he could accept, severe enough to acknowledge that no conception of a hidden morality in nature can remove the fact that, as he phrases it in the *Life*, "Pain has been, and pain is."[113]

The Need to Believe: Wallace Stevens

Among the writers considered in this chapter as literary atheists, Stevens may seem the one least to belong, for the word God was congenial to him. "The major poetic idea in the world," he declared, "is and always has been the idea of God."[114] But to write also, and no less characteristically, "God is merely a poetic idea even if the supreme poetic idea" or "God and the Imagination are one" (*S* 674) is to aestheticize it. Stevens leaves no doubt as to the relative importance of the poetic and religious use of the word: "We no longer think that God was, but was imagined....The idea of God is only one of the things of the imagination."[115] The words he most often associated with it were "nobility" and "elegance," themselves suggestive of an aesthetic bias.

Although not a believer, Stevens did have a religious sensibility. He was devout in his attentions to the physical world and to his feelings about what he saw and heard in nature, and he said things like: "[Poets] purge themselves before reality...in what they intend to be saintly exercises" (*S* 790); "[M]y own way out toward the future involves a confidence in the spiritual role of the poet...in restoring to the imagination what it is losing at such a catastrophic pace."[116] Not surprisingly he rejected the label of atheist, which must have seemed bleakly rationalistic. He was seeking a humanism of an expansive type—Emersonian, Whitmanian, Nietzschean—one that, without committing him to transcendence, was responsive to the suggestiveness of a word like "beyond." The poet asks the muse of Fictive Music for the power to express what is "near" but "not too near," "like" but "not too like," the human. Meditating on "the man with the blue guitar," the poet would make a song "of" ourselves yet "beyond us." The singer who creates an idea of order at Key West mediates between her human audience and the "inhuman" ocean. The mountain Chocorua finds "acutest speech" to inhere in the *height* and *depth* of the human. "Nuances of a Theme by Williams" turns Williams's parable of human courage in loneliness into one about the strength to live with an alien heaven.

Stevens' stance, then, extends the idea of humanism. But it is naturalistic from beginning to end, from "Divinity must live within herself" ("Sunday Morning") to "God is in me or else is not at all" ("Adagia II"). The religious mythology that invokes Heaven may be mocked ("The Worms at Heaven's Gate," "Cortège for Rosenbloom"), dismissed as "colossal illusion" ("Landscape with Boat"), or put aside as "an exhausted culture" unable to produce poetic power ("Adagia II"). Our revelations today "are not the revelations of belief, but the precious portents of our own powers" ("The Relations Between Poetry & Painting"). We cannot go back to a religious age, Stevens everywhere assumes, even though our disbelief may trouble us. Nor can we adopt a non-Christian divinity, for "the death of one god is the death of all" (*S* 329), and, in any case, the poet inevitably shares the disbelief of his time (*S* 847).

Stevens is sometimes called an agnostic, but if agnosticism is understood as doubting rather than disbelieving the Christian idea of God, the word is really not accurate. In style Stevens makes much use of conditionality and tentativeness in order to meditate with exquisite precision on elusive shades of feeling. Like Nietzsche he shuns *the* truth—"The the," as he puts it memorably at the end of "The Man on the Dump." But theological uncertainty is absent from his work. Unlike such last-gasp Victorian doubters as Twain and Hardy, Stevens takes a position firmly beyond any debate about the existence of God. For him, "loss of faith...is growth (*S* 911)." What remains is the need to believe.

The crux issue for Stevens is not God but belief, and belief he attaches to poetry, which "must take the place/ Of empty heaven and its hymns (*S* 137)." Such phrasing suggests an affinity with with the nineteenth-century religion of art that we discussed in Chapter One. And so does each of the following declarations: "After one has abandoned a belief in god, poetry is that essence which takes its place as life's redemption" (*S* 901); "In the absence of belief in God, the mind turns to its own creations and examines them, not alone from the aesthetic point of view, but for what they reveal, for what they validate or invalidate, for the support that they give" (*S* 916). But Stevens the modernist is subscribing to a religion of art very much on his own terms. To say "The final belief is to believe in a fiction, which you know to be a fiction" (*S* 903) is to make belief voluntary. That is somewhat different from an involuntary belief in a God or God-substitute, as Stevens himself implied when he said, in "Imagination as Value," that "poetry does not address itself to beliefs."

I think we can best gauge the distinctiveness of his thought here if we ask how his idea of believing in a fiction differs from, even as it resembles, similar speculations on the part of his important teachers, William James and George Santayana. In *The Will to Believe*, published in 1897 (a book much discussed during his Harvard years although Stevens did not meet the author), James is at pains to defend the *right* to believe against the aggressive agnosticism of writers like Huxley and Clifford, which he took to be antagonistic to this right, no different really from dogmatic atheism. Although not himself a believer, James was convinced that believing was psychologically and morally advantageous, and so argued that one could and should adopt belief as hypothesis in the same way that a scientist adopts hypothesis as an investigative tool. Stevens alludes to James's phrase in a letter written years later, with a slight but significant change of wording, altering the word "will" to "need": "Underlying it [i.e., the poem he was calling Notes Toward a Supreme Fiction] is the idea that, in various predicaments of belief, it might be possible to yield, or to try to yield, to a declared fiction. This is the same thing as saying that it might be possible for us to believe something that we know to be untrue. Of course we do that every day, but we don't make the most of the fact that we do it out of the need to believe, what in your day, and mine, in Cambridge was called the will to believe."[117] James himself, I think, would have found strange the idea of believing in a declared fiction. For James, a hypothesis, unlike a fiction, *may be true*, and that possibility was important for him. He wanted to argue the case for religious belief on grounds that would make sense to a scientist, not to a poet whose need to believe could be satisfied by poems.

Stevens' idea of believing a declared fiction is closer in spirit to Santayana's linking of religion and *poetry* than to James's linking of religion and *science*. In *Interpretations of Poetry and Religion* (1900) Santayana had written, "religion and poetry are identical in essence," and "differ merely in the way they are attached to practical affairs."[118] Like Stevens, he considered the old Christian mythology exhausted, but he was still seeking poetry *in* religion rather than *instead of* it, which was perhaps why Stevens, who did know Santayana at Harvard and always admired him, shied away from nominating him for the projected Poetry Chair. More subtly, it may be why, in his tribute poem, "To an Old Philosopher in Rome," Stevens, in Harold

Bloom's words, "for once allowed himself to repress his strong awareness that the mind could never be satisfied."[119]

Perhaps the closest analogue to Stevens' idea of believing in a fiction is to be found in the idea of "literary belief" proposed by his fellow-poet and contemporary, Robert Frost. Frost makes it clear that the speech of poets (and of scientists as well, if they but knew it) is inseparable from metaphor: it "is enthusiasm tamed by metaphor." But he is also at pains to explain that poems "are written not by cunning, but by belief." They are "believed into existence," beginning "in something more felt than known." And he ventures to add that "the art-belief" is "closely related to "the God-belief...a relationship you enter into with Him to bring about the future."[120]

Religion in Stevens' mind stood for unchangingness, as is clear in "A High-Toned Old Christian Woman" and in "Sunday Morning." It could not therefore serve well as a vehicle for the kind of belief that interested him. Believing *in* a fiction will seem to some a curious idea, but what Stevens meant was an emotional commitment that, though inevitably temporary and changeable, was total at the moment. He knew well, as did Frost, that "if you don't believe in poetry, you cannot write it."[121] He knew like Nietzsche, and perhaps learned from him, that fiction or illusion can have a strong truth value, especially for the creative mind. One striking way he expressed this was: "We never arrive intellectually. But emotionally we arrive constantly (*S* 911)." "Thought is false happiness" (in "Crude Foyer") was another, a statement that would not have won the assent of James or even Santayana.

The most important working out of the idea of fiction-and-belief in Stevens is of course "Notes Toward a Supreme Fiction" (1942), which we must approach by way of a brief excursus on those crucial terms, Reality and Imagination. I cannot here do justice to their multiple uses throughout Stevens' work, but an outline will help us read the poem.

Reality and Imagination are both what David R. Jarraway calls "subjective poles," and so are not logically separable.[122] For Stevens, reality is nothing other, nothing more metaphysical, than the succession of appearances given to the mind's eye, and imagination is nothing other than the making of metaphor and poetry out of this material. Stevens can collapse the distinction at any time, as when he writes: "Reality Is an Activity of the Most August Imagination"; or "Poetry and materia poetica are interchangeable terms"; or "Things seen are things as seen." But he wants to think of them as contraries because he values the pressure that each—the given world and the made world—exerts on the other. Lest we think of his use of these contraries as drily abstract, we should understand that their interaction is mediated by what Frank Kermode aptly called "the urgency of need" and Helen Vendler "passionate feeling."[123] In a summery mood the pressure exerted by Imagination is ascendant, in a wintry mood the pressure of Reality dominates, but Stevens is constantly aware of the danger of thinking in such a way that one loses touch with the other. "Sometimes I believe most in the imagination for a long time and then, without reasoning about it, turn to reality and believe in that and that alone. *But both of these things project themselves endlessly and I want them to do just that* [my emphasis]."[124]

The supreme fiction for Stevens is poetry, but poetry in what sense? It cannot be identified quite with the poem because there will always be another poem, and for Stevens another poem is often written out of dissatisfaction with the last. (Asking himself why he wrote poetry, he answered, "because one grows tired of the monotony of one's imagination" [*S* 785]). But neither can poetry be identified simply with the poet's *oeuvre* because that would make it a definable monument, not an ongoing activity. The poet is "under the daily necessity of getting the world right" (*S* 913). The mind tries to counter its own "final no" with "a yes," but the mind "can never be satisfied...never" (*S* 224). The imagination cannot make any image "chief" because *it* is "the irrepressible revolutionist" (*S* 736). The closest Stevens can come to pinning down the meaning of supreme fiction is by indicating that its originating power lies in the mind, in the self. That, I think, is why there are so many efforts in Stevens, especially in his hero phase (which includes "Notes") to mythicize this self, giving it such names as central man, major man, miraculous man, giant, and glass man without external reference. In one poem, the sun itself is called "that brave man" (*S* 112). But this is something more—or less—than divinizing the poet, as Emerson and Whitman did: "We do not say the poet is to take the place of gods" (*S* 842). A supreme fiction must be human but must also be open to a less familiar and comfortable something beyond humanity.

The poem necessarily begins by posing (tentatively, as the words "Notes" and "Toward" in the title imply) an originary fiction that clears away accumulated fictions, and this it calls "the first idea." The first idea is perhaps best understood as the power of metaphor, and touching base with it oscillates in the poet's concern with the generated particulars. The first of the three sections is called "It Must Be Abstract." The word abstract here, as Joan Richardson suggested to me in conversation, probably has the sense it had for James and Henri Bergson, something drawn off from concrete imagery but not categorically distinct from it. Thus the "ignorant man," who by virtue of his freedom from preconceptions can perform this abstraction, finds the "sun" both inconceivable and reconceivable.

The second part is called "It Must Change" and is the necessary complement of the first. The first section of this part tries to find the originary within language, and speaks of the difficulty of what it is to be. The second begins by punning on "bee"/"be," the humble bee serving as an amusing symbol of ceaseless movement, necessary and refreshing: hence "the President ordains the bee to be." Stevens has thus established his cycle: the first idea generates the "exhilaration of changes," and these very changes, when they eventually become monotonous, revive our thirst to know the origin of change. But Stevens' "exhilaration" does not simply turn from Coleridgean "joy" into "dejection." Because of that "wintry temperament," his imagination thrives on a sense of alienation in the natural world: "From this the poem springs,/ That we live in a place that is not our own/ And much more not ourselves/ And hard it is in spite of blazoned days." This is sublime pathos, yet it too does not resolve anything. If there is any resting point at the end of the second part, it lies only in the very idea of cycle, an alternate reduction to and expansion from the first idea.

The third and last part, "It Must Give Pleasure," has received varied readings. I see it as an effort to show that, in the working out of this cycle, there is some danger of getting stuck at one end or the other. On the one hand there is the danger of becoming obsessed by a single idea of self, like the sparrow with its "Be thou me"; on the other, there is the danger of becoming imaginatively untethered, like the too enthusiastic Canon Aspirin, who is not likely to find what will suffice. The "I" of the poem finds some satisfaction in the fiction of an angel but implies a distinction between its own belief in this fiction and the Canon's. The "I" knows, as the Canon does not, that its believing is a product of its *own* poverty: "There is a month, a year, there is a time/ In which majesty is a mirror of the self:/ I have not but I am, and as I am, I am." The Canon seems to forget that "not to have is the beginning of desire"; he could not say "as I am, I am" in a spirit of humility, only in a spirit of pride.

The coda to such a poem cannot choose finally between "the mind" and "the sky," but it can say with some finality that there is a "war between" them and always will be. Yet that alone would sound too unresolved for a poem that is after all trying to validate, however tentatively, a supreme fiction, which is why, I think, the "Soldier" is brought in. In an earlier poem

Stevens had referred to a soldier's death as "absolute and without memorial (*S* 81)," and certainly his disbelief in an afterlife had not changed. But he could also imply now that the words generated by the activity of poetry have some value in the world, that there is a connection between the fictive and the real, between the hero as poet and the hero as soldier, and that therefore the soldier, "with proper words," can die gladly if he must.

Before we move toward a conclusion, one other longer poem deserves at least passing attention here, for "Esthétique du Mal" (1944) tries to deal directly with the general problem of pain or evil that has fueled so much unbelief.

It tells us that the "too too human God" we have created must be discarded. Based on pity for man, this conception sentimentalizes suffering. For Nietzsche, who clearly influenced Stevens' thinking in this poem,[125] it was Epicurus who provided the model for the noble response to suffering, but this nobility was corrupted by the theology of Christianity. Stevens, less specific historically and more in sorrow than in the spirit of rejection, writes of "the death of Satan"—i.e., of a vigorous and vital idea of evil—as "a tragedy for the imagination." In "Sunday Morning," "a ring of men...shall chant...their boisterous devotion to the sun," but men are now pictured as "children of poverty" who have only language to support them. "The greatest poverty is not to live/ In a physical world, to feel that one's desire/ Is too difficult to tell from despair," and this is the nub of what is equivocal in "Esthétique du Mal." In Stevens' hedonistic phase the physical world seemed to provide almost endless delight, although there are melancholy undercurrents in *Harmonium*, as Kermode reminds us.[126] But after "Farewell to Florida" and the resumption of his poetic career in a new key, Stevens endorses the sufficiency of the physical world in a somewhat stoic fashion, making it difficult for us to distinguish *his* desire from despair. "Esthétique du Mal" eloquently evokes the idea of a new "adventurer in humanity" conceiving "a race/ Completely physical in a physical world." Its conclusion rises to a height of eloquence:

> And out of what one sees and hears and out
> Of what one feels, who could have thought to make
> So many selves, so many sensuous worlds,
> As if the air, the mid-day air, was swarming
> With the metaphysical changes that occur,
> Merely in living as and where we live.

But it is difficult not to read this celebration of richness and responsiveness as a kind of wish-fulfillment, and the impression is heightened if one takes into account the two poems that follow "Esthétique" in *Transport to Summer*, "The Bed of Old John Zeller" and especially "Less and Less Human, O Savage Spirit," which contains the frightening lines: "It is the human that is the alien,/ The human that has no cousin in the moon./...If there must be a god in the house, let him be one/ That will not hear us when we speak."

In Stevens' final phase, Reality more than Imagination became "the necessary angel," as Vendler implies when she comments, in sharp contrast to the received idea of Stevens the hedonist, that "his fundamental donnée [was] the disappointments of desire."[127] The tension between imagination and reality, the war between the mind and sky, never really ceased for Stevens, but in his great last period he developed remarkably subtle ways of expressing their interaction. In "The Course of a Particular" (according to Vendler the poem he was born to write[128]), the human meaning of the repeated "cry of the leaves" diminishes to point zero ("until, at last, the cry concerns no one at all"), yet, we may add, the cry itself, not only the verdict of its final meaninglessness, lingers in our minds. "Final Soliloquy of the Interior Paramour" works from the other pole, consoling us with the knowledge of what is enough, but it is suffused with pathos evoked by the image of our retreat "Out of all the indifferences, into one thing...a single shawl/ Wrapped tightly round us, since we are poor." The late poem that perhaps most subtly connects the contraries is "Of Mere Being," which concludes the *Collected Poems* and has been called his "death-poem."[129]

> The palm at the end of the mind,
> Beyond the last thought, rises
> In the bronze decor.
>
> A gold-feathered bird
> Sings in the palm, without human meaning,
> Without human feeling, a foreign song.
>
> You know then that it is not the reason
> That makes us happy or unhappy.
> The bird sings. Its feathers shine.
>
> The palm stands on the edge of space.
> The wind moves slowly in the branches.
> The bird's fire-fangled feathers dangle down.

Gold coloring, palm, bird, and fire are familiar images evoking desire in its more youthful manifestations, but the poem is seeking the end of desire, the mereness of being. The bird sings, the palm stands, the wind moves. And the last line captures one last gaudy flourish, "fire-fangled feathers," in order to check it by another alliteration suggestive of sexual finality, "dangles down." Stevens' "mere being" with its absence of "human meaning" contains no hint of transcendence, protest, or even acquiescence. Yet it moves us by extending our sense of the human into the space of the inhuman. By this kind of radical humanism does Stevens finally satisfy his need to believe.

In the essay "Imagination as Value," Stevens had written, "the great poems of heaven and hell have been written and the great poem of the earth remains to be written." A poem like "Sunday Morning" looks like a direct response to this challenge, but when we consider the whole poetic career, the response comes to look more indirect, a celebration not so much of earth or even of poetry as such but of poetic power. Stevens' range is said to be very limited since all his poetry is about poetry, but this subject matter is somewhat less specialized than it seems if we realize that poetry for him is equivalent finally to the creative human imagination. Kermode had it about right when he wrote: "In the end that is the subject of Stevens: living without God and finding it good, because of the survival of the power that once made Him suffice."[130] I would only add that the humanism embraced at last is perhaps a bit less comforting, a bit more austere, than Kermode implies. "Imagination," we are told in "Relations Between Poetry & Painting," "is to be regarded not as a phase of humanism but as a vital self-assertion in a world in which nothing but the self remains."

Samuel Beckett and the Bastard Who Doesn't Exist

Beckett found his audience with *Waiting for Godot*, written in 1948–49, published in 1952, and first produced in Paris in 1953, the US in 1954, and the UK in 1955. Somewhat unfortunately, the moment coincided with the emergence of a fashion (lasting about fifteen years) for Death of God theology, and so a play that deliberately avoided specification and that maximized uncertainty[131] was subjected to allegorical interpretation. Those hungry for moral significance were of course not satisfied by the author's insistence that he himself did not know who or what Godot was or even if he existed.[132]

But a teasing name like Godot cannot simply be ignored, especially in view of the publication in 1943, a few years before the play was composed, of Simone Weil's *Attente de Dieu*, translated as *Waiting for God*. In fact the name is a typical Beckettian tease of the 1940s, like Mr Knott in *Watt* or Moran's boss Youdi, names that have been rightly taken by critics to be parodic of Yahweh. The *ot* suffix mocks or cancels our expectation of significance, the way Molloy's addition of the letter *g* to "Ma" "abolished" and "spat" on a name that ought to be honored.

In his magisterial biography, *Damned to Fame*, James Knowlson describes Samuel Beckett as an agnostic.[133] This makes good sense because the *oeuvre* thematizes not knowing. Moreover, as Porter Abbott argues in *Beckett Writing Beckett: The Author in the Autograph*, Beckettian skepticism actually requires a "metaphysical openendedness" expressing "a fascination with possibilities," in contrast to the certainty of "a skepticism that accepts the absolute absence of knowledge outside of the text."[134] But if agnosticism is understood as a commitment to unbelief, it is a misleading description of Beckett's stance as a writer. Atheism would of course also be misleading and for the same reason, implying a commitment to unbelief and thus the flipside of a commitment to belief. Seeking more precision, Mary Bryden, in her recent book *Samuel Beckett and the Idea of God*, summons to her aid an "atheist mystic," Jean Claude Bologne, who describes his own writerly stance as "a state…not a statement of position."[135] This is helpful. If we can think of atheism not as a principled denial of God's existence but as a characteristic imaginative movement whereby theological and religious allusions are evoked and then turned in a subversively ironic direction, the term describes Beckett's way of doing things pretty well. Such allusions abound in his work. As he told Colin Duckworth, "Christianity is a mythology with which I am perfectly familiar, so I make use of it."[136] Make use of it he did, for his religious and theological allusions are almost always occasions for irreverent wit.

It is important to understand that Beckett's witty use of these allusions is characteristically aggressive. The intention is not merely to scale down the comforts and consolations of faith but to puncture them as a cheat and a delusion. Trying to keep Beckett at least marginally within the Christian fold, Bryden comments, "Even when repeatedly stamped upon, the *idea* or hypothesis of a Godhead keeps growing back in Beckett's texts."[137] It would more accurate to reverse these clauses and say, even though the idea of God keeps growing back in Beckett's texts, it is repeatedly stamped upon. This does not mean, however, that Beckett wants to define himself as non-Christian. As Shira Wolosky acutely observed in her book *Language Mysticism: The Negative Way of Language in Eliot, Beckett, and Celan*, "Beckett does not work so much within or out of theological tradition as reflect back upon it."[138]

The wit of Beckett's theological allusions requires that God's existence be in some way postulated so that it can be attacked, much the way a bowling pin must be set up in order to be knocked down. A quintessential example is Hamm's bitter comment when he and his little group in *Endgame* must abandon their attitude of prayer as fruitless: "The bastard! He doesn't exist!" The word "bastard" acknowledges, albeit rudely, God's existence. The denial of this existence is then witty because, combined with the personifying word "bastard," it is illogical, but this very illogic reveals its cutting, passionate force. This is emotional repudiation, not intellectual doubt. No wonder that, when the Lord Chamberlain wanted "the bastard" removed while allowing the atheistic (but, by itself, dull) little sentence to stand, Beckett dug in his heels, writing to his director, Alan Schneider, "'He doesn't exist' without 'the bastard' is inacceptable [*sic*] to me."[139]

His real target is not Christianity as such but, rather, any deceptive spiritual comfort—which, to be sure, Christianity and other religions offer and advertise as stock in trade. For this enemy of false consolation, a phrase like "first love" (the title he gave to a cynical story) or like "joy forever" is irritating. Youdi's messenger alters Keats's famous line to "life is a thing of beauty and a joy forever" so that Moran can deliver the punch: "do you think he meant human life?" "The Lord upholdeth all that fall" declared the biblical psalmist, but the bitter humor of the radio play titled "All That Fall" exposes not the Bible as such but our readiness to hope that its language can still support us.

It helps to keep in mind this larger target when we encounter such theological allusions as these: "incorruptible, uninjurable, unchangeable"—Augustine's exalted tribute to God applied to Belaqua's rather different love object, the Smeraldina in *Dream of Fair to Middling Women*; "And now abideth these 3: Doubt, Despair & Scrounging" (from the *Dream* notebook); "apathia" and "athambia" (traditional terms in negative theology, as Wolosky reminds us[140]) juxtaposed in Lucky's tirade with "aphasia," a psychiatric term denoting the inability to speak or understand. Some critics have taken "aphasia" to mean merely "not answering prayers," but this keeps the terms on the same plane and spoils the wit.[141] When Bryden isn't anxious to mitigate Beckett's irreverence, she understands this aspect of Beckett's style very well, commenting nicely: "A sometimes searing awareness of different or sundered planes is for Beckett infinitely preferable to a...reassuring synthesis of them. Hence his distaste for the fluidity of the Ich-Gott relation in Rilke's poetry."[142]

The sharpness of Beckett's literary atheism may be better appreciated if we contrast *his* skeptical use of an Augustinian phrase, "honey of heaven," to that of Wallace Stevens. Stevens wrote, in "Le Monocle de Mon Oncle," "the honey of heaven may or may not come," a *politely* skeptical sentence because the poet's loyalty is clearly to the honey "of earth [that] comes and goes at once." Beckett, on the other hand, jumps up and down on the phrase. Augustine described his pre-conversion self, in Book 9 of the *Confessions*, as "a pestilent person, a bitter and a blind bawler against those writings, which are honied with the honey of heaven." In the notebook for *Dream of Fair to Middling Women*, Beckett had copied this along with other quotations from the *Confessions*, and interjected irritably, "against the honey what honey bloody well you know the honey." And, still irritated, in the novel he twice uses the word "honey" in connection with the relationship between Belacqua and Alba, and twice turns round on it to say, "What honey?" The solacing sweetness of a phrase like "honey of heaven," rather than Augustine or Christianity as such, could not be tolerated.

Beckett saw the human situation not in terms of faith, hope, and charity but in terms of suffering, which means, perhaps paradoxically, that there was one Christian image that he could actually welcome and exploit—crucifixion. Making use of the possibilities in this case required him to shift his ironic strategy a bit, and show that a *painful* Christian image was not painful *enough*. The strategy of allusion still involves irony, but now the point is to show that the horror of Christ's crucifixion can be overmatched in everyday experience by "the suffering of being," to use a key phrase in his early monograph on Proust.[143] Creating a kind of black humor, Beckett suggests that crucifixion, for all its horror, might be thought of as an easy way out of the suffering of being. Estragon has only the vaguest recollection of the Bible, is bewildered by notions of repentance, sin and salvation, but he understands punishment very well indeed and readily identifies with Christ as fellow sufferer—"All my life I've compared myself to him"—but of course Christ's suffering in a land where "they crucified quick" was merciful compared to his own lifelong crucifixion. Molloy, similarly, describes his painful progress on crutches as "a veritable calvary, with no limit to its stations and no hope of crucifixion." ("No hope of crucifixion" is a wonderful touch.) Clov begins *Endgame* with an allusion to words spoken by Christ on the cross ("It is finished"), but, remembering his own situation, he backs off from this formulation as too comforting: "Finished, it's finished, nearly finished, it must be nearly finished....I can't be punished any more."

It has been said, notably by Georg Lukács, that Beckett's work is unable to protest against social injustice.[144] Theodor Adorno has rebutted the charge adroitly by indicating that Beckett's work paradoxically enables a more just society precisely by the thoroughness of his disengagement from the existing one, the strength of his negation thus compelling rather than merely asking for a change of attitude.[145] Adorno's argument is subtle and debatable but has the merit of calling attention to Beckett's by no means inert political consciousness. Pictures of cruelty and bullying pervade his work. What obscures our perception of this fact is less the lack of social reference than the writer's unwillingness to *explain* brutality (for example, the why or wherefore of the "they" who beat Estragon overnight), as if he would say, in Bryden's words, "brutality...simply happens."[146] In all the drafts of *Godot* up until the last, Beckett's name for Estragon was Lévy, a sufficiently clear indication that he was thinking of his Jewish friends recently killed by the Nazis but also that he wanted, finally, not to say this in the play, for the sake of universalizing his theme. In Hamm's stark words, "you're on earth, there's no cure for that!" Abbott's analysis goes to the heart of the matter:

> From beginning to end, Beckett's art is one long protest. It is written out of a horror of human wretchedness and a yearning that this wretchedness be lessened. But the overriding sense in Beckett is not that there is something wrong with society...but something massively wrong with the entire arrangement, from birth to death. Beckett's social protest is always shadowed by his metaphysical bafflement.[147]

This is worth keeping in mind when we hear of the unpolitical Beckett. And it also alerts us to a danger and an opportunity in Beckett's use of the idea of God. Since the artist does not really seek to stamp *out* the idea, he has to be careful, at the risk of seeming to air a grievance, that the suffering of his characters not appear to derive from supernatural malevolence. Perhaps in only one minor instance, the mime play attached to *Endgame*, does he yield to this temptation—at any rate I cannot disassociate the frustrations of the figure on stage from a sadistic agency manipulating them from behind the scene. But Beckett regularly succeeds in eluding and indeed capitalizing on this danger because of his uncanny art of of what Abbott calls "recollection by invention."[148] That is, fragments of memory rich in pathos are drawn up into an experience in present time; the emotion is there but deflected by the formal fascination of interlocking frames and planes. In this way, I think, an incipient grievance against God expressed through Winnie (*Happy Days*), Mouth (*Not I*) or the Rooneys (*All That Fall*) is transformed.

Nietzsche mused marvelously, "I am afraid we are not getting rid of God because we still believe in grammar."[149] It would be difficult to think of another writer who has come closer than Beckett to undermining our faith "in grammar." He has done so mainly in two ways. One is what Abbott described as "a narratricidal need to undo the masterplot of death and procreation."[150] Plot is traditionally a progressive action moving to a significant close, a piece of a masterplot involving origins and destinies, hence gods or fates. *Waiting for Godot* goes a great way toward undermining this tradition, showing human beings in a state of waiting without beginning or end, and even folding a traditional plot, Pozzo's fall from high to low degree, inside of this "action." The other major strategy undermines our faith in an essential self made in the image of God, and this the art does by its strenuous and unavailing effort (not only in *The Unnamable*) to find a pronoun equivalent to the self. Beckett's speakers feel keenly that they have never been entirely *there*, never entirely *born*, and thus are unable to become identical to themselves. They are distressingly trapped in language, and so their dream of an ultimate source or end can never be realized.

The latter problem reminds us of what a number of philosophers have also been saying, perhaps most notably Jacques Derrida. But the resemblance between Beckett and Derrida on this matter entails an important difference. Derrida relishes the infinite play of language, considering it mere illusion or nostalgia to imagine an escape from it. One of the most impassioned ideas in Beckett's work, however, is the desirability of the silence or peace or nothingness that *is* imagined as existing before or beyond language. (He once advised a critic who wished to write about his work to start from two of his favorite quotations: Democritus' "Nothing is more real than nothing" and the Descartes disciple Arnold Geulincx's "Where you are worth nothing there you do want nothing.")[151] Beckett *knows* that the dream is illusory, but his art energetically bends every resource of language to attempt to reach the unreachable. Perhaps this contrast with Derrida demonstrates that the artist has an advantage over the philosopher, even a philosopher who works in the area between philosophy and literature. Beckett can be indifferent to logical consistency, giving his conflict of emotions full expression, but Derrida is working in a mode that does not quite give him this freedom.

It has proved difficult for many readers to confront squarely Beckett's thematic pessimism. Christopher Ricks's *Beckett's Dying Words* is a significant exception, a book that succeeds not only because of its candor but because Ricks has enough learning to show how the theme of contempt for life fits into a long and serious literary tradition.[152] Critics who want to combat this idea on a thematic level can do little more than to try to mitigate it, like Bryden, or to stress the countervailing theme of stoicism implied by phrasing like "I can't go on, I'll go on." But Beckett has pretty thoroughly emptied out the resonance of "the Victorian trope of onwardness."[153] And the famous "go on" at the end of *The Unnamable* refers more to speaking than living, to the determination to go on failing as daringly as possible in the vain hope of getting beyond words.

If we want to discover the excitement of reading Beckett we must try not to soften his "nothing" but to see that his originality is bound up with it. His nothing is "the nourishing murk that is killing me" (as Malone puts it), where "nourishing" and "killing" are inextricably connected. In her final chapter, "Solitude, Stillness, Silence and Stars," Bryden, recognizing that Beckett privileges these images, seeks to link his art with the tradition of mysticism inherent in the *via negativa* and in negative theology. She finds that his silence, like Jean Claude Bologne's, is where "atheism" and "mysticism" meet.[154] But, as Shira Wolosky has strongly demonstrated, Beckett is in fact a "counter-mystic," *negating* the negative way. He uses the methods of negative theology to achieve different goals.[155] When we look a second time at passages in his work that suggest this theology, we catch clearly the tone of irony—as when the Unnamble says, "First I'll say what I'm not, that's how they taught me to proceed," or as when the narrator of *Watt* asserts:

> The only way one can speak of nothing is to speak of it as though it were something, just as the only way one can speak of God is to speak of him as though he were a man, which to be sure he was, in a sense, for a time, and as the only way one can speak of man…is to speak of him as though he were a termite.

In Beckett the dynamic relation between negation and invention is all-important. And it has been spelled out best, I believe, by two of his numerous critics. One is Porter Abbott, who shows that the more reduced Beckett's art became, the more mind-bending became its originality. He unpacks the double and triple loops of the short "A Piece of Monologue," a work so intricately balanced between narrative and drama that it resembles an Escher graphic, one genre sliding back and forth into the other. When you look at it closely, the "dramatic universe...contains the narrative universe, and the narrative universe contains the dramatic universe." Equally impressive is Abbott's analysis of the short late play, "Ohio Impromptu," in which the artist "creates a complex experience in which both author and audience are at once inside and outside the art, participants and observers." This, of course, he demonstrates in detail; phrased comprehensively, the point is that "the counter tropes of reduction, negation, cancellation, and despair—always parts of the Beckett signature—invariably set off the vigor of that productivity."[156]

The other critic who writes especially well about negation and invention is Shira Wolosky, who sees the connection in terms of language theory rather than of form and effect. She cites many other critics who are committed to the idea that Beckett is exposing the inadequacy of language and seeking to attain the wordless truth beyond language. Her contrary idea is that Beckett's relentless reductions expose instead the fact that there *is* no human world beyond language, and that his own language is thereby triumphantly asserting its success. To imply that only unspeaking can assert truth hardly implies the inadequacy of one's language if one never ceases to speak—and speak inventively. Wolosky sums up her comprehensive analysis with admirable pithiness: "[Beckett's] use of negative tradition is finally ironic, presenting its paradoxically plethoric nothingness as in fact a void. His own negative modes, in contrast, convert nothingness into a fertile source of continuous imaginative effort."[157]

"No lack of void" appalled poor Estragon, but it stimulated Beckett and Nietzsche to extraordinary achievement.

NOTES

In the notes on Nietzsche I follow the practice of most scholars and use section rather than page numbers in references to his aphoristic books. In the notes on Stevens I quote frequently from a single text—Frank Kermode and Joan Richardson, eds., *Stevens: Collected Poetry & Prose* (New York: Library of America, 1997)—and therefore have placed in parenthesis after each quotation an italicized *S* and a page number, unless the poem or essay quoted from is already adequately identified in the text.

1. Unless otherwise indicated, quotations from Diderot's writings are based on the twenty volume *Oeuvres complètes*, edited by J. Assézat and M. Tourneux, originally published in 1875, reissued in 1966.
2. Lester G. Crocker, ed., *Diderot's Selected Writings*, trans. Derek Coltman (New York: Macmillan, 1966), 21.
3. Diderot, *Correspondance 1713–1757*, 74–8. Diderot returns to the subject of this letter in a late piece, "Conversations with Abbé Barthélemy," in which he claims to the Abbé that he wrote what he did to please Voltaire, and adds: "This is what happens, Abbé: when I am with atheists...all the arguments in favour of the existence of God spring up in my mind; when I happen to be with believers, it's just the opposite." See Diderot, *Interpreter of Nature: Selected Writings*, trans. Jean Stewart and Jonathan Kemp (Westport, CT.: Hyperion Press, 1937), 202-03. This is to repeat the same mixture of tact and candor but perhaps in a more disingenuous spirit since the Abbé is not quite a Voltaire.
4. Diderot, *Interpreter of Nature*, 43. For other examples, see Arthur M. Wilson, *Diderot* (Oxford: Clarendon Press, 1972), 144–45.
5. Quoted in Carol Sherman, *Diderot and the Art of Dialogue* (Geneva: Librairie Droz, 1976), 53.
6. Herbert Josephs, *Diderot's Dialogue of Gesture and Language* (Columbus: Ohio State University Press, 1969), vii.
7. John Hope Mason, *The Irresistible Diderot* (London: Quartet Books, 1982), 12.
8. Wilda Anderson, *Diderot's Dream* (Baltimore: Johns Hopkins University Press, 1990).
9. Aram Vartanian, "Diderot or the Dualist in Spite of Himself," in *Diderot: Digression and Dispersion: A Bicentennial Tribute*, eds. Jack Udank and Herbert Josephs (Lexington, KY: French Forum Publishers, 1984), 250–58.
10. P. N. Furbank, *Diderot: A Critical Biography* (New York: Knopf, 1992), 135–38.
11. Rüdiger Safranski, *Nietzsche: A Philosophical Biography*, trans. Shelley Frisch (New York: Norton, 2002), 176.
12. Wilson, *Diderot*, 666.
13. Wilson, *Diderot*, 663.
14. Denis Diderot, *Jacques the Fatalist and His Master*, trans. Michael Henry (New York: Penguin, 1986), 21–22.
15. Quoted in Otis Fellows, *Diderot*, rev. ed. (Boston: G. K. Hall, 1989), 126.
16. Furbank, *Diderot*, 354–55. The French of the problematic distich, which may be found in vol. 9, p. 16, of the *Oeuvres complètes*, reads: "*Et ses mains ourdiraient les entrailles du prêtre,/ Au défaut d'un cordon pour étrangler les rois.*"

17 This includes three dramatic works (*Danton's Death, Leonce and Lena, Woyzeck*), one polemical pamphlet ("The Hessian Messenger"), and a story ("Lenz").
18 Carl Richard Mueller, Introduction, in Mueller, ed., *Büchner: Complete Plays and Prose* (New York: Hill and Wang, 1963), xv.
19 Mueller, *Büchner*, xiii.
20 Victor Price, Introduction, in Price, ed., *Danton's Death, Leonce and Lena, Woyzeck by Georg Büchner* (Oxford: Oxford University Press, 1971), x.
21 Herbert Lindenberger, *Georg Büchner: Modern Critiques* (Carbondale, IL: So. Illinois Univerity Press, 1964); Victor Brombert, *In Praise of Antiheroes: Figures and Themes in Modern European Literature 1830–1980* (Chicago: University of Chicago Press, 1999).
22 Lindenberger, *Büchner*, 26.
23 Lindenberger, *Büchner*, 30.
24 Ronald Hauser, *Georg Büchner* (Boston: Twayne, 1974), 46.
25 Crocker, ed., *Diderot's Selected Writings*, 87.
26 Maurice Benn, *The Drama of Revolt: A Critical Study of Georg Büchner* (Cambridge: Cambridge University Press, 1976), 70.
27 Letter of 1834, quoted in Mueller, *Complete Plays and Prose*, xvi.
28 Michael Hamburger, Introduction, in Hamburger ed., *Georg Büchner: Leonce and Lena, Lenz, Woyzeck* (Chicago: University of Chicago Press, 1972), xii.
29 Quoted in Lindenberger, *Büchner*, 15.
30 Especially useful texts for background on Nietzsche's reading are Walter Kaufmann, *Nietzsche: Philosopher, Psychologist, Antichrist*, 4th ed. (Princeton: Princeton University Press, 1974); and Bernd Magnus and Kathleen M. Higgins, eds., *The Cambridge Companion to Nietzsche*, (Cambridge University Press, 1996), 1–68.
31 Typical of his oblique admission of debt is this sentence-opening from the early notebooks: "Darwinism (which by the way I consider to be true)...." See Nietzsche, *Philosophy and Truth: Selections from Nietzsche's Notebooks of the Early 1870s*, edited and translated by Daniel Brezeale (Atlantic Highlands, NJ: Humanities Press, 1979), p. 43. The quotation in my text is an unpublished translation by Burton Pike of a passage in Nietzsche, *Werke in drei Baenden*, vol. 3, ed. Karl Schlecta (Munich: C. Hanser, 1954–56), p. 894.
32 Friedrich Nietzsche, "History in the Service and Disservice of Life," in *Unmodern Observations,* ed. William Arrowsmith, trans. Gary Brown (New Haven: Yale University Press, 1990), pp. 88–91.
33 Friedrich Nietzsche, *Daybreak: Thoughts on the Prejudices of Morality*, trans. R. J. Hollingdale, (Cambridge: Cambridge University Press, 1982), #91.
34 Nietzsche, *Daybreak*, #95.
35 Friedrich Nietzsche, *On the Genealogy of Morals*, trans. Douglas Smith (Oxford: Oxford University Press, 1998): Third Essay, #5–6.
36 Friedrich Nietzsche, *Twilight of the Idols*, trans. Duncan Large (Oxford: Oxford University Press, 1998) sec. IX: 5.
37 Friedrich Nietzsche, *Beyond Good and Evil: Prelude to a Philosophy of the Future*, trans. Walter Kaufmann (New York: Vintage, 1966), #108.

38 Arthur C. Danto, *Connections to the World: The Basic Concepts of Philosophy* (Berkeley: University of California Press, 1997), 52.
39 Robert C. Solomon, "Nietzsche *ad hominem*: Perspectivism, personality and *ressentiment*," in *The Cambridge Companion to Nietzsche*, 198–201.
40 Friedrich Nietzsche, *The Will to Power*, trans. Walter Kaufmann and R. J. Hollingdale (New York: Vintage, 1968), p. 493.
41 Friedrich Nietzsche, *Human, All Too Human: A Book for Free Spirits*, trans. Marion Faber with Stephen Lehmann (University of Nebraska Press, 1984), #251. See also the section headed *Long live physics* (#335) in *The Gay Science: with a Prelude in Rhymes and an Appendix of Songs*, trans.Walter Kaufmann (New York: Vintage, 1974).
42 Safranski, *Nietzsche*, 200.
43 Friedrich Nietzsche, *Twilight of the Idols* and *The Anti-Christ*, trans. R. J. Hollingdale (Baltimore: Penguin, 1968), p. 172.
44 Friedrich Nietzsche, *Thus Spoke Zarathustra: A Book for None and All*, trans. Walter Kaufmann (New York: Penguin, 1966), p. 87.
45 Nietzsche, *On The Genealogy of Morals*: Second Essay, #20.
46 Nietzsche, *The Gay Science*, #343.
47 Nietzsche, *The Will to Power*, p. 9.
48 Martin Heidegger, *Nietzsche*, vol. 1, translated by David Farrell Krell (San Francisco: Harper and Row, 1961), 26.
49 Rorty, *Contingency, Irony, and Solidarity*, 20.
50 Nietzsche, *Beyond Good and Evil*, #146.
51 Quoted in Kaufmann, *Existentialism from Dostoevsky to Sartre*, 194.
52 Alexander Nehamas, *Nietzsche: Life as Literature* (Cambridge: Harvard University Press, 1985): 98, 8.
53 Peter Berkowitz, *Nietzsche: The Ethics of an Immoralist* (Cambridge: Harvard University Press, 1995), 275n.
54 Nehamas, *Nietzsche*, 222.
55 Quoted by George J. Stack, *Nietzsche and Emerson: An Elective Affinity* (Athens, OH: Ohio State University Press, 1992), 44.
56 C. G. Jung, *Psychology & Religion* (New Haven: Yale University Press, 1966), 103.
57 *Genealogy of Morals*: First Essay, #12.
58 Friedrich Nietzsche, *The Birth of Tragedy* and *The Case of Wagner*, trans. Walter Kaufmann (New York: Random House, 1967), p. 144.
59 See *Genealogy of Morals* (Third Essay, # 6) and *The Will to Power*, pp. 84ff.
60 *The Gay Science*, #135.
61 The pathology of this three-way relationship is brilliantly presented in Joachim Köhler's *Nietzsche & Wagner: A Lesson in Subjugation*, trans. Ronald Taylor (New Haven: Yale University Press, 1996).
62 Nietzsche, *Thus Spoke Zarathustra*, p. 265.
63 *Zarathustra*, p. 255.
64 Friedrich Nietzsche, *Ecce Homo: How One Becomes What One Is*, trans. R. J. Hollingdale (Harmondsworth, England: Penguin, 1979), p. 68.
65 Nietzsche, *Birth of Tragedy*, p. 22.

66 Nietzsche, *Unmodern Observations*, p. 350.
67 Nehamas, *Nietzsche*, 133.
68 Twain, *The Autobiography of Mark Twain*, ed. Charles Neider (New York: Harper and Row, 1975), 44.
69 Twain, *The Bible According to Mark Twain*, eds. Howard G. Baetzhold and Joseph B. Mc-Cullough (New York: Simon & Schuster, 1995), 319–20.
70 *The Bible According to Mark Twain*, 238–39.
71 Twichell is quoted in Kenneth R. Andrews, *Nook Farm: Mark Twain's Hartford Circle* (Cambridge: Harvard University Press, 1950), ch. 2.
72 Quoted in Stanley Brodwin, "Mark Twain's Theology: The Gods of a Brevet Presbyterian," in *The Cambridge Companion to Mark Twain*, ed. Forrest G. Robinson (1988), 242.
73 Mark Twain, "Reflections on Religion," ed. Charles Neider, *The Hudson Review* 16:3 (Autumn 1963), 343–46.
74 Quoted in Brodwin, "Mark Twain's Theology," 222.
75 Twain, *Autobiography*, 298.
76 Brodwin introduced the idea of the unjust banishment of Eden as Twain's central theme in "Mark Twain and the Myth of the Daring Jest," in *The Mythology of Mark Twain*, eds. Sara deSaussure Davis and Philip D. Beidler (University of Alabama Press, 1978). The concept of a "countertheology" he developed in "Mark Twain in the Pulpit: The Theological Comedy of *Huckleberry Finn*," in *One Hundred Years of 'Huckleberry Finn': The Boy, His Book, and American Culture*, Centennial Essays edited by Robert Sattelmeyer and J. Donald Crowley (Columbia, MO.: University of Missouri Press, 1985).
77 Twain's phrases are quoted in Brodwin, "The Theology of Mark Twain: Banished Adam and the Bible," in *The Mississippi Quarterly*, vol XXIX, No. 2 (Spring 1976), 167.
78 Mark Twain, *Pudd'nhead Wilson* (New York: Signet, 1980), 26.
79 *The Bible According to Mark Twain* ("Eve's Diary"), 70.
80 Chapter V of *Huckleberry Finn*. While working on this novel, Twain wrote a piece called "Recent Crime in Connecticut" (1876) that exposes the "natural man" as a killer.
81 Stanley Brodwin, "Wandering Between Two Gods: Theological Realism in *A Connecticut Yankee in King Arthur's Court*," *Studies in the Literary Imagination* 16:2 (Fall 1983), 57–82.
82 Bernard De Voto, "Mark Twain and the Great Valley," in Harold Bloom, ed., *Mark Twain: Modern Critical Views* (New York: Chelsea, 1986), 26.
83 James D. Williams, "Revision and Intention in Mark Twain's *A Connecticut Yankee*," *American Literature*, v. 36 (1964–65), 288–297.
84 Alfred North Whitehead, *Adventures in Ideas* (New York: Macmillan, 1933), 24.
85 Judith Fetterley, "The Anxiety of Entertainment," in Bloom, ed., *Mark Twain: Modern Critical Views*, 90.
86 F. R. Leavis comments perceptively on the quiet but telling astringency of this conclusion. See "Mark Twain's Neglected Classic," in Bloom, ed., *Mark Twain: Modern Critical Views*, 43.
87 Twain, *Mark Twain's Mysterious Stranger Manuscripts*, ed. with introd. by William M. Gibson (Berkeley: University of California Press, 1969), 166.

88 From the manuscript of *A Tramp Abroad*, reprinted in Twain, *Letters from the Earth: Uncensored Writings of Mark Twain*, 183.
89 Twain, *Autobiography*, 18.
90 Gibson, Introduction, in Twain, *Mark Twain's The Mysterious Stranger Manuscripts*, 19.
91 Twain, *Letters from the Earth*, 7ff.
92 The phrase is quoted by De Voto in Bloom, ed., *Mark Twain*, 15.
93 *Twain's Mysterious Stranger Manuscripts*, 405. Twichell's comment is quoted in Gibson's Introduction, 30.
94 Prefatory Note to *Poems Past and Present* (1901), in *Thomas Hardy: The Complete Poems*, ed. James Gibson (New York: Macmillan, 1976), 85.
95 General Preface to the Wessex edition of 1912, reprinted in Martin Seymour-Smith, ed., *The Mayor of Casterbridge* by Thomas Hardy (London: Penguin, 1985), 417.
96 Introductory Note to *Winter Words in Various Moods and Metres*, in Thomas Hardy, *The Complete Poems*, 834.
97 Florence Emily Hardy, *The Life of Thomas Hardy* (New York: St. Martin's Press, 1962), 285.
98 A. N. Wilson, *God's Funeral*, 13.
99 *Life of Thomas Hardy*, 224.
100 *Life of Thomas Hardy*, 296.
101 See James Persoon, "*Dover Beach*, Hardy's Version," in Harold Orel, ed., *Critical Essays on Thomas Hardy's Poetry*, (Boston: G. K. Hall, 1995), 96–97.
102 *Life of Thomas Hardy*, 376.
103 Thomas Hardy, *The Complete Poetical Works of Thomas Hardy*, Vol. V, ed. Samuel Hynes (Oxford: Clarendon Press, 1995) Part Third: I:v, 31.
104 Hardy's fullest statement of his meliorist intentions is found in his "Apology" to *Late Lyrics and Earlier*. See Thomas Hardy, *The Complete Poems*, ed. James Gibson (New York: Macmillan, 1976), 556–562.
105 Hardy, *The Complete Poetical Works*, ed. Samuel Hynes, V, 255. Hardy's earnestness about meliorism is evident also in several passages of the *Life* (335, 387, 449, 454). But he is said to have regretted writing the upbeat close of *The Dynasts* when World War I broke out. See Roy Morrell, "*The Dynasts*," in Harold Bloom, ed., *Thomas Hardy: Modern Critical Views* (New York: Chelsea, 1987), 35.
106 Martin Seymour-Smith, ed., *The Mayor of Casterbridge*, 417–18, 16.
107 Kenneth Millard, "*The Dynasts*: words...to hold the imagination," in Harold Orel, ed., *Critical Essays on Thomas Hardy's Poetry*, 179.
108 Margaret Mahar, "Hardy's Poetry of Renunciation," in Bloom, ed., *Thomas Hardy* (New York: Chelsea, 1987), 164ff.
109 Irving Howe, *Thomas Hardy* (New York: Macmillan, 1967), 145.
110 D. H. Lawrence, *Study of Thomas Hardy*, in *Phoenix: The Posthumous Papers of D. H. Lawrence*, ed. Edward McDonald (London: Heinemann, 1936), Ch. IX.
111 Gillian Beer, *Darwin's Plots*, 257–58.
112 George Levine, "Darwin and Pain: Why Science Made Shakespeare Nauseating," *Raritan* XV:2 (Fall 1995), 97–114.
113 *Life of Thomas Hardy*, 315.

114 Holly Stevens, ed., *Wallace Stevens: Letters* (New York: Knopf, 1966), 378.
115 *Letters*, 369.
116 *Letters*, 340.
117 *Letters*, 443.
118 George Santayana, *Interpretations of Poetry and Religion*, eds. William G. Holzberger and Herman J. Saatkamp, Jr. (Cambridge: MIT Press, 1989): 3, 20.
119 Harold Bloom, *Wallace Stevens: The Poems of Our Climate* (Ithaca: Cornell University Press, 1977), 363.
120 Robert Frost, "Education by Poetry: A Meditative Monologue," in Edward Connery Lathem and Lawrance Thompson, eds., *Robert Frost: Poetry and Prose* (New York: Holt, Rinehart, and Winston, 1984): 332–33, 338–39.
121 *Letters*, 500.
122 David R. Jarraway, *Wallace Stevens and The Question of Belief: Metaphysician in the Dark* (Baton Rouge, LA: Louisiana State University Press, 1993), 67.
123 Frank Kermode, *Wallace Stevens* (New York: Grove Press, 1961), 27; Helen Vendler, *Wallace Stevens: Words Chosen Out of Desire* (Knoxville, TN: University of Tennessee Press, 1984), 10.
124 *Letters*, 710.
125 The influence of Nietzsche was largely unacknowledged by Stevens. But some critics—especially Harold Bloom (in *The Poems of Our Climate*), Milton J. Bates (in *Wallace Stevens: The Mythology of the Self*), and David R. Jarraway (in *Wallace Stevens and The Question of Belief*)—have made a point of it. See also Patrick Bridgewater, *Nietzsche in Anglosaxonry*, (Leicester University Press, 1972), ch. 15.
126 Kermode, *Stevens*, 29.
127 Helen Vendler, *On Extended Wings: Wallace Stevens' Longer Poems* (Cambridge: Harvard University Press, 1971), 47; Vendler, *Words Chosen Out of Desire*, 4.
128 Vendler, *On Extended Wings*, 5.
129 Bloom, *Poems of Our Climate*, 98.
130 Kermode, *Stevens*, 127.
131 One little example of just how conscientiously Beckett maximized uncertainty may stand for many more. In Matthew 25:33–34 Jesus intimates that in the kingdom of heaven the obedient "sheep" will be blessed while the disobedient "goats" will definitely not be. But the Boy in *Waiting for Godot* reports that Mr. Godot beats his brother who minds the *sheep* but not himself who minds the *goats*. The only inference we can make is that our desire to make one has been baffled.
132 Beckett answered a question from one correspondent as follows: "I do not know who Godot is. I do not even know if he exists. And I do not know if they believe he does or not, those two who are waiting for him." See Beckett, "Letters: Who is Godot?" *New Yorker Magazine*, 24 June and 1 July 1996, 136. Similarly, his director Alan Schneider reported (in the *Chelsea Review* of Autumn 1958) that Beckett had told him: "If I knew [who or what Godot is] I would have said so in the play." Quoted by Colin Duckworth, ed., *Samuel Beckett: En attendant Godot* (Walton-on-Thames, Surrey: Thomas Nelson, 1985), xxv.

133 James Knowlson, *Damned to Fame: The Life of Samuel Beckett* (New York: Simon and Schuster, 1996).
134 H. Porter Abbott, *Beckett Writing Beckett: The Author in the Autograph* (Ithaca: Cornell University Press, 1996): 55, 183.
135 Mary Bryden, *Samuel Beckett and the Idea of God* (New York: St. Martin's Press, 1998), 4.
136 Quoted in Bryden, *Samuel Beckett and the Idea of God*, 35.
137 Bryden, *Beckett and the Idea of God*, 1.
138 Shira Wolosky, *Language Mysticism: The Negative Way of Language in Eliot, Beckett, and Celan* (Stanford: Stanford University Press, 1995), 93.
139 Quoted by Dan Gunn, "The beam of Sam's light," in *Times Literary Supplement*, 15 January 1999, 4. "Bastard" may also allude to Jesus' highly unusual conception, although Christ's crucifixion is an image that Beckett's people in some sense *embrace*. To appreciate better the force of Hamm's witty exclamation, one might compare it to similar but weaker attempts by Prosper Mérimée and the Marquis de Sade. Mérimée wrote: "His only excuse is that He doesn't exist." Sade wrote: "I wish that for a moment you could exist/ To have the pleasure to better insult you."
140 Wolosky, *Language Mysticism*, 90.
141 See, for example, Duckworth, *En attendant Godot*, cvii.
142 Bryden, *Beckett and Idea of God*, 22.
143 Samuel Beckett, *Proust* (New York: Grove Press, 1957), 8.
144 Georg Lukács, *The Meaning of Contemporary Realism*, trans. John Mander and Necke Mander (London: Merlin Press, 1962).
145 Theodor Adorno, "Commitment," in *The Essential Frankfurt School Reader*, ed. Andrew Arato and Eike Gebhardt (New York: Continuum, 1990), 314–15.
146 Bryden, *Beckett and Idea of God*, 139.
147 Abbott, *Beckett Writing Beckett*, 147.
148 Abbott, *Beckett Writing Beckett*, 29.
149 Nietzsche, *Twilight of the Idols*, 19.
150 Abbott, *Beckett Writing Beckett*, 70.
151 Letter to Sighle Kennedy, reprinted in *Disjecta: Miscellaneous Writing and Dramatic Fragments*, edited by Ruby Cohn (New York: Grove Press, 1984), 113.
152 Christopher Ricks, *Beckett's Dying Words* (New York: Oxford University Press, 1993).
153 Abbott, *Beckett Writing Beckett*, 32–42.
154 Bryden, *Beckett and Idea of God*, 185–86.
155 Wolosky, *Language Mysticism*, 93.
156 Abbott, *Beckett Writing Beckett*: 156, 174, 108.
157 Wolosky, *Language Mysticism*, 134.

CHAPTER THREE
Literature and Religion

"Narrative corrugates dogma, puts truth in motion."
James Wood, "Writing Under God"

Questioning religion's tendency to absolutize moral judgments directs our attention toward the institution of religion as well as toward abstract theology, but the continuing concern of this study will be the interplay between liberal and literal uses of God and certain related words. My understanding of the word literature throughout this study, but especially in this chapter, includes not only individual written works and bodies of work but also an activity of mind alert to the fact that the meanings of words are not constant, although our strong moral convictions incline us to believe that they are. The social authority of religion is to some extent bound up with the erroneous belief that God, itself a word, can be used to stabilize language and hence morality. Speaking of God as *beyond* language is, at best, only a rhetorical device indicating the strength of subjective belief. One of the tasks of the modern atheist is to remind us that the word should always be understood within quotation marks.

The languages of literature and religion are allied in the modern world insofar as each understands that it is not a transparent medium for whatever truth it seeks to convey. But they become rivals when religion assumes what before the Enlightenment it could take for granted, that its language belongs to a higher order of truth because it deals with things sacred rather than profane. The issue at stake between them is the relation of Language to the Question of Belief, which becomes my chapter's first subtopic.

I move then to the topic of Literature, Religion, and Human Need. This segment focuses on three profound needs: for social cohesion and ideals that confer an experience of group identity; for a sense of being related to the universe, sometimes called an experience of totality; and, thirdly, for an overview, typically in the form of stories of collective origins and ends, of explaining how and why we are here. These needs are served especially well by religion, whose very business, one might say, is to adapt itself to them, whereas literature is a much more variegated affair, concerned with all kinds of material and sometimes (whether sophisticatedly or vulgarly) quite averse to serious purpose. But when in the spirit of John Dewey we apply the adjective "religious" to experience rather than to doctrine, rivalry between the languages of literature and religion does not come into question. Religious *experience* is equally available to poet, philosopher, and scientist, and requires no institutional support. This alliance is most apparent with regard to the first two specified needs. When we come to stories of origins and destinies, the relation between literature and religion is confused by the intervention of a third element, the prestige and authority of science, for the stories that exert the greatest influence on us today are often inspired by science.

My third subtopic, then, is Literature and Religion in the Age of Science. Insofar as science and its objective perspective have achieved for many a privileged status during the last century or two, the language and value of art, ethics, and religion—which are nothing if not products of a subjective perspective—have been subordinated. Some scientists acknowledge and respect an alternative perspective, but some who have reached a wide audience tend to fold art, morality, and philosophy into a unified view governed by science. I think, therefore, that we need to clarify the difference between *explaining* consciousness, a scientific endeavor, and *expressing* it, which is the inevitable modality of both literature and religion.

One curious result of science-inspired speculation in our time, especially in the area of evolutionary biology, is the emergence of an updated version of a pre-Kantian deity, a power beyond human understanding that nonetheless determines human nature—but genetically rather than supernaturally. The apotheosis of blind process is hardly comforting, but, as evolutionary process is in a very limited sense purposeful and thus can be appear to be directed toward moral goals, it has stimulated some theists to welcome scientific speculation and some agnostics to fear religion in a new way. The old debate between science and religion has taken on a new look, which could use a little skeptical attention from the modern atheist.

The underlying tension between literature and religion has also been heightened by new challenges to an assumption little questioned fifty years ago, namely that modern Western societies, American society especially, are in our time basically secular, their politics and regulations more or less independent of religion. So it becomes important finally in this chapter to raise the topic of Literature and Religion in a Secular Age. My argument in Chapter Four, which challenges the very notion of "sacred writing," becomes difficult if not impossible to pursue if our political leaders are able to make successful appeal to divine authority. I do not quite believe that dissolution of the vitally important boundary between church and state is, in the United States, imminent, but certain developments in recent years have weakened my confidence that it isn't. Some consideration of the secular-sacred debate with particular reference to the American situation will clear ground for my discussion of the sacred text, in which I bring to bear my understanding of the literary imagination on the representation of Yahweh (and to some extent of Jesus) in the Bible.

Language and the Question of Belief

In his *Rhetoric of Religion* Kenneth Burke wrote: "Theological doctrine is a body of spoken or written w*ords*. Whatever else it may be, and wholly regardless of whether it be true or false, theology is preeminently *verbal*. It is *words* about 'God.'"[1] This may seem obvious yet it is likely to startle us a little, which presumably accounts for Burke's use of emphasis.

The word God itself might be called an idea-word rather than a thing-word but different from other idea-words like, say, omnipotence or omniscience, in that it has been personalized, sacralized, invested with religious aura. Even modern secularists cannot fail to acknowledge the presence of this aura and cannot be entirely free of it, evidenced by the fact that they sometimes resort to superstitious utterances. (I'll finish this book, *deo volente*.)

The joke is told of a learned professor, who, when at last he finds himself in heaven, encounters two signs at a crossroad, one pointing to "God," the other to "Lecture on God," and from old habit turns in the latter direction. Presumably the joke is on the professor, but it could be understood another way as well, for the only access to God is by way of words. We laugh not only at the lecture-ridden old professor but also because the joke suddenly releases and relieves an incompletely repressed fear that there really might be someone up there after all, making a mockery of our adult judgment. The idea of a personal, caring God I take to be a legacy of our Judeo-Christian culture, reinforced in varying degrees by the psychological need of human beings who were once helpless, dependent children. Adult atheists and agnostics, in my view, have put the idea away *inside* their minds.

What is likely to annoy the sophisticated unbeliever is not the idea of God as such but a certain rigidity in its expression and promotion. I for one am wholly in sympathy with the spirit of humane skepticism voiced by writers like Montaigne and E. M. Forster, neither of whom was opposed to religion. Rather, they were averse to believing in belief for its own sake. Montaigne understood that our minds are fluid and various, rejoicing now in one thing, now in another. Religion at its best serves as a check on human arrogance, but if "man fabricates a thousand ridiculous associations between God and himself...the world is filled and soaked with twaddle and lies."[2] Forster wrote of faith as "a sort of mental starch, which ought to be applied as sparingly as possible. I dislike the stuff. I do not believe in it, for its own sake, at all." "My law-givers," he affirmed, "are Erasmus and Montaigne, not Moses and St. Paul."[3] The general subject of Poetry and Belief, which their mode of skepticism opens up, is one I will turn to shortly.

To understand theology as "preeminently verbal" is to be wary of its tendency to attach to its crucial word God the literal sense of a supernatural being, a being that must not be understood as metaphor, symbol, or myth. Many believers understand God's existence in this literal sense, and take language for granted as the vehicle of that belief. At the other extreme stands a radical skeptic like Jacques Derrida, who celebrates metaphorical language for eluding any fixity imposed by religious or indeed by philosophical doctrines.[4] We need, I think, to modify his purely linguistic orientation with some *psychological* account of the *power* that words can have in evoking feelings and convictions. "God" to a sophisticated reader is *understood* as myth but is still *experienced* as what George Steiner calls, presumably with a nod to the Catholic doctrine of Eucharist, "real presence." Such an idea could help to establish a middle ground between illusion and reality, between literal and metaphorical meaning. Coleridge, we remember, thought his contemporaries could not read the Bible well because they could not discover this ground. That a passionate and sincere believer like Flannery O'Connor should say about the Eucharist, "If it's a symbol, to hell with it," is beguiling because she does not so much confuse as override the distinction between objective and subjective judgment, and so the question of literal *versus* metaphorical meaning does not arise.[5] But the concept of *middle* ground is important here because, just as Derrida's attack on logocentrism goes to one extreme in ignoring the power of words to evoke feelings, Steiner, attacking

Derrida for failing to appreciate the "immanence" achieved by great art, goes to the *opposite* extreme in claiming that such immanence *must* lead us back into a metaphysics of transcendence.[6] This it need not do.

It is useful to consider how a tendency toward literalmindedness might arise. The psychoanalyst Melanie Klein taught that successfully developing children learn to think symbolically only at the cost of learning to be depressed, accepting the fact that they can only have a substitute for what they want. Perhaps, then, literalmindedness about the meaning of words helps ward off depression—but at an intellectual price. The higher tolerance for the sliding meaning of words that usually accompanies intellectual sophistication may well complicate the process of mental growth, but it may also foster a more complex and boldly creative form of maturity and expression. Perhaps Cardinal Newman was right to fear, on behalf of his religion, John Stuart Mill's ringing endorsement of the free play of intellect, for such play can loosen and break the bonds of faith. The Catholic theologian Hans Küng betrays some anxiety on this score when he first concedes that religious imagery is not to be taken literally but then assiduously gathers support from all sorts of unorthodox testifiers—Spinoza, Einstein, and Wittgenstein among them—who have used the word God in a positive sense, no matter exactly what that sense is.[7]

Believers seeking an unmediated truth are sometimes tempted to circumvent language, and to say, as Karen Armstrong does, that "the reality we call 'God' exceeds all human expression" or, again, that "language is a limiting faculty [because] God is beyond speech or description."[8] Armstrong is clearly attracted to mysticism, which is all very well insofar as she does not imply that such statements as these are literally true. How could they be? What would mysticism mean if it could not even be communicated by means of language?

William James taught that mystical experience was distinctive in its "ineffability," but Walter Kaufmann found this criterion inadequate, persuasively arguing that there is "no essential difference between mystic and non-mystic experience."[9] On the question of mysticism, Santayana was nearer the mark than James, describing it as an abandonment of imagination in pursuit of the mirage of absolute truth.[10] Santayana was no enemy of religion, but he saw it as a kind of poetry, poetry in which we let ourselves believe rather than a higher order of truth. There is an idealizing strain in Santayana's view of both religion and poetry, but the important point he makes, as we saw in

Chapter Two, is that their languages are essentially alike. He conceded only (and sensibly) that religion has greater bearing upon conduct.

It is helpful, I think, to introduce a long historical perspective before going any further in a discussion of religious versus poetic truth. For the biblical writers a distinction between religion and poetry did not exist, obliging the modern sophisticated reader to put this distinction aside for the sake of an empathetic response, even though she cannot forget that Yahweh is at the same time a *representation* and that the Bible must therefore also be read from a secular point of view. (I shall discuss in Chapter Four the difficulties involved in this double response to the sacred text.) For Aquinas and Dante in the high middle ages, the distinction *did* exist, and what Aquinas called the "allegory of the theologians" based on *fact* was absolutely superior to the "allegory of the poets" based on *fiction*. Because the poet Dante wanted to claim for his *Commedia* the *highest* truth, he presented his fiction, the scholar Robert Hollander explains, as though his poetic journey into afterlife worlds were actual and historical, fact not fiction. He sought to write not a competition with scripture but an "adjunct to Scripture," and Hollander gives us fascinating evidence of Dante's subtle ways of being heretical in this endeavor without seeming to transgress at all (for example by treating Ovid as a writer of fiction *unlike* himself whereas John the Evangelist's truth and his own are of the *same* kind).[11] Poets of the modern era, by contrast, cannot really disavow the fictionality of their vision, however religious that vision may be. Frost and Stevens, for example, knew that metaphor or fiction was inescapable, but they stressed the importance of emotional commitment, of giving oneself to language whose truth was, in Frost's words, "more felt than known." The neuroscientist Antonio Damasio, in *Descartes' Error,* has made a similar point with regard to our very ability to act in the world: we need things to matter to us before we can make choices, and it is our emotions that make things matter.

Modern students of theology influenced by developments in literary criticism and philosophy do often indicate their awareness of language as an inescapable mediator of religious (or any other) truth. In anthologies like *Critical Terms for Religious Studies* or *The Postmodern God: A Theological Reader*, one regularly finds the word God called a "metaphor" or a "symbol." Innovative theologians are likely to make the point obliquely. In Chapter One we noticed, for example, how Jean-Luc Marion's used the distinction between "idol" and "icon" as a kind of substitute for the distinction between literal and metaphorical. A more preemptive maneuver is Barth's appropriation of language on *God's* behalf. Barth seems to have understood that the obstacle to be got round is language itself, but, disdaining fellow theologians who seek to accommodate secular sensibilities (like Rudolf Bultmann who would remove transcendence from divinity or like Paul Tillich who would equate it with "ultimate concern"), he makes God and not man the maker and master of language, declaring: "Our words are not our own property but His....We use our words improperly and pictorially...when we apply them within the confines of what is appropriate to us as creatures. When we apply them to God, they are not alienated from their original object, therefore from their truth, but, on the contrary, are restored to it."[12] This would stop my argument in its tracks if I did not understand such appropriation of the human imagination as itself an act of the human imagination.

Doubtless it is easier for poetry than for theology to regard belief as a species of fiction, for the very medium *builds in* a sense of play. As Stevens puts it, "A man with a [firm] faith in the meaning of words should not bother to listen to poetry (S 25)." A reader of poetry expects words to dance whereas a reader of texts deemed religious expects them not to and tends to distrust poetry as a result. But poets and literary critics are not exempt from the common problem of becoming attached to words and arrangements of words, to jargon and dead metaphors, and therefore may find themselves having to make an effort to dislodge habits that pin meaning down.

Our learning to use phrases like "idea of God" or "myth of God" is, as I indicated in Chapter One, a salutary legacy of Romanticism. But we are also heirs of the Enlightenment tradition, which, while it did a pretty thorough job of knocking out the props of the traditional arguments for the existence of God, generated a wide distrust of imaginative products like myth. Although the Enlightenment helped greatly to advance modern science, it has also left us a positivist legacy that impedes the secular intellectual's ability to appreciate the common ground between literature and religion. It is a bit too easy—too positivistic—to say with the philosopher Jerry Fodor that "God died of the Enlightenment."[13] We need a finer understanding of the Romantic modification of its achievements.

For example, the Romantics often incorporated the vocabulary of theology within a naturalistic framework, absorbing more than discarding religious tradition. Samuel Johnson on behalf of the classical sensibility had insisted (in his "Life of Waller") on the separation of theology from fiction, declaring magisterially that "The ideas of Christian Theology are too simple for eloquence, too sacred for fiction." But, as Harold Bloom points out on behalf of Romanticism, William Blake knew that "forms of worship are always drawn from poetic tales," and Emerson knew that "religion is imagined and always must be reimagined."[14]

I have been using the words metaphor, symbol, and myth more or less interchangeably, but in connection with "God" this can be a problem. Fodor, very sophisticated and urbane in his disdain of God-talk, explains that the word cannot express a metaphorical truth because "metaphorical truths have to 'supervene on' literal truths." That is, he goes on, the relevant respects in which God is like something "have to be somewhere in the background, and they have to be literal if what is said metaphorically is true. Perhaps God is like a father because he is figuratively kind to his figurative children. But then his being figuratively kind must depend on his being literally something or other else…sooner or later he has to go to ground…it's just how metaphors work."[15] Fodor may be right about metaphor, yet the God who "died of the Enlightenment" has not died altogether, even for intellectuals. The traditional idea has proved to be remarkably resilient, evidence that this particular cultural legacy, while it may be revised or opposed, cannot be quite discarded. It continues to respond to certain needs.

But if metaphor is not quite the right designation for the word God, "symbol" also presents difficulties. Its indefiniteness of reference (making it comparable to Marion's "icon") is an advantage, but, because symbolism can suggest a transcendental realm, I would prefer to use the term myth. Myth is the preferable term for another reason as well. It is tempting to think of God as metaphor or symbol because it is a single word, and an anthropomorphic God is a single image. But this obscures the important fact that the idea of God always entails, however faintly, a measure of narrative, a story of human origin and destiny or of encounter between human and superhuman. Perhaps it is best to think of the word God as an elliptical myth.

Myth, furthermore, can help us out of a persistent difficulty as to the truth-status of fictions. We are prone to draw too sharp a distinction between a positivistic view of fictional texts, according to which they contain no truth-value, and a purely aesthetic view, according to which they are said not to refer to the real world at all. Paul Ricoeur has very helpfully suggested that the dichotomy is a false one because fictions refigure a *possible* world, and thereby may be both referentially revealing and formally satisfying. He gives as an example van Gogh's painting of peasant shoes, an emblem of working class life in late nineteenth-century France but also one that is meaningful in aesthetic terms. In his later work, Ricouer suggests that myth is particularly effective in this respect because it gathers together a narrative that is "constitutive of personal identity," a narrative we all need in order to make some sense of our lives.[16] We tend to think of history as true or real and fiction as false or unreal, but myths of origins and destinies elude this dichotomous judgment.

Use of the word myth in this sense does, it is true, resemble Frank Kermode's use of the word "fiction" as opposed to myth. Kermode describes myth as fiction that has hardened into belief, like the Nazi myth of racial superiority, which was taken for literal truth.[17] That is a valuable distinction, but his "fiction" and my sense of "myth" (adapted from Ricoeur) are really getting at the same thing, a defense of the metaphorical and literary against the doctrinaire and literal. Kermode's myth is equivalent to what I have called dogmatic belief, always a danger in the moral life of a community. Myth has also been distinguished from literature by Herbert Schneidau (in *Sacred Discontent: The Bible and Western Tradition*) because it exerts a conservative and stabilizing social influence whereas great literature seeks to "make it new," but the two are linked as metaphorical rather than literal uses of language. In actual cases, of course, it is not easy to determine the degree of a writer's awareness of figurative language, hence to distinguish sophisticated from naïve belief, but one sure sign of the latter is the claim of literal truth for one's particular perception of things together with the denigration of metaphor or poetry, as when Teilhard de Chardin defends his mystical theology with the statement: "This is no metaphor; and it is much more than poetry."[18] My present concern is to dispel the dichotomy between false fiction and true reality. Toward this end, it helps to keep in mind that certain nineteenth-century writers who became acutely aware of it, like Coleridge and George Eliot, were at pains to make a claim for the *veracious imagination* in contrast to mere fancy or mere imitation, a claim for the mind's power to *reframe* the world rather than simply ignoring or reflecting it.

We have been circling the topic known for some time in criticism as Poetry and Belief. It is a topic that, for two major reasons, emerged after the Enlightenment. One is that the increased authority of science—sharply increased after Darwinism in effect routed natural theology—made religion and poetry allies in opposition to the challenge of a newly prestigious scientific model of truth. In the opinion of some, the reverence for fact bred by science effectively drove religion into the arms of poetry. This is what Matthew Arnold meant when he said, in "The Study of Poetry," that religion has run aground because it "it has attached its emotion to the supposed fact...whereas "poetry attaches its emotion to the idea," so that "the strongest part of our religion to-day is its unconscious poetry." Arnold like Nietzsche recognized that spiritual need was bound to persist even in an age of science, and both critic and philosopher, influenced alike by the Romantic tradition, looked for satisfaction of that need in aesthetic terms. To be sure, as Terry Eagleton pointed out, commenting on Arnold's view, poetry "is nothing like as capable as religion of furnishing an anxious age with spiritual uplift and social cohesion" because it "touches only a select few" whereas "religion is that rarest of phenomena, an aesthetic ritual which involves millions of ordinary people."[19] But Arnold was right to suggest that the literalmindedness of religion had cost it the allegiance of many who cared about poetry.

The second reason is that an increasing number of serious readers were becoming more secular in their interests yet inherited a literary tradition that was indebted to religious (primarily Christian) tradition, and this presented a problem for the guardians of literature. For students of poetry, the specific questions that arose were, first, what sort of truth does poetry embody, and, second, how should nonbelievers read and respond to literature that took for granted certain religious beliefs.

These questions only became inescapably important when criticism itself became professionalized in the second quarter of the twentieth century with the ascendance of "New Criticism." Allen Tate represented the new movement when he declared that the question of belief is today "the chief problem of poetic criticism."[20] A number of these New Critics were overtly Christian in their religious sympathies, but this only made them more concerned to keep the controversial issue of belief away from poetry, in the hope, clearly derived from Matthew Arnold, that poetry itself could provide some of the satisfactions of religion. I. A. Richards sharply distinguished the pseudo-statements of poetry from the truth-claims of science not in order to denigrate poetry but to suggest that poetry must take over the function of ordering our emotional life. Readers, he implied, should come to poetry without ready beliefs, and let the poem help them balance their emotions. T. S. Eliot said we must "read poetry as poetry and not another thing" and "must assume that the reader can obtain the full literary or aesthetic enjoyment without sharing the beliefs of the author." Delmore Schwartz believed that the right way to appreciate Thomas Hardy's poetry was "to keep Hardy's beliefs *in* his poetry [securely locked in by their "concreteness"] and our own beliefs outside." And Cleanth Brooks asserted that all statements in poetry are made through formal elements; content and form are inseparable; and therefore a poem's truth derives from its internal unity rather than from its correspondence to an external world.[21]

Samuel Johnson had said in his "Life of Gray," "we are affected only as we believe." The New Critics were trying to say something very different, although they did imply at times that the reader who was a believer had an advantage. Douglas Bush wrote that "no doubt" readers "would be happier and richer if they held a firm dogmatic faith" than if they "wandered between two worlds."[22] (Presumably Arnoldian melancholy was the only alternative to "firm faith.") And a contempt for "heresy"—hard to distinguish from a contempt for liberalism or even from anti-Semitism—unfortunately mars the work of Eliot and Tate. I am not trying to suggest that the New Critics were hypocrites. The matter is more interesting than that. They were sincerely worried about how readers with different beliefs could arrive at some consensus as to the meaning and value of a poem. (Richards' *Practical Criticism,* inaugurating New Critical *explication de texte*, highlighted this anxiety very clearly.) And when they could not locate a normative element inside the poem, they sought it in the reader, in the wishful dream of a basically homogeneous readership. So they wrote about "centrally human beliefs and values," "the same set of general responses," "patterns of human nature," "the same basic notions about conduct," and of "humanity's unchanging fundamental oneness."[23] There may seem to us now a touch of paranoia in all this, but in fact Brooks's nightmare fantasy of social diversity and cultural relativism causing a breakdown in consensus has become reality. What Brooks did not foresee was that many in the academic world would become adjusted to the new situation, and generate new critical procedures out of the very absence of consensus.

M. H. Abrams, editing and leading off in the volume I have quoted from, wondered if some of the contributors were not drawing distinctions between poetry and belief too sharply. Poetry, he said, "depends for its efficacy on evoking a great number of beliefs,"[24] making it in practice quite different from most religious discourse. Readers of poetry, I would add, also need to be flexible and various in their response, sharing something of Montaigne's healthy respect for the ever-changing human mind. In the century after Montaigne's, Hobbes made a good distinction between "believing" and "believing in"—to believe is to trust whereas to believe in is to accept on faith—and, in the next, Hume distinguished similarly between trust and revelation. Perhaps the Hobbes-Hume distinction helps to offset a weakness in Coleridge's otherwise splendid phrase, "willing suspension of disbelief," for in reading empathetically we do not so much start from a posture of disbelief as from a neutral and open readiness to trust for a time. We then slide into the spirit of whatever beliefs are effectively evoked and expressed. Yet the reader continues to remain alert to other possibilities. A poem is like a religious ritual in creating a temporary magic, but it is also different because, in religious ritual, performative stability is desirable and the participant welcomes sameness and the quieting of thought rather than variation and the stimulation of thought.

In the last chapter of his *God and the Poets*, a chapter called "Poetry and Belief," David Daiches throws some interesting light on the New Critical anxiety about belief when he observes that Christian faith is more demanding than many other systems of belief. (We are never troubled by the gods in Homer, for example.) It may be best, he writes, "to stand outside all closed systems of belief if we wish to be able to respond to the way the poet builds up meaning out of the system he believes in." Daiches goes on to suggest that such an uncommitted and open-minded observer may be the one best situated to appreciate belief as an aspect of poetic language and how it works, and perhaps even "the one capable of the most generous response to poetry of different ages and cultures...[the one best able to share] the dilemmas of those he responds to."[25] Daiches does not mean that less committed readers will be free of bias—an impossible ideal—but they will be freer to move in and out of the dilemmas of others.

The Jesuit critic Walter J. Ong challenged the non-Christian reader of a Christian poem when he asked, "how can one share Donne's beliefs emotionally [in the *Holy Sonnets*] without sharing them intellectually?"[26] The answer is in part provided by the New Critics themselves—by Winters who doubted that there was a good devotional poem that did not stress moral universals, by Brooks who discovered a fusion of form and content in all good poems, by Eliot who distinguished between telling and showing belief. Perhaps Ong's psychology was too simple, for the distinction between thought and feeling, head and heart—although it can never be clean and neat—is a very familiar one in criticism. We are all capable as writers and readers of moving back and forth between layers of mind, from a more detached, considered and objective point of view to a more passionate and imaginative one that draws on emotion. As Gillian Beer keenly puts it in her book *Open Fields*, human beings live in multiple and conflicted epistemologies or they couldn't survive—wisdom that the Christian critic D. Bruce Lockerbie fails to appreciate when he states flatly that "disbelief makes the appreciation of religious art impossible."[27]

Father Ong's tendency to stress what good poems have in common *thematically* may obscure an important part of the problem at hand. The nonbeliever, faced with Donne's "Batter my heart, three-personed God," responds not only to the accessible theme clothed in a religious vocabulary, namely a conflict between rebellious and submissive desire, but also to the dramatic aspect of the style and the brilliant patterning of sound and sense. So, although Donne's poem could be called Christian thematically, we are able to delight in its original use of language. And part of its originality is the very boldness of the sexual imagery in which the speaker's pleading is couched, a boldness verging on blasphemy. I am not suggesting that the poem *is* blasphemous, but language is a slippery thing, and Julia Kristeva's point is well taken—that, while poetic language may be complicitous with religious language, it "may also set in motion what dogma represses."[28] In a similar vein, the critic James Wood describes the novel as inherently a secular rather than religious form because "narrative corrugates dogma, puts truth in motion."[29] The relevance of both remarks reaches beyond the single genre—poetry or narrative—to which each is applied. Consider the "subversiveness" of Coleridge's "Rime of the Ancient Mariner," both a poem and a narrative. Its story dramatizes a lesson of redemption from sin but it displays also a different story and lesson, the horror of perpetual punishment for a gratuitous act.

As New Historicists like to say, imaginative literature *contains* its subversive energy, but, as they also like to show, that energy nonetheless comes through to the reader, and it does so in the originality of style as well as of thought. It is not surprising, then, that institutional religion and establishment politics are frequently suspicious of poetry and of the arts in general, whose effects on their audiences are unpredictable. "The literary," as Eagleton observed, "is not a good custodian of the moral."[30] That of course makes the unfettered imagination somewhat problematic. Good moral custodianship, one infers from formal religious services, requires not fresh but familiar and repetitive language in a fixed form and tone, and many attend them to find such language. The kind of comfort and consolation sought by worshipers comes not simply from the lessons imparted to them but also from ritual language repeated from week to week, providing the illusion of stable and secure meaning. We should not deny the practical advantages of ritual language, apparent to us on many occasions and used during many ceremonies, joyous as well as solemn. The freedom of imaginative literature, let us admit without condescension, is not something we want every time we read or listen to words.

Literature, Religion, and Human Need

Literature and Religion are not only concepts but material practices and institutions that bear on our everyday life. Religion is by far the stronger of the two in this respect. Indeed, literature hardly seems an institution at all. Harry Levin called it one because he sought to modify Taine's general notion of literature as an "expression of society [that] controls a special body of precedents and devices [and] must translate...the impulsions of life...into its own terms and adapt them to its peculiar forms."[31] Derrida called literature "a strange institution." By this he meant that, because it "allows one to say everything," it has no determinable existence and so appears to be "inconsequential."[32] But religion is something else. Churches and sects are often well organized and politically potent. By virtue of its extraordinary liberty (the source of its power for individual readers) literature is socially disorganized and so rather ignorable in practical everyday life. In contrast, religion, even in our so-called secular society, cannot be ignored by anyone.

It has been the fond hope of many liberal thinkers since the Enlightenment that, as secular institutions and practices spread, religions themselves would wither away. This had been the dream of utopian humanists like Marx and Comte, and in our day it has been revived by pragmatic thinkers like Richard Rorty, inheriting Whitman's and Dewey's vision of a truly liberal democracy. In the years after World War II, as a new prosperity encouraged the pursuit of secular goals, it looked to many observers, whatever their bias, that religious institutions were indeed losing their strength, irrevocably. One can almost date the moment at which the perception of religion's loss of prestige peaked—perhaps 1968, when the United States Supreme Court struck down a ban against self-declared atheists running for public office. At about that time, some writers with a journalistic flair were trying out slogans like "post-Christian" and "post-religious" to describe the new age. Now at the beginning of the next century that vision has faded. Rorty himself admitted in 1998 that it is not likely to be realized.[33] Today, the dream of the *end* of religion seems as naïve as did religion itself to many intellectuals of and after the Enlightenment.

Indeed, the question is not whether institutional religion has a future because it all too clearly has. Even though the needs religion responds to may be satisfied without institutional support, most people prefer that support, and seem to require it. The question we should ask, then, is what *are* those needs and how are they satisfied by the two different institutions of religion and literature. I have selected three crucial ones that are often cited: the need for social cohesion and for group-identification secured by moral ideals; the need to experience a sense of totality in one's relation to the universe; and the need for compelling narratives of human origins and ends.

The need to belong to a group codifying the moral ideals that make it cohesive is what Emile Durkheim, in his classic work, *The Elementary Forms of the Religious Life*, saw as the heart of religion.[34] Of course there are non-religious groups that approximately satisfy this need but not so effectively, for the authority of religion is widely perceived as rooted in something permanent. Typically, this is expressed by a moral code handed down by a leader, a quasi-divine figure or one in touch with divinity—like Moses, Jesus or Mohammed. Belonging to a religious group makes many people feel chosen, which in practice too often means that members of such a group feel bound to one another while showing intolerance toward those in other groups. A religion's moral ideals may be charitable in principle but are usually much less so in practice because cohesion and group identity require exclusions as well as inclusions.

There have been many attempts since the time of Kant and his inner moral law to separate the admirable ethical content of religious teaching from theologies that result in exclusivity and intolerance. But believers are likely to think that God is necessary to defend absolute truth against a feared moral breakdown, against a slide into relativism. This is true even of sophisticated believers. Reviewing A. N. Wilson's conflicted account of the loss and yet persistence of God and religion in nineteenth-century Britain, the Victorian scholar Gertrude Himmelfarb, as deft as she is conservative, brought forward to her readers the book's reassuring message. God may be dying or dead yet "he is always resurrected, perhaps not in his original incarnation but (for Mr. Wilson, at any rate) in a reasonable facsimile thereof."[35] In other words, all that really matters is that the God-idea remain stable enough so that morality remain firm. A more naïve but more typical example is provided by the Colorado State Board of Education that recently encouraged its schools to display the words "In God We Trust" in their classrooms, and defended the practice on the grounds that it would only enforce morality: "the issue has nothing to do with religion."[36] Like most moral guardians, these Colorado educators would probably find puzzling or repellent Rorty's keen insight that "all efforts to seek rational grounding for moral claims...are futile hangovers from immature longings for religious certitude."

Yet firmness of belief, although it might contribute to social cohesion in a simpler society, cannot in ours be satisfactorily correlated with a high level of conduct. As the physicist Steven Weinberg fairly commented, "People ought to be religious or not religious according to whether they believe in the teachings of religion, not because of any illusion that religion raises the moral level of society."[37] Nor can it be established that nonbelievers are less "law-abiding or productive than believers of the same socioeconomic class," to use E. O. Wilson's criteria of moral behavior.[38] In spite of this, nonbelievers have for centuries been suspected of bad conduct.

Believers, in fact, often seek an explicit moral code, like the Ten Commandments, on the assumption that people require moral reasons in order to behave morally. The American school administrators who now place the Commandments in constant view of their students forget that codes of conduct have never prevented misconduct and in fact have merely identified the major modes of misconduct.[39] Unimpressed by the decalogue, W. H. Auden memorably quipped that there's nothing so wonderful about merely observing human nature and adding, 'Thou shalt not.' Some religious wag recently put up signs across America signed by "God," one of which reads "Which of the Ten Commandments exactly don't you understand?" I may be taking this buffoonery too seriously, but it seems worth pointing out that it was never a question of *understanding* the commandments, only of *obeying* them. We don't behave very well but not because moral rules and reasons are lacking.

If moral rules rooted in religious belief cannot be relied on, perhaps we can turn to a universal and binding inner law, Kant's substitution for God. But the authority of conscience, understood through the long nineteenth century to be God's law inscribed in our hearts, has since Freud become thoroughly suspect, for we have learned how easy it is to fit our conscience to our inclinations. James Q. Wilson supports the belief that human nature contains an inherent moral sense by, among other arguments, the claim that even those who behave badly will justify their behavior with moral reasons.[40] He is right, they often do. Adolf Hitler, for example, wrote a whole book to justify the race hatred he was soon to have the opportunity of expressing so horribly. This proves, first, that Hitler had a moral sense, and, second, that a moral sense can be worse than useless because it can be used to justify thoroughly criminal behavior.

The surprising fact is that we don't on the whole behave worse than we do. But there are no clear—or too many—reasons for this: early education in both self-esteem and guilt, fear of reprisal, sympathy, the wish to gain or impress, genetic determination. In any case, we are not doomed to behave badly without religion any more than we are guaranteed to behave well with it. Our moral sense operates at varying levels, as a rule unconsciously, within the scope of our individual characters. Seldom do we deliberately follow moral rules. I cited in Chapter One the report by a teacher of Religious Studies that his students wanted to remove "theology" from their curriculum, but the desire to ground religious morality in theology proves to be strong. Elsewhere in the volume where that report is quoted, an essay on "God" tells us that "the heart of all religion" is "the proper name 'God,'" which provides an "ultimate point of reference [that] *relativizes* all present human practices, ideologies, and institutions" (my emphasis).[41] That is to say, the heart of religion may be the wish to believe that there is no disagreement as to what is right and no uncertainty as to what is best—the wish in short to preserve an absolute that relativizes all else. Social cohesion is to a degree necessary to any functioning group but it may be achieved at too high a price. The inner flexibility that makes for tolerance requires a willingness to see one's own position as one among others.

Conservative moralists often understand instinctively that a negative attitude toward God is not simply another point of view to be tolerated but a threat to social order of an obscure kind (obscure because, while adversarial, it is rarely violent). Hence the nicely ironic moment in Albert Camus' *The Stranger* when the magistrate protests agitatedly against Meursault's indifference to God, crying out, "Do you want my life to have no meaning?"—leaving Meursault to wonder what the magistrate's *raison d'être* has to do with his own unbelief. An American high school student wanted to start up an atheist club just like the religious clubs in existence, and was surprised when the school authorities took a dim view of the project.[42] They must have sensed that atheism was not just another affiliation to be granted equal opportunity but something oppositional to existing affiliations. A niche publishing company like Prometheus Books seeks to make atheism a virtual synonym for "secular humanism," and understands the word accordingly as an alternative religion in the spirit of Charles Bradlaugh or Robert Ingersoll. But atheism can never itself be a faith. It is always a posture of opposition. In recent polls a majority of Americans have said they could accept a female or Jewish or black political leader, but the majority dwindled when it came to "gays" and disappeared for "atheists." This general distrust of atheism as alternative *belief* is not, I think, misguided.

For thoughtful theists, suspicion of unbelievers often falls not so much on their conduct as their state of mind. A number of theologians tell us that those who do not believe in God must lead lives of despair. Even William James supposed we would fall into "the religious disease" of pessimism without a belief in the salvation of the world. This statement appears in an essay called "Is Life Worth Living." It might be more accurate to wonder whether people are not drawn to religion *by* despair. This was the view of Freud, at any rate, who observed somewhere that people do not worry a question like whether life is worth living *unless* they are ill.

One other aspect of this subject, the relation between religious belief and a desirable state of mind, needs to be raised at this moment when evolutionary psychology is in the air. We hear it said that believing is an advantage in terms of survival because it permits a more efficient use of one's resources. The statement is plausible but perhaps too easily so. There must be cultural as well as genetic reasons why, say, devout persons tend to have more children and increase the survival chances of their genes. And, although one may arrive at one's goal more efficiently if one is less beset by conflict and uncertainty, it is also true that those who spare themselves conflict and uncertainty usually accomplish less valuable work. Conflict can cripple but it can also stimulate.

Obviously I cannot do justice to so complex a subject *en passant*, so let me turn to a contemporary novelist, Ian McEwan, who in *Enduring Love* sets out the argument concisely and not without some intellectual respect, yet in a tone and a context that effectively generate satire as well, exposing the limits of the claim:

> Might there be a genetic basis to religious belief, or was it merely refreshing to think so? If faith conferred selective advantage there were any number of possible means and nothing could be proven. Suppose religion gave status, especially to the priestly caste. Plenty of social advantage—that. What if it bestowed strength in adversity, the power of consolation, the chance of surviving the disaster that might crush a godless man? Perhaps it gave believers passionate conviction, the brute strength of singlemindedness.
>
> Possibly it worked on groups as well as individuals, bringing cohesion and identity and a sense that you and your fellows were right, even—or especially—when

you were wrong. With God on our side, uplifted by a crazy unity, armed with a horrible certainty, you descend on the neighboring tribe, beat and rape it senseless, and come away burning with righteousness and drunk with the very victory your gods had promised. Repeat 50,000 times over the millennia, and the complex set of genes controlling for groundless conviction could get a strong distribution.

McEwan reduces to absurdity the idea of religious belief's genetic advantage. The satirical thrust is even cleverer in context. The meditating character is musing on a phrase ("can't be in two places at once") used by the policeman whose aid he has enlisted against a male stalker. Then he remembers making love to his wife the night before, while reading a book. He is impressed by having engaged separate but overlapping functions of the brain simultaneously (of having indulged "two of life's central, antithetical pleasures, reading and fucking"), and boasts to his wife, "Don't you think...I'm some kind of evolutionary throw forward?" But she is not impressed. Having earlier in the novel characterized the neo-Darwinian evolutionary psychology as "rationalism gone berserk" and "the new fundamentalism," she now adds with affectionate mockery, "And anyway, evolutionary change, speciation, is an event that can only be known in retrospect."[43]

The second need that, in the opinion of many observers, religion responds to uniquely is providing human individuals, who often enough feel themselves obscure specks, with a sense of belonging in the universe, giving them a sense of totality, of oneness. Some would say this need can only be satisfied by a belief in cosmic purpose, which comes down to a belief in the old personal and providential God. In the spirit of Hume, I suspect that those who are reasonably satisfied with their individual lives do not worry much about cosmic meaninglessness. Moreover, even when scientific speculation demotes the cosmic importance of the human being, it inevitably *promotes* the role of human consciousness in grasping that idea.

This isn't to deny that many people today feel that their lives have fallen into a spiritual drabness, an uninspired moral mediocrity. But since this feeling often prompts a longing for an age of religious faith, it is important to remind ourselves that any past age, looked at closely, cannot by any agreed upon measure be counted superior or inferior to the present. Deploring the inferiority of the present—and Lord knows there is much to deplore and much to make one anxious—is based on a comparison of past *peaks* and present *averages*. (It is also, I realized after hearing the superb monologue in Tony Kushner's play, *Homebody/Kabul*, the result of thinking of events in recent decades as somehow alterable whereas we think of more distant events as part of the unalterable shape of history.) The kind of melancholy that Andrew Delbanco finds distinctive of the present age, in his thoughtful meditation *The Real American Dream,* seems to me to have always been around in one form or another, and the kind of collective idealism he seeks, again in different forms, to be as available today as formerly. One odd thing proved by 9/11 is that a time of war and conflict, although in one sense less desirable than a time of peace and cooperation, also heightens our sense of significance, relieves the sense of spiritual drabness, showing just how difficult it is to judge the spirit of a whole age by an agreed upon standard.

The desire for an experience of totality, for feeling connected to the universe, is, we might agree, a common if fitful need of the human spirit. When fulfilled, it might well be called a religious experience, and certainly the rituals of institutional religion provide it for many. But it is accessible also through aesthetic experience, intellectual work, friendship, and a wondering relation to the natural world. For me, something like religious experience occurs when in the presence of trusted friends or amid the vastness of alien nature, I feel that my bounded and responsible personal self has dissolved for a moment. Or again when I lose the sense of time and place during intensely absorbing work. I would be inclined to offer a psychological explanation of these totalizing, "oceanic" experiences, but I do not object to describing them as religious. I see no contradiction at all, as does Robert Coles, between "the secular mind" and a sense of awe in relation to the mysteriousness of life.

I draw support for such a view from John Dewey, who in "Religion Versus the Religious," made a valuable distinction between the noun form of the word associated with supernaturalism and the adjective form describing an "attitude that may be taken toward every object and every proposed end or ideal." Dewey's "natural piety," "free of "scheme, doctrine and creed," endorsed "a quality of experience that could be aesthetic, scientific, moral, political" as well as religious.[44] Similarly, the physicist Richard Feynman described eloquently how his thinking about atoms sometimes ended "in awe and mystery, lost at the edge in uncertainty." He demurred from the idea that experience so "deep and impressive" must involve God, but he made a significant acknowledgment: "Some will tell me that I have just described a religious experience. Very well, you may call it what you will....[Perhaps] the God of the church isn't big enough....Everyone has different opinions."[45] The importance of Feynman's testimony lies in showing not only that such experience is available to a nonbeliever but that a nonbeliever who is unanxious about belief will not be intimidated by the word "religious."

Certainly literature and literary criticism are full of what may be called religious experience of a kind that might engage any serious reader. When for example I read Emily Dickinson or T. S. Eliot (or the critic Alfred Kazin's luminous comments on those writers in *God and the American Writer*), I make no distinction between what is and isn't religious. I am caught up in the energy of belief, which is indistinguishable from the energy of imagination as it shapes a possible world.

On this ground, the pragmatic view of William James continues to have importance today. Although not himself able to believe, James persuades us that belief even in a supernatural God may provide the believer with an ability to act in the world, and should not therefore be called mere illusion. In *Omens of Millennium*, Harold Bloom builds interestingly on James's middle ground between supernaturalism and empiricism, asserting (with assistance from the Islamic scholar Henry Corbin) that "the mediating power of the imaginal is a cognitive force in its own right. Empiricists and supernaturalists alike may dismiss this middle sphere as fiction but imaginative men and women, whether literary or not in their orientation, will recognize that the imaginal world exists, and is not *fantasy or wish-fulfillment*."[46] This is a particularly useful amplification of James's idea because it links religious with aesthetic experience, something that James himself was not quite prepared to do.

What Bloom is rightly skeptical of is the tyranny of the scientific model of truth requiring that "the imaginal," which reveals truth for the subject, be judged as *either* literal truth *or* illusory fiction. The epistemologist Susan Haack, who recognizes only one meaning of truth but who quite understands that science like literature employs imagination, tries to get around this kind of argument by making a distinction between *imaginative* science on the one hand and *imaginary* fiction on the other.[47] But this relegates fiction to the scrapheap of the untrue. Similarly, her book *Evidence and Inquiry*, although it makes telling and subtle arguments against a dogmatic foundationalism in epistemology, still works from the assumption that truth can only mean conclusions reached on the basis of objective evidence, and so cannot include subjective truth attained through aesthetic or religious experience.

This leads into the third need distinctively served by religion, the need for mythic stories of how and why we are here. Stories of this kind are really collective versions of the personal mythmaking we construct all the time in the process, Paul Ricoeur suggests, of building our individual identities. We think of these myths as explanatory and so give them special value. That is to say, they are not only literary but also religious myths. The association of the two has been strengthened during the last 150 years by the increased prestige of science, which has thrown these two kinds of mythmaking into the same camp.

After observing that one of the functions of religion is to compose a story of how and why we are here, E. O. Wilson's *Consilience* makes an appropriative move, true to the spirit of his subtitle, The Unity of Knowledge: "Perhaps science is a continuation on new and better-tested ground to attain the same end [attempted earlier by Holy Writ]. If so, science...is religion liberated and writ large."[48] Now, myths of origins and destinies are always going to be influenced by the science of their time (as Richard Feynman implied), but that is not quite what Wilson is saying. He doesn't see religious or literary myth as working from its own direction to articulate the experience of being in the world; rather he sees the scientific perspective as capable of controlling the narrative, as if modern literature replaces older literature in the same way that modern science replaces older science. This would imply that older literature and ancient myths are untruthful, are myths in a purely pejorative sense. Such a view misunderstands what needs the literary or religious imagination responds to in making narrative, and overestimates the reach of scientific hypotheses and models. But Wilson's remark opens up the subject of literature and religion to another line of investigation.

Literature and Religion in an Age of Science

Given the importance of science in the modern world, it is no wonder that the arts, religion, and philosophy are attracted to its theories and speculations. Although the Bible will not be replaced any more than *King Lear* will be replaced, the stories of origins and ends that matter most to us now are likely to be influenced by science. In recent decades we have moved beyond the "two cultures" problem as quite a few novelists, dramatists and poets have drawn on and made serious use of the sciences, especially physics and biology. But these fields have also attracted the more dubious interest of "theo-scientists" (as I will call them), who find "evidence" that moral purpose or "intelligent design" informs the material processes of nature. Theo-scientists do not admit to making a myth nor do they seek to test a hypothesis with scientific rigor. Rather, they claim as objectively true what they strongly wish to be so.[49]

One of the most cunning theo-scientific arguments, deployed for example by Phillip Johnson, tries to use science against itself. Johnson claims that science refuses to consider all possibilities impartially, the supernaturalistic as well as naturalistic. He asserts that, in so doing, science is atheistic, dogmatically atheistic. But this is to misunderstand the scope of science. As Niles Eldredge puts it, "Science does not say that the supernatural does not exist; it simply says that the supernatural is not part of its territory."[50] A *poet can* say, in effect, that the supernatural exists because he knowingly adopts a subjective perspective as the scientist adopts an objective one, unlike Johnson who confuses the two.

Another influential theo-scientific tactic is to assert that the designs of nature are just too complex to have evolved by merely natural processes. This tactic draws support from the biochemist Michael Behe whose *Darwin's Black Box* argues that the stunning complexity of cell machinery requires us to hypothesize a purposeful designer. His argument has been effectively discounted by a number of biologists, among them Michael Ruse who points out (in his book *Can A Darwinist Be A Christian?*) that natural selection can cobble together over time some amazing results and that a God who works *through* natural selection, implicated in the details of design, would be not only scientifically embarrassing, since it could neither be proved nor disproved, but morally embarrassing as well when systems go tragically wrong. Ruse's counterargument is particularly telling because he gives a positive answer to the question raised in his title, meaning by "Christian" a learned moral intelligence that allows us to go beyond the natural limits imposed by the evolutionary imperative.[51]

Hungry for overall moral significance, writers from the early days of Darwinism to the present have yielded to the temptation to find a guiding moral purpose in natural process itself. Spencer's Social Darwinism represented a nineteenth-century version of this fusion, and something like it has appealed to quasi-scientific visionaries ever since—to George Bernard Shaw with his Creative Evolution, to Teilhard de Chardin with his evolution as an ascent of consciousness working forward to Supreme Consciousness,[52] to Holmes Rolston, III, who in a book published in 1999 uses up-to-date molecular biology to demonstrate that a gene-driven universe is a God-driven universe. "The secular evolves into the sacred" is one of Rolston's inimitable formulations.[53]

It is of course true that many distinguished moralists since the time of Plato have found it very difficult to abandon teleological thinking—that is, reasoned belief that there exists, apart from our desire for it or our individual ability to patch one together, some discernible goal or aim for human life in general, some universal moral purpose. Darwin marks the most important turning point in our ability to put aside this weighty, traditional assumption. The philosopher and psychoanalyst Jonathan Lear, linking Darwin and Freud, clarifies neatly what is at stake here:

> Darwin explained away the appearance of teleology by showing that, although disruptions in nature may be occasions for the evolution of the species, that is not why they are occurring. Similarly, a disruption in the mind may be an occasion for growth [or, as Lear indicates, may fail to be, resulting in a repetition of the past] but that is not why it is occurring.[54]

Such disruption, according to Lear, has no content; it is only possibility; whether or not it is a move forward depends on what happens next. He shows that Freud himself, in his late formulation of the death drive as a *principle* of aggression in human life, could not resist the lure of teleological thinking and obscured his own insight into the contentlessness of unconscious disruptions, just as Plato and Aristotle, in deciding that "the good" or "happiness" was the ultimate aim of life, obscured their own awareness of what he calls "the remainder of life," i.e., residue open to possibilities and not end-oriented. Darwin's thought, not centered on man, is less constrained than Freud's in this way, showing us that, although species in struggling to survive behave purposefully in this way or that, mutations that initiate change in the very capacities of species are not themselves expressive of purpose.

Some students of evolution, like Robert Wright, object to others, like Stephen Jay Gould, for overlooking evidences of direction. The Darwinian world ruled by natural selection, as Gould presents it, is purposeless, accidental, without moral goals. Superficially, Wright's objection, which emphasizes the learning derived from feedback, makes sense since species do behave purposefully to survive, to reproduce, etc. But Gould's basic argument about the lack of moral purpose of nature itself is not undermined.[55] And such lack is even more apparent in a nonbiological science. As Steven Weinberg famously remarked, "The more the universe seems comprehensible, the more it also seems pointless."[56]

Since theological thought pivots on teleology, facing a Darwinian world is especially difficulty for philosophers with a theological bent. Thus Heidegger, in *An Introduction to Metaphysics*, raises with a great air of mystery the "fundamental question"—why is there something rather than nothing?—suggesting a unity-of-knowledge argument from a *religious* point of view. It is, however, not impossible for a modern philosopher, even one with a religious sensibility but not as prejudiced against science as Heidegger, to keep subjective and objective perspectives apart. Wittgenstein, for example, wrote, "It is not *how* things are in the world that is mystical, but that it exists," a somewhat similar statement but one that implies a distinction between scientific and poetic points of view, between *how* and *that* things are.[57] How it all began is a question at the edge of science, and if not handled with care can slip into theological speculation, which is the case when Creationists invoke the Heideggerian question as if it were rhetorical, implying the *probability* of divine existence.

What is now called in theoretical physics a Grand Unified Theory (GUT), misleadingly also called a Theory of Everything (TOE), a system of interlocking equations that aspires to bring together quantum theory and relativity, has a vaguely theological resonance, though this has been wisely resisted by most scientists. One of the most interesting caveats comes from a physicist who is also a theologian, John Polkinghorne, who declares: "if they ever do find the GUT it won't be the TOE because the only TOE is theology."[58] His book *Belief in God in an Age of Science* clearly indicates that he does not simply seek from science equal time for theology (as do some Creationists) but seeks to set science "within a wider and more profound context of understanding." Here again is the unified view from the religious end. As Polkinghorne puts it, "We are not now looking to the physical world for hints of God's existence but to God's existence as an aid for understanding why things have developed in the physical world in the manner that they have."[59] Now, since theology, like literature, typically seeks an embracing myth, he has a point, although he would not like the way I am going to rephrase it. Scientific theory is not by its nature imperialistic (only excited into being so) but theological myth is. In this respect it is like great literary theodicies, *The Divine Comedy* or *Paradise Lost*. But the works of Dante and Milton know themselves to be myths whereas Polkinghorne's theology does not.

Other scientists today are excited into theo-science by the very scope of physical theory. Among them are the mathematical physicist Paul Davies (*The Mind of God*), the astronomer Robert Jastrow (*God and the Astronomers*), the physicist Gerald Schroeder (*Genesis and the Big Bang*), and the cosmologist Frank Tipler (*The Physics of Immortality*). Stephen Hawking, it is well known, concluded his *Brief History of Time* with a flourish about "the Mind of God," but seems to have regretted it since. (He says he wants to stay on the scientific side of the divide between science and theology, and declines to respond to questions about God.)[60] We might wonder whether these writers have been a little encouraged by Einstein's flirtation with the metaphor of God, expressing his awe at the reach of his own theory, at the intelligibility of the universe. But Einstein surely meant to convey only the sense of wonder anyone might feel in successfully pursuing an ambitious goal in any field. "The individual," he wrote, "wants to experience the universe as a single, significant whole," and "this kind of religious *feeling*" [my emphasis] is "the strongest and noblest motive for scientific research."[61] It is possible, however, that Einstein carried his fancy a step too far in linking the word God to his awe of the very intelligibility of the universe. This neglects the fact, mentioned by Freud among others, that a world quite alien to human understanding, a world in which human consciousness plays no part, would have no conceivable interest for us.

On the contemporary intellectual scene, it is especially the science of evolutionary biology that has proved most imperialistic, most seductive in implying that our very ability to think about the relation of brain to mind is genetically determined, so that we are in effect wholly contained by material process, as nature in pre-Enlightenment theology was contained by God. Richard Lewontin, himself a molecular biologist, overstates only a little in asserting that "molecular biology is now a religion, and molecular biologists are its prophets."[62] The philosopher Thomas Nagel in *The Last Word* also takes note of this "religious flavor" and has written wryly about it: "Darwin enabled modern secular culture to heave a great collective sigh of relief, by apparently providing a way to eliminate purpose, meaning, and design as fundamental features of the world," but the "overuse of evolutionary biology to explain everything about life," even our ability to think about and judge it, arouses in us "the fear of religion." It is an odd situation, the secular intellectual newly frightened by religion. Nagel's own helpful counterargument is that we cannot in practice avoid believing in the "independent validity of our reasoning," so "there is no alternative but to try to decide what to believe and how to live."[63] Perhaps this doesn't quite confront the *fear* of religion, which seems to draw forth old feelings of helplessness. (A version of this fear—a controlled version, capable therefore of affording us pleasure—seems to be at work, for example, in science-fictions about invasions from outer space.) But I will soon call on Nagel for his excellent defense of the subjective perspective from a philosopher's objective point of view.

I turn now to three very persuasive and influential authorities on the moral dimensions of contemporary biological theory, who are all aware of the difference between scientific and humanistic thought but who blur this awareness in an ambitious reaching for a unified view, a view that folds moral *into* physical knowledge, mind *into* brain. E. O. Wilson, Richard Dawkins, and Daniel Dennett degrade art, religion, and philosophy in so doing, although they do not seek to, because they pursue what Wilson calls "the unity of knowledge" from the scientific perspective alone.

Let me make clear that the fundamental assumption of Wilson, Dawkins, and Dennett is not in question here. I doubt that anyone today sees mind as an entity quite separate from brain (in the old Cartesian manner) rather than an aspect of it, although Dennett seems to argue against those who do. The question at issue, rather, is whether the scientist's unified view of knowledge that necessarily *subordinates* culture to biology constitutes an intellectual overreaching, however useful it might be as a heuristic device. At times, Wilson, the very experienced and knowledgeable biologist, clearly indicates the limits of science. Science, he tells us, is "neither a philosophy nor a belief system [but an effective] combination of mental operations."[64] Moreover, he shrewdly admits there is a danger of falling in love with one's own theories, a danger that scientists are no more exempt from than other people. But, excited by the idea that mind must have a physical basis, he is impelled to say things like: "*Ought* [i.e., morality] is the product of a material process."[65] Since any thought-event is the product of a material process, this doesn't say much by itself, and what Wilson really seems to mean is that morality is not an independent subject of inquiry. In his attempt to fold Ought into Is, morality into nature, Wilson not only ignores the healthy skepticism on this issue of Hume, Poincaré, Feynman, and Gould but circumvents the extensive cultural tradition that explores and expresses moral questions. To argue that moral reasoning is "consilient" with natural science sounds innocuous, but it belittles the significance of ethics, religion, and the arts.

At another point Wilson characterizes our sense of free will, of "freedom from the constraints imposed by the physiochemical states of one's own body and mind," as an "illusion created by the hidden preparation of mental activity," but a useful illusion, true in an "operational sense" because "confidence in free will is biologically adaptive."[66] Now, one does not want to fall into the trap of denying those physiochemical constraints, but Wilson is obliged to use a pejorative word like "illusion" because he would not want to say that, from one point of view, free will is an illusion whereas, from another, it is not. And there is no way of *merging* these perspectives! They can only be coordinated by philosophical abstraction or partnered by means of an ironic wit that dramatizes their incongruity, as when Isaac Bashevis Singer wonderfully remarked, "Of course I have free will—do I have a choice?"

Perhaps Wilson should have read more deeply in his Diderot, one of the Enlightenment figures he so much admires. Although Diderot embraced a materialist position, he also understood the incongruity that arose when the materialist and humanist perspectives were juxtaposed. Significantly, Wilson, in his enthusiasm for the Enlightenment, has not a kind word to say about Romanticism, ignoring the fact that one of the things Romanticism distrusted was the grandly unified answer. "We also owe to Romanticism," Isaiah Berlin wrote, "the notion that a unified answer in human affairs is likely to be ruinous, that if you really believe there is one single solution to all human ills...you must impose this solution at no matter what cost."[67] True, Berlin is thinking of political utopianists, but scientific hegemony can lead to a comparable deprecation of moral uncertainty.

Richard Dawkins' *The Selfish Gene* is another fascinating exploration of this interdisciplinary territory, and its speculations are also informed by a strong sense of what science is and is not. Dawkins indicates clearly that he is using the word "selfish" metaphorically, as a way of making accessible to human understanding the idea that the only "purpose" of the gene is to survive and that individuals are only pawns in the game: "We are survival machines, robot vehicles blindly programmed to preserve genes."[68] There is no hidden will, nothing wants to evolve, evolution just happens. "Natural selection is...blind because it does not see ahead, does not plan consequences, has no purpose in view."[69] So, "if there is a human moral to be drawn, it is that we must *teach* our children altruism, for we cannot expect it to be part of their biological nature."[70] Steven Weinberg recently made the same point, saying that science itself offers no basis for establishing values and so it is up to us to "write the script."[71]

I am particularly grateful to Dawkins for dispelling the confusion, generated as a rule by *humanists*, concerning two concepts that are prominent in discussions of Darwinian theory, Chance and Determinism. Realizing that he had explained Chance too casually in *The Selfish Gene*, he clarifies this somewhat complex concept at length in *The Blind Watchmaker*. One factor in evolution, mutation, is indeed random, but natural selection, the cumulative process that is fundamental in evolution is "the very opposite of random."[72] No natural law has been suspended in either case. As for determinism, "genes 'determine' behaviour only in a statistical sense."[73] Again there is no hidden will at work. Nonscientists are inclined to invest the words chance and determinism with theological resonance, making chance mean that the gods are indifferent to our fate and determinism mean that the gods necessitate our fate. Such statements may be misleading, though poets like Hardy can make successful literary use of their resonance because poems, unlike propositions, express the feeling of what happens.

But such is the imaginative energy released by the breakthroughs in evolutionary biology—the arts, philosophy, and religion can show nothing comparable—that Dawkins, too, succumbs to the temptation to fold an explanation of culture inside of it. He does so in his chapter on "Memes, the new replicators," in which he speculates that the cultural transmission of ideas proceeds by a totally involuntary replication of "idea-memes," which function *like* genes. (In *The Blind Watchmaker* he admits that "cultural evolution is not really evolution at all if we are being fussy and purist about our use of words, but there may be enough in common to justify some comparison of principles."[74] This in effect is to withdraw his own admission so he can continue to ride his hobbyhorse.) Thus, for example, there is "a religious meme complex...called faith. It means blind trust, in the absence of evidence, even in the teeth of evidence."[75] The sarcasm of the last sentence clearly enough indicates that Dawkins is not content with scientific agnosticism but, like Huxley, is using science to deny the very validity of theological and by extension other non-scientific imagining. "I am sceptical of all myths," he writes, dismissing Tennyson's memorable phrase "nature red in tooth and claw."[76] He cannot believe, I am sure, that Tennyson's phrase is making a scientific claim rather than expressing effectively a shared feeling. It is a little part of culture, without which we would lack the moral energy to rebel, as Dawkins would have us rebel, against "the tyranny of the selfish replicators."

My scruple here is not to be confused with the argument of Holmes Rolston, III, *contra* Dawkins, that the very fact we can say 'we should teach altruism' shows that altruism is inherent in the evolutionary process, for how else are we one able to express such a thought?[77] Rolston merges morality into natural process whereas my query assumes, as Dawkins himself elsewhere assumes, that we should not. But Dawkins doesn't make himself quite clear on this point. In his 1996 introduction to *The Blind Watchmaker*, he is evidently responding to the kind of objection I am raising: "I do not mean that history, literary criticism, and the law should be recast in a specifically Darwinian mould. Far from it, very far. But all human works are the products of brains, brains are evolved data processing devices, and we shall misunderstand their works if we forget this fundamental fact."[78] Very well, but he gives no indication as to how we are to understand, except in a specifically Darwinian mould, those products of brain that constitute the so-called humanities. For him as for Wilson, a shift to the humanistic *perspective* would apparently threaten the hegemony of the scientific point of view.

Before we turn to Daniel Dennett's *Consciousness Explained*, it would in fact be clarifying if we take a moment to call on Nagel for a philosophically grounded formulation of the perspectival premise, which will help us make better sense of science's relation to religion, philosophy, and the arts.

The basic problem addressed by Nagel in *The View from Nowhere* is "how to combine the perspective of a particular person inside the world with an objective view of that same world, the person and his viewpoint included." His basic claim is that "the pursuit of a highly unified conception of life and the world leads...to the refusal to recognize part of what is real." Full human reality consists of "the interplay of these two uneasily related types of conception [subjective and objective] and the essentially incompleteable effort to reconcile them." Nagel wants us to understand that objectivity as a method of understanding is a matter of degree: "To acquire a more objective understanding of some aspect of life or the world, we step back from our initial view of it and form a new conception which has that view and its relation to the world as its object. In other words, we place ourselves in the world that is to be understood." We can carry this process further but only so far because there is the danger of what Nietzsche called false objectification when an appearance produced by a subjective perspective "cannot be better understood from a more objective standpoint." One limit we encounter in seeking this standpoint becomes clear when objectivity "tries to encompass subjectivity in its conception of the real." This is to ignore the fact that our personal perspective belongs to the world too.

Thus for Nagel science "is bound to leave undescribed the irreducibly subjective character of conscious mental processes, whatever may be their intimate relation to the physical operation of the brain," and without this subjective consciousness "we couldn't do physics or anything else." Nagel's risky word "irreducibly" does *not* postulate a dualism of brain and mind nor does it mean that subjectivity situates a *fixed* point of view or *essential* self.

What Nagel wants to make clear (as did Nietzsche in his day) is that no one type of human understanding, scientific or ethical, "is in charge of the universe and what can be said about it."[79]

In his elaborate and impressive treatise *Consciousness Explained*, Daniel Dennett is aware of Nagel's argument and makes some attempt to refute it, unsatisfactorily in my opinion. His avowed target is what he calls the Cartesian theater of mind, the rooted prejudice that mind stuff is unique and separate from the material brain, but Nagel's perspectivism is not to be confused with this Cartesian dualism. Shifting his ground somewhat, Dennett then quotes Nagel—"It may be impossible for us to abandon certain ways of conceiving and representing ourselves, no matter how little support they get from scientific research"—and replies: "it is indeed difficult but not impossible."[80] He asserts that first person accounts of the phenomenology of experience are not inevitable, for we can imagine other minds and give third-person accounts of them, a process he calls "heterophenomenology." When we do this, we see that we are no longer dealing with a Self or Central Meaner but with a fiction edited through multiple drafts or with a Center of Narrative Gravity, more closely resembling the model of the Computer than any traditional model of Mind. Dennett contends, *contra* Nagel, that we *can* get away from a level of phenomenology to a level of physiology, and "explain consciousness" according to it, but that many people resist this out of "fear that such explanation will cause them to lose their moral bearings."[81]

It *is* disconcerting to think of consciousness as operating quite like the artificial intelligence of a computer, but fortunately there is a good deal of skepticism around to keep that fear at a distance. This skepticism proceeds along two lines. The first concedes to brain enthusiasts like Paul Churchland and Jonathan Weiner that (in Weiner's words) "in the long view, molecular genetics bids to unite all of the sciences, all of philosophy, and all of the arts."[82] But it would underline "long view." That is to say, there are so many causal pathways involved in human behavior (many concerned with our complex lives as social beings) that the idea of fully explaining culture biologically is too remote to be worth consideration. As Lewontin pertinently reminds us, "it takes a certain moral courage to accept the messages of scientific ignorance and all that it implies."[83] The second line of skeptical thinking goes farther and asserts that certain questions—like the meaning or purpose of life, the facing of death—are simply not scientific questions at all and never will be. In Nagel's language, the effort to unite the two kinds of thinking at issue here is necessarily "incompleteable." Necessarily, at any rate, in the modern world, after the crucial separation occurred between science and religion, between explanatory and expressive languages. The physicist Roger G. Newton evokes very well the pathos of this separation: "We must settle for the delight of knowing how Nature works. The various kinds of truths that have been torn asunder—scientific and religious, rational and emotional—can never be joined together again."[84]

Beyond such general scruples, my skeptical response to Dennett's book involves two points deriving from my literary background. One is that Dennett's attack on the Self and the Central Meaner is not exactly news to those of us long exposed to literary theory. It is almost a commonplace for us that the self, as distinct from the empirical person, is best imagined as a function or a nexus or an evolving and never fully integrated sense of identity. Dennett's "Center of Narrative Gravity" captures this last sense well enough, although I prefer Antonio Damasio's formulation: "the body, as represented in the brain, may constitute the indispensable frame of reference for the neural processes that we experience as the mind"; "at each moment the state of self is constructed [in this] body-minded brain."[85] Nor do students of literary theory think of meaning as *controlled* by an author; it is, rather, distributed in texts and certainly depends in part on the varying responses of readers. Dennett praises Nietzsche and Freud for appreciating the superficiality of consciousness, but he fails to make clear that this was because they had such an enormously rich conception of mind apart from surface consciousness.

My other scruple about Dennett's work touches on my earlier critique of Wilson and Dawkins, and is aimed as well at other unified-field theories. His ambitious book never seems to recognize that consciousness might be understood according to any other than a strictly scientific model, that any other model of truth is operative, that the vast accumulation of eloquent testimony produced by philosophy, religion, and the arts has any meaning or importance at all. Wilson and Dawkins pay these fields the compliment of condescending to them. Dennett doesn't even do that.

Wilson, Dawkins, and Dennett are at least well worth quarreling with, but there are in fact many spokesmen for science who respect its limits, and do not condescend to religion, the arts, and moral philosophy, and I will here cite two who are sufficiently representative.

One is Richard Feynman, who recognized that there is a gap between scientific and religious understanding, and whose commitment to the former did not blind him to its limits or to the importance of engaging the latter.

"From science alone," he wrote, "we do not know what is the meaning of life and what are the right moral values...no discussion [of which] can be made...without coming to the great source of systems of morality and descriptions of meaning, which is the field of religion." He frankly admitted that "most scientists do not believe in God," and implicitly included himself in the group, but since science cannot disprove God's existence, he could say there is no inconsistency between believing in God and doing science. Science and religion do interact but loosely and uncoercively: "Science makes, indeed, an impact on many ideas associated with religion, but I do not believe it affects, in any very strong way, the moral conduct and ethical views." With an air of simplicity and genial flexibility, Feynman thus relaxed some of the knots that have led both morality and science into a competition prompting each to attempt to subsume the other.[86]

A second spokesman is Stephen Jay Gould, well known for his ability to discuss the implications of evolutionary theory for a general audience, who made the same point in response to the decision by a school board in Kansas to remove evolution from the science curriculum (a decision since revoked, though only on practical grounds). Gould wrote: "no factual discovery of science (statements about how nature 'is') can, in principle, lead us to ethical conclusions (how we 'ought' to behave) or to convictions about intrinsic meaning (the 'purpose' of our lives). These last two questions—and what more important inquiries could we make?—lie firmly in the domains of religion, philosophy and humanistic study. Science and religion should be equal, mutually respecting partners, each the master of its own domain, and with each domain vital to human life in a different way."[87]

But I do not wish to rule out the legitimacy and interest of speculation into the gray areas between such widely diverse fields as neurology or evolutionary psychology on the one hand and literary or ethical theory on the other. It isn't a question here of perfectly balancing the two, for it would scarcely be possible for someone to have a highly developed knowledge of both. It is a question rather of working from one end and engaging the other in some mutually suggestive way. Two brief examples. In *The Feeling of What Happens* Antonio Damasio handles evidence like the neurologist he is, but his book is alert throughout to the *quality* of experience. In explaining how mind functions in terms of brain, he is alert to the kinds of questions reflective persons (even poets, whom he pertinently quotes) actually ask themselves—how they experience the spatiotemporal world, how bodily images and emotions work in their experience of consciousness.[88] My other exemplar here is H. Porter Abbott whose specialty is the theory of literary narrative. Given the reach of a concept like narrative, he is able to use the work of such cognitive scientists and evolutionary psychologists as Jerry Fodor and Merlin Donald, offering fascinating suggestions linking the origin and development of the sense of time in narrative to the origin and development of the human mind.[89]

Despite its flirtations with religion in recent years, it is probably still true that, by the nature of its method, science is the most self-critical of the three fields of endeavor I am triangulating. A scientific theory is constructed so as to welcome challenge. That is hardly true of theological or poetic myths, which are constructed so as to gain emotional assent. But I have also been arguing that the language of literature is more self-conscious, more self-aware, than that of religion. The literary imagination, then, is in some ways allied to the religious against science and in some ways allied to the scientific imagination against religion.

The influence of science in the modern world, inspiring a certain degree of fear, may well be one of the reasons why the word God (without those understood quotation marks) has gained ground in our debates about the place of religion in civil society. In any case, we are faced today with a resurgence of religious enthusiasm, obviously in the Islamic world but to some extent in the West too, particularly in the United States, where it is intertwined with conservative politics. It is strange that the US should be, on the one hand, the most entrepreneurial and forward-looking among the Western democracies and yet, on the other, the most constrained by religion, the most retrograde in its social morality, especially in regard to sexuality and criminal justice.

Some attempt to place (and keep in place) religion in a secular society is in order here because my running argument concerning the importance of the literary imagination depends upon the assumption that our society is not dominated by religious practices, institutions, and modes of thought. It would be futile to conduct such an argument within a society more religious than secular. The danger of religious influence can be exaggerated, but there have been rather alarming trends in recent decades, in the United States much more than in Western Europe, toward more entanglement of religion with social and political life. I cannot analyze in depth this complex situation, but an assessment of the general tension between religious and secular components in contemporary society will help to clear ground for what I have to say in the final chapter concerning the sacred text.

Literature Versus Religion in a Secular Age

"By the middle of the twentieth century," writes Karen Armstrong in *The Battle for God*, "most Western people assumed that religion would never again play a major part in world events."⁹⁰ This was indeed the opinion of many candid observers in those post-War decades, and, accordingly the term "secular" as a description of everyday lives that are no longer organized by religious observances and institutions was widely used in a more or less neutral and non-controversial sense. The word seemed merely to acknowledge the fact that religion was playing a smaller role in the modern world, due to advances in technology and education, increased material prosperity, and the consequent relaxation of certain social restraints, especially those concerning sexual behavior. Thus the evangelist Billy Graham could describe the United States as "a secular country in which thousands of Christians live and have substantial influence," and Gabriel Josipovici, from a very different background, could write as late as the 1980s of "our predominantly secular age, an age where religious authority has lost its hold on all but a very few."⁹¹ "Secular" was in fact formally defined in a reference work of religious terms published in the 1990s as "officially neutral and benevolently disinterested in questions pertaining to religion."⁹²

Then something happened—or was happening all along without our realizing it at the time—a complex process of polarization between liberals riding the momentum of the sixties on the one hand and, on the other, increasingly frustrated Christian conservatives who wanted to express their resistance to liberalism and to modernism in general. The pull on one side was perhaps most concisely represented by a number of American Supreme Court decisions during the 1960s and 1970s, especially those striking down "any law whose purpose [intentional or otherwise] is primarily to advance the cause of religion...or that results in the entanglement of government in the affairs of religion."⁹³ The pull on the other is perhaps best illustrated by the remarkable growth of the Christian Right, spurred by evangelical sects spreading from the South and small-town Midwest, an anti-liberal culture that felt threatened by, and began to crusade against, the liberal consensus loosely forming among Protestants, Catholics, Jews, and secularists.

Modern American evangelicalism (unlike nineteenth-century varieties in both the United States and Britain that supported the abolition of slavery) has become increasingly consolidated in its opposition to liberal policy in general and particularly to liberal attitudes regarding such issues as civil rights, abortion, school prayer, feminism, and homosexuality. An evangelical now is to some extent a fundamentalist, a term that had been understood to refer to religious separatism and belief in the inerrancy of scripture but that today is better defined as someone "who is in militant opposition to liberal theology in the churches or to changes in cultural values and mores, such as those associated with 'secular humanism.'"[94] Another scholar defines current fundamentalism as *"orthodoxy in confrontation with modernity."*[95]

I focus on the Christian right, radical in its opposition to secularism, because it has begun to exert a significant political influence, accounting in no small part for the disturbing tendency in America's last half century to introduce God into politics. An important change occurred during the Eisenhower presidency of the 1950s. Lincoln and other presidents before that time invoked God, to be sure, but kept the borderline between church and state reasonably clear. Eisenhower blurred the line, probably in response to the dread of godless communism. He approved both the adding of "under God" (following "this nation") to the Pledge of Allegiance required from schoolchildren and the inscribing of "In God We Trust" on American currency; he also declared rather fatuously, "Our government makes no sense unless it is founded on a deeply felt religious belief—and I don't care what it is."[96]

At the same time the evangelist Billy Graham began to launch his crusade, and Graham was to become spiritual counselor to Richard Nixon. Kennedy and Johnson during the sixties did not politicize religion, but almost every president since Nixon has described himself as a born-again Christian. One presumes that a measure of political expediency influenced these declarations. (As Edward Gibbon observed concerning the various modes of worship prevailing in ancient Rome, they were "considered by the people as equally true; by the philosopher as equally false; and by the magistrate as equally useful.")[97] Still, the overall picture is surprising.

What are we to make of the fact that every poll conducted in recent years shows that more than 90% of Americans say they believe in the existence of a personal God and that a large majority say they attend church regularly?[98] Probably some respondents were more comfortable answering yes than no to the questions asked, but the figures drawn from American surveys are much higher than those drawn from countries in Western Europe.[99]

A backward glance is helpful here, with particular reference to American understanding of the Constitution's First Amendment that ensured the disestablishment of the Anglican or Episcopal Church. The American public today appears not to be agreed on the aim or intention of that amendment. It used to be said that its principal aim was to guarantee freedom *of* religion for various competing sects that feared a state religion. But recently we have heard that the aim was rather to guarantee freedom *for* religion, freedom to promote religion. And the interest in doing so was apparently active during the Revolutionary era, as is shown in Jon Butler's *Awash in a Sea of Faith*, which accumulates evidence of an "explosion of efforts at religious renewal and revival" from 1700 onward. Butler shows that, although Jefferson and Madison believed religion should not demand assistance from the state, sects in their day were vying for political influence.[100]

Martin E. Marty, a prolific historian of American religion, has developed the subtle and suggestive argument that Enlightenment in the already pluralistic colonies did not, as in Europe, curb religious zeal (witness The Great Awakening of the 1730s and 1740s) because each sect thought of its own beliefs as universally true yet respected other earnest sects. The distinctive American factor for Marty, as for Tocqueville, was that people felt themselves free to choose their religion, rather than feeling simply born into one faith, and so became zealous and even competitive in their adherences.[101]

In his classic of the 1830s, *Democracy in America*, Tocqueville touched on a crucial distinction between the American and European experience of religion. After observing that "the religious atmosphere of the country was the first thing that struck me on arrival in the United States," he suggested that the main reason for the "sway of religion over their country was the complete separation of church and state."[102] This sounds paradoxical but he meant that, in the absence of a *state church* to which people accommodate themselves as a birthright and more or less take for granted, there are in America numerous *sects* seeking to increase the number of their voluntary adherents, all infused by the Protestant individualistic spirit that shook off the authority of the Pope and acknowledged no other religious supremacy. And he underlined the great importance in this connection of the fact that political sovereignty in the American federalist system was not centralized but divided between a central authority and far from passive state authorities.[103]

Very useful development of Tocqueville's insight may be found not only in Marty but also in Seymour Martin Lipset's *American Exceptionalism: A Double-Edged Sword*. Lipset cites G. K. Chesterton who wrote that "America is the only nation in the world that is founded on a creed," the elements of which are liberty, egalitarianism, individualism, populism, and laissez-faire. Extending this idea, he explains that American society differs from that of European countries (and from Japan and even Canada) because the latter are "postfeudal" and so place more emphasis on obedience to political authority and deference to superiors. In contrast, writes Lipset, the elements of the American creed (all of them "liberal" in the classic anti-statist sense) add up not simply to a nationality but also an ideology. American sectarian religions unlike European state religions *moralize* politics, think of the conflicts of nations in terms of good and evil more than of practical interests. Influenced by this ideology, Americans typically believe their nation is morally exceptional among the nations of the earth. Lipset calls the sense of American exceptionalism a double-edged sword because, if on the one hand it leads to a more anarchic and moralistic political atmosphere than what is found in Europe, it also inspires more effective moral protest against what are perceived as state-sponsored evils.[104]

What observers like Tocqueville, Lipset, and Marty enable us to see is that it is false to describe American society *either* as tenaciously secular *or* as tenaciously religious: both are true because the two powerful forces of religion and secularism are in ever-present contention. Marty fairly argues that, just as we underrated the strength of religion fifty years ago, the new danger may be to underrate the strength of American society's secularism, to forget the fundamentally pluralist character of that society. "Unless theorists and theologians reckon with *both* all-pervasive religiousness *and* persistent secularity," he cautions us, "they will again be left stranded with each cultural shift in search of theories to match their perceptions."[105]

My concern in this segment of the present chapter is the robustness of secularism in the West, and particularly in America where it is most attacked. And so, although not forgetting Marty's caution, I turn in the direction of my fear, to the most direct challenges to secularism.

The American pollster George Gallup, offering his statistics, concluded that "such a nation cannot by any stretch of the imagination be described as secular in its core beliefs."[106] Even if this is overstated, there is little doubt that during the last few decades political power in the United States has shifted to the right. In the present atmosphere, the word secular, always a bugbear for the Christian right, has now become demonized, even among intellectuals. I first became aware of this degradation only a few years ago when my attention was directed to a sophisticated volume of essays titled *Post-Secular Philosophy*. The phrases "post-religious" and "post-Christian" had been in the air for several decades, but they suggested a conceptual limbo whereas "post-secular" seemed to lead nowhere but back to religion, an impression not dispelled by reading into the volume. Then I came across a quotation from the journals of the liberal literary critic Alfred Kazin, and was surprised to find the word secularism used in a pejorative sense: "When I pray to You to give me some peace, to cease this endless clamor of anxiety, which consists always in asking, 'Oh Lord, what am I supposed to do next?' I am really asking for relief from my overstrained will, from the determination to do and even to do over what is expected of me. That is what secularism is—the triumph of the individual will—no matter what the cost to everything crying out in you for another realm of being."[107] And soon after, I read *The Secular Mind* by Robert Coles, a trained psychoanalyst with some background also in English literature, and realized that the word was carrying some very heavy baggage indeed. According to Coles, the secular mind is "hateful," "pernicious," the product of "inward despair." It is responsible for all the ills of the twentieth century including Hitler—and perhaps the ills of all centuries, for Jeremiah and Jesus were scolding societies gone "secular." It is in his view a synonym for egoism and for an indifference to the mystery of otherness. "Scientific materialism is the heart of secular thinking," and the heart of scientific materialism is a dangerous "wondering" and search for "mastery."[108]

Coles distinguishes very sharply between secularism and religion. It is true that a sharp distinction between them is in some sense traditional—Mircea Eliade believed, for example, that the sacred fell *outside* the secular, and Emile Durkheim imagined it a dimension of our lives not subject, like every other part, to change. But does this clean separation express anything today but nostalgia for an age of faith? It seems to me that Coles is polarizing attitudes in contemporary American life that overlap, that indeed are commonly found, uncomfortably combined it may be, in the same person. The journalist Michael Novak deplores "a totally secular frame of reference," but is there such a thing in fact? A religious American in some respects has a secular orientation, and those leading a secular life inevitably share interests and orientations with religious members of society. Indeed, that there is some tension between these two viewpoints *within individuals* is an assumption of this book. Moreover, I see no reason why a capacity for wondering is ruled out by secularism or why humility, if that is the virtue it supposedly lacks, cannot mean humility before nature, before the processes that govern us all, as well as humility before God. Nor do I see why mastery cannot also mean self-mastery, self-esteem, a good protection *against* egoism.

The threat to secularism in America that I most fear comes not from intellectuals or from the mainline (sometimes called oldline) Christian sects that are generally liberal and avoid stridency but from the fast-growing evangelical sects, whose members now make up, according to a recent report, "about 25 percent of the American population," a very large figure.[109] Add fundamentalists, numbering 4%, along with politically active conservatives among Catholics and Jews, and you have a formidable bloc.

Polls show that sharp increases in the evangelical population have gone along with decreasing membership in oldline religious affiliations. According to figures published a few years ago measuring increase and decrease over the last 30 years as a proportion of the population, the percentage changes are as follows: Episcopal, down 44%; Methodist, down 38%; Roman Catholic, down 3%; Jewish, down from 3% to 2% of the population (mainly due to intermarriage); Southern Baptist, up 8%; Mormon, up 96%; Jehovah's Witnesses, up 119%; Assemblies of God (the Church of Attorney General John Ashcroft), up 211%; Church of God in Christ, up 863%.[110] From the oldline point of view, one could (like John Updike, reflecting on "The Future of Faith"[111]) lament the decline of interest in religion, but if we take into account the fast-rising evangelical sects, the overall picture looks different.

Evangelicalism causes me alarm not only because of its rapid growth but also because it fosters a certain kind of uncompromisingness that puts its positions beyond debate. Evangelicals do not merely hold strong convictions but, like Ashcroft, seem unwilling to differentiate between law and morality. George Marsden gives us a sharp insight into this cast of mind. He says those militant evangelicals he calls fundamentalists do not think of themselves as anti-science even though they are anti-modern. Theirs is an older science, pre-Darwinian, a science associated with the confident empiricism of Francis Bacon. They subscribe, in other words, to Common Sense, to what is "plainly evident" and therefore ought to be universal. They consider themselves, in Jerry Falwell's well-known phrase, the Moral Majority. To outsiders the evangelicals seem intolerant but, in their own view, liberals seeking to change a God-sanctified history are perverse. At the same time, they have learned to be adaptive and innovative in playing the political game. Whatever one thinks of figures like Pat Robertson and Jerry Falwell, it is clear that they are not politically naïve.

I will therefore consider finally in this chapter the particular aspects of contemporary American evangelicalism that seem most prominent and most capable of influencing the general climate of opinion.

In *American Evangelicalism: Embattled and Thriving*, Christian Smith and his sociologically trained associates analyze the vitality of this movement. A major point made by them is that, after the fiasco of the Scopes trial in 1925, Evangelicalism separated itself from the retrograde Fundamentalism that insisted on biblical inerrancy, then regrouped and gradually learned to adapt itself to a pluralistic society, thereby becoming able to thrive as an embattled segment of that society. The emergence of Billy Graham and his crusade in the 1950s marked its coming of age.[112]

I think we can specify three principal ideas, loosely derived from Smith, to which modern American evangelicalism is most committed.

The first is the commitment to Jesus as personal Lord and Savior, the belief that there is no other path to salvation except through a strong personal connection to Jesus. Harold Bloom calls "an emotional immediacy of unmediated...encounter with Jesus" a crucial element of the American Religion,[113] and this appears to be the case. It is not so much Jesus as exemplar, counselor or friend that is important but Jesus as a presence with whom one identifies very closely and with whom identification is sustained by frequent, hypnotic invocation. Robert Duvall's brilliant film *The Apostle* captured very well the mixture of extraordinary empowerment and equally extraordinary psychic deformation that this identification induces. Traditionally, the divine Christ came into the human world to share our suffering and redeem us from sin. But in evangelical Christianity, suffering and a sense of human unworthiness receives much less stress than the joy of becoming one with Jesus.

The second element is the absolutistic morality, the acute feeling of self-righteousness and of others' sins, usually sexual sins (homosexuality, reproductive choice, and the like). Bloom's emphasis on the importance of feeling "born again" is very relevant here. Baptist worship, for example, is notably different in style from worship found among, say, Episcopalians, Presbyterians, or Reform Jews. Its theme is praise and its tone enthusiastic, as if one were being asked to participate in a new state of innocence, with Jesus as the American Adam. The others feature quieter reminders of our weaknesses and strengths, and with little more than token consideration of some ultimate redemption. The sense of not being burdened by the past has always been an important element in American experience, and in the evangelical context it has gained new strength.

Finally, there is a third evangelical commitment, the winning of others to Christ, the felt obligation to "witness," to proselytize. What is striking here is that this zeal in some ways goes against America's traditional tolerance for the religions of others and the expectation of like tolerance in return. It seems to override that consideration. This can make contemporary evangelicalism look insidious. On a walk with friends in California, we passed an evangelical church enclosed by a fence with a gated entry. Just inside the gate I could see a sign on a post dug in the earth, its lettering facing inward, as if intended for those exiting rather than entering the church. My friends told me the sign read: "You are now entering the Mission Field." That is to say, the rest of the world is there to be conquered.

One more supporting detail, this drawn from the newspaper of the day I write this paragraph. It reports that a certain Rev. Paige Patterson, president of a Southern Baptists' denomination and its seminary in North Carolina, defended his group's mission, which was an (unwelcome) effort to proselytize Jews. He quoted John 14:6 in which Jesus said, "no one comes to the father except through me," and commented: "If Jesus was telling the truth, He's Lord and we have to do what he says, which includes witnessing."[114] It's difficult to judge whether Rev. Patterson is naïve or cunning, but against that kind of hard literalmindedness there is no effective civilized weapon. He dares us to call Jesus a liar, and, if we won't, he is ready to assert that the conversion of the Jews has the very highest imprimatur.

One's tolerance for the religion of others is strained if their intolerance is insistently forced on one's attention, as when at President Bush's inauguration a certain Pastor Caldwell offered his "humble prayer in the name that's above all other names, Jesus the Christ," and added ominously, "Let all who agree say Amen." No non-Christians, presumably, were being invited to welcome the new president. Modern atheists therefore find themselves not only drawn to irony in literature but also, as political animals, under pressure to clear more space for freedom of expression. I take heart, however, from the fact that there are many strong voices on the American scene who also find the turn today toward God-in-government deplorable but less of an immediate threat than those who fear it suppose it to be, confident that the secular spirit is indeed robust despite the challenges to it now much publicized. I take heart also from the fact that American society is really the anomaly among the Western democracies in this whole area of religion and politics. Perhaps Americans will learn a little in the coming years from other and older national experiences that have resulted in a different outcome.

NOTES

1 Kenneth Burke, *The Rhetoric of Religion: Studies in Logology* (Boston: Beacon Press, 1961), vi.
2 Michel de Montaigne, *The Complete Essays of Montaigne*, trans. Donald M. Frame (Stanford: Stanford University Press, 1965): 399, 403.
3 E. M. Forster, "What I Believe," in *Two Cheers for Democracy* (San Diego: Harcourt Brace, 1966), 67.
4 See Jacques Derrida, "White Mythology: Metaphors in the Text of Philosophy," in Derrida, *Margins of Philosophy*, trans. Alan Bass (Chicago: University of Chicago Press, 1982), 207–71.
5 O'Connor is quoted in Hilton Als, "A Critic At Large: This Lonesome Place," *The New Yorker Magazine* (29 January 2001), 87.
6 George Steiner, *Real Presences: Is there anything in what we say?* (London: Faber and Faber, 1989).
7 Hans Küng, *Does God Exist? An Answer for Today*, trans. Edward Quinn (Garden City, NY: Doubleday Anchor, 1980), 655ff.
8 Armstrong, *History of God*: xxi, 211.
9 Walter Kaufmann, "The Core of Religion," in Angeles, ed., *Critiques of God*, 129–34.
10 Santayana, *Interpretations of Poetry and Religion*, 66.
11 Robert Hollander, "Lecture Thirteen: Justice and Poetry: Dante's Book of the Dead," *The Great Courses on Tape: The Bible and Western Culture, Part II*, (Springfield, VA.: The Teaching Company, 1998), 4–5.
12 Quoted in Ward, ed., *Theology and Contemporary Critical Theory*, 17.
13 Jerry Fodor, "Workings of the Spirit," *Times Literary Supplement* (29 January 1999), 20.
14 Harold Bloom, *The American Religion: The Emergence of the Post-Christian Nation* (New York: Simon and Schuster, 1992), 24.
15 Fodor, "Workings of the Spirit."
16 Paul Ricouer, *Figuring the Sacred: Religion, Narrative, and Imagination*, trans. David Pellauer, ed. Mark I. Wallace (Minneapolis: Fortress Press, 1995). See especially 8–12 and Parts III and IV.
17 Frank Kermode, *The Sense of An Ending* (New York: Oxford University Press, 1967).
18 Pierre Teilhard de Chardin, *The Phenomenon of Man*, in Appleman, ed., *Darwin*, 339.
19 Terry Eagleton, "Giants Refreshed: Matthew Arnold," *Times Literary Supplement* (21 January 2000), 14.
20 Quoted in M. H. Abrams, ed., *Literature and Belief* (New York: Columbia University Press, 1958), vii.
21 See Abrams, ed., *Literature and Belief*: 8, 20, 54, 59. See also Delmore Schwartz, "Poetry and Belief in Thomas Hardy," in *Hardy: A Collection of Critical Essays*, ed. Albert J. Guerard (Englewood Cliffs, NJ: Prentice-Hall: 1963), 134. Eliot, to be sure, could make sour remarks about the corrupting influence of secularism on modern literature, as in "Religion and Literature," in T. S. Eliot, *Selected Essays* (London: Faber and Faber, 1972). But, as Louis Menand has pointed out, he kept his literary criticism largely in-

dependent of his larger religious and political commitments. See *The Cambridge History of Literary Criticism*, Vol. 7, Chap. 1 (Cambridge University Press, 2000).
22 Douglas Bush, "Tradition and Experience," in Abrams, ed., *Literature and Belief*, 35.
23 Abrams, ed., *Literature and Belief*: xi, xii, 61, 70.
24 M. H. Abrams, "Belief and the Suspension of Disbelief," in Abrams, ed., *Literature and Belief*, 5.
25 David Daiches, *God and the Poets*, 214–17.
26 Walter J. Ong, S.J., "Voice as a Summons for Belief," in Abrams, ed., *Literature and Belief*, 92.
27 Gillian Beer, *Open Fields: Science in Cultural Encounter* (Oxford: Clarendon Press, 1996), 200. See also D. Bruce Lockerbie, *Dismissing God: Modern Writers Struggle Against Religion* (Grand Rapids, MI: Baker Books, 1998), 14.
28 Julia Kristeva, *Revolution in Poetic Language*, trans. Margaret Waller (New York: Columbia University Press, 1984), 61.
29 Wood, "Writing Under God," *The New Republic* (26 February 2001), 28.
30 Eagleton, "Giants Refreshed: Matthew Arnold."
31 Harry Levin, *The Gates of Horn: A Study of Five French Realists* (New York: Oxford Galaxy, 1966), 21.
32 Jacques Derrida, "This Strange Institution Called Literature," in Attridge, ed., *Acts of Literature*, 37–8.
33 Richard Rorty, "Beliefs: Interview with Richard Rorty," *New York Times* (11 July 1998), B6. Peter Steinfels' interview concerns Rorty's book, *Achieving Our Country*.
34 Emile Durkheim, *The Elementary Forms of The Religious Life*, trans. Joseph Warren Swain (New York: Free Press, 1965).
35 Gertrude Himmelfarb, "Deity and Doubt," *Wall Street Journal Bookshelf* (15 June 1999).
36 Michael Janovsky, "Colorado Asks: Is 'In God We Trust' a Religious Statement," *New York Times* (3 July 2000), A9.
37 Steven Weinberg, "Five and a Half Utopias," *Atlantic Monthly* (January 2000), 112. Documentation for the widespread and unsupported belief that people cannot be "good" without "God" has been brought up to date by Natalie Angier, "Confessions of a Lonely Atheist," *New York Times Magazine* (14 January 2001), 34–38.
38 E. O. Wilson, *Consilience*, 269.
39 Dirk Johnson, "Schools Seeking to Skirt Rules That Bar Ten Commandments," *New York Times* (27 February 2000), sec. 1:24.
40 James Q. Wilson, *The Moral Sense* (New York: Free Press, 1993): 25–26, 194.
41 Francis Schüssler Fiorenza and Gordon S. Kaufman, "God," in Mark C. Taylor, ed., *Critical Terms for Religious Studies*, 154.
42 Micah White, "Atheists Under Siege," *New York Times* (21 June 1999), A15.
43 Ian McEwan, *Enduring Love* (London: J. Cape, 1997): 170–73, 74–75.
44 John Dewey, "Religion Versus the Religious," in Angeles, ed., *Critiques of God*, 189.
45 Richard Feynman, *The Meaning of It All: Thoughts of a Citizen Scientist* (Reading, MA: Helix Books, 1998), 39–40.
46 Harold Bloom, *Omens of Millennium: The Gnosis of Angels, Dreams, and Resurrection* (New York: Riverhead Books, 1996), 167.

47 Susan Haack, "Commentary," *Times Literary Supplement* (9 July 1999), 13.
48 E. O. Wilson, *Consilience*, 7.
49 It is not a recent problem only. Nietzsche (in *Human, All Too Human*, #110) was already scoffing at "the theologian's trick of mingling scientific knowledge and edifying speculation." Readers interested in the trick's current versions will want to read Frederick Crews' evisceration of a dozen books concerned with so-called Intelligent Design. See his "Saving us from Darwin, Parts I and II," in *New York Review of Books*, 4 October 2001, 24–27; and 18 October 2001, 51–55.
50 Eldredge, "More Corn from Kansas," *Times Literary Supplement* (18 February 2000), 9.
51 Michael Ruse, *Can A Darwinist Be A Christian?* (Cambridge: Cambridge University Press, 2000).
52 Teilhard de Chardin, in Appleman, ed., *Darwin*, 334–42.
53 Holmes Rolston, III, *Genes, Genesis and God: Values and Their Origins in Natural and Human History* (Cambridge: Cambridge University Press, 1999), 362.
54 Jonathan Lear, *Happiness, Death, and The Remainder of Life* (Cambridge: Harvard University Press, 2000), 112.
55 Robert Wright, "The Accidental Creationist," *The New Yorker Magazine* (13 December 1999), 56–65.
56 Quoted in James Glanz, "Nobelist Ponders God, Truth and 'Final Theory,' *New York Times* (25 January 2000), F2.
57 Ludwig Wittgenstein, *Tractatus Logico-Philosophicus*, trans. D. F. Pears and B. F. McGuiness, rev. 2nd ed. (New York: Humanities Press, 1972), sec. 6:44.
58 Polkinghorne is quoted in Hugo Williams, "Commentary," *Times Literary Supplement* (26 February 1999), 16.
59 John Polkinghorne, *Belief in God in an Age of Science* (New Haven: Yale University Press, 1998): 10, 13.
60 According to Michael Shermer, *How We Believe*, 102.
61 Albert Einstein, "The Religious Spirit of Science," in *Ideas and Opinions* (New York: Crown, 1956), 38–40.
62 Richard Lewontin, *It Ain't Necessarily So: The Dream of the Humane Genome and Other Illusions* (New York: New York Review Books, 2000), 137.
63 Thomas Nagel, *The Last Word* (New York: Oxford University Press, 1997), 127–43.
64 Wilson, *Consilience*, 49.
65 Wilson, *Consilience*, 275.
66 Wilson, *Consilience*, 130–31.
67 Isaiah Berlin, "Commentary: The Romantics and Their Roots," *Times Literary Supplement* (19 February 1999), 15.
68 Richard Dawkins, *The Selfish Gene*, new ed. (New York: Oxford University Press, 1989), 3.
69 Dawkins, *The Blind Watchmaker*, 21.
70 Dawkins, *Selfish Gene*, 139.
71 Weinberg, "The Future of Science and the Universe," *New York Review of Books* (15 November 2001), 63.
72 Dawkins, *The Blind Watchmaker*, 41.

73 Dawkins, *Selfish Gene*, 267.
74 Dawkins, *Blind Watchmaker*, 216.
75 Dawkins, *Selfish Gene*, 198.
76 Dawkins, *Selfish Gene*, 233.
77 See Dawkins, *Selfish Gene*, 139; and Rolston, *Genes, Genesis and God*, 265.
78 Dawkins, *Blind Watchmaker*, x. See also *Selfish Gene*, 218.
79 Thomas Nagel, *The View from Nowhere* (New York: Oxford University Press, 1986), 3–10.
80 Daniel C. Dennett, *Consciousness Explained* (Boston: Little Brown, 1991), 424.
81 Dennett, *Consciousness Explained*, 448.
82 Quoted in Helen Epstein, "The Fly in the DNA," *New York Review of Books* (24 June 1999), 16.
83 Lewontin, *It Ain't Necessarily So*, 197.
84 Roger G. Newton, *The Truth of Science: Physical Theories and Reality* (Cambridge: Harvard University Press, 1997), 223.
85 Antonio Damasio, *Descartes' Error: Emotion, Reason, and the Human Brain* (New York, Putnam, 1984): xv, 240, 229.
86 Feynman, *The Meaning of It All*: 34, 41.
87 Stephen Jay Gould, "Viewpoint," *Time Magazine* (23 August 1999), 59.
88 Antonio Damasio, *The Feeling of What Happens: Body and Emotion in the Making of Consciousness* (New York: Harcourt Brace, 1999).
89 H. Porter Abbott, "What Do We Mean When We Say 'Narrative Literature?' Looking for Answers Across Disciplinary Borders," *Style* 34:2 (Summer 2000): 260–73; H. Porter Abbott, "The Evolutionary Origins of the Storied Mind: Modeling the Prehistory of Narrative Consciousness and its Discontents," *Narrative*, 8:3 (October 2000): 247–56.
90 Karen Armstrong, *The Battle for God* (New York: Knopf, 2000), 199.
91 Gabriel Josipovici, *The Book of God: A Response to the Bible* (New Haven: Yale University Press, 1988), 27. Billy Graham is cited in a dissertation by Leo Prengeman, "Absent Fathers, Ambiguous Father: Walker Percy and the Scandal of Christendom" (City University of New York Graduate Center, 1999).
92 Taylor, ed., *Critical Terms for Religious Studies*, 57.
93 Steve Bruce, *The Rise and Fall of the New Christian Right: Conservative Protestant Politics in America 1978–1988* (Oxford: Clarendon Press, 1988), 40. In preceding paragraphs, Bruce shows how these rulings developed from the Schempp v. Murray decision of 1963 prohibiting bible reading and religious exercises in public schools.
94 George M. Marsden, *Understanding Fundamentalism and Evangelicalism* (Grand Rapids, MI: William B. Eerdman's, 1991), 1.
95 James Davison Hunter, "Fundamentalism: An Introduction to a General Theory," in Laurence J. Silberstein, ed., *Jewish Fundamentalism in Comparative Perspective: Religion, Ideology, and the Crisis of Modernity* (New York: New York University Press, 1993), 28. Armstrong's *Battle for God* is really an elaboration of Hunter's thesis.
96 Cited in Joan Didion, "God's Country," *New York Review of Books* (4 October 2000), 76.
97 Quoted in Roy Porter, *Gibbon: Historians on Historians* (New York: St. Martin's Press, 1988), 119.

98 For example, George Gallup, Jr. and Jim Castelli, *The People's Religion: American Faith in the 90's* (New York and London: Macmillan, 1989): 4, 90; Jack Miles, "Belief by the Numbers," statistics compiled by Russell Shorto, in *New York Times Magazine* (7 December 1997), 60; and Natalie Angier (citing further polls), "Lonely Atheist," 34–35.

99 For example, Geoffrey Wheatcroft writes: "Fewer than one French person in 10 goes to church even once a year....[In] my country, we have a Church of England by law established [whose] services are now regularly attended by a mere 2 percent of the population." Wheatcroft, "Politics Without Piety," *New York Times* (9 September 2000), A15.

100 Jon Butler, *Awash in a Sea of Faith: Christianizing the American People* (Cambridge: Harvard University Press, 1990), 164 and *passim*.

101 Martin E. Marty, *Religion and Republic: The American Circumstance* (Boston: Beacon Press, 1987), 53–76.

102 Alexis de Tocqueville, *Democracy in America*, trans. George Lawrence, eds. J. P. Mayer and Max Lerner (New York: Harper & Row, 1966), 271–72.

103 For commentary, in sociological language, on the religious consequences of the difference between centralized authority in Britain and decentralized authority in America, see Steve Bruce, *The Rise and Fall of the New Christian Right*, especially 69–70.

104 Seymour Martin Lipset, *American Exceptionalism: A Double-Edged Sword* (New York: Norton, 1996), especially 19–26 and 62–67.

105 Martin E. Marty, *Religion and Republic*, 22.

106 Gallup, *The People's Religion*, 90.

107 Quoted from Alfred Kazin's Journals, in David Remnick, "A Critic at Large: In the Capital of Words," *New Yorker Magazine* (22 June 1998), 142.

108 Robert Coles, *The Secular Mind* (Princeton: Princeton University Press, 1999).

109 Margaret Talbot, "A Mighty Fortress," *New York Times Magazine* (27 February 2000), 36.

110 *New York Times Magazine* (7 December 1997), 60.

111 John Updike, "Reflections: The Future of Faith," *New Yorker Magazine* (29 November 1999), 84–91.

112 Christian Smith, *American Evangelicalism: Embattled and Thriving* (Chicago: University of Chicago Press, 1998).

113 Bloom, *American Religion*, 238.

114 Gustav Niebuhr, "Baptists' Ardor for Evangelism Angers Some Jews and Hindus," *New York Times* (4 December 1999), A10.

CHAPTER FOUR
From Sacred Writing to Heightened Reading

"Our age is an age of criticism....If the sacredness of religion and the authority of legislation are exempted from critical examination, they become the subjects of just suspicion."
  Immanuel Kant, 1781 Preface to *The Critique of Pure Reason*

The phrase "literary atheism" owes a traceable debt to my rabbinical father, the dedicatee of this book, who died many years ago. On the one hand, my adolescent hostility toward his role as man of God and defender of institutional religion is still in some sense active, though complicated by maturer understanding and separated from my memory of him as a person. On the other hand, my love of literature, also dating from adolescence, was never a rebellion but rather an extension of my father's own strong love of books and learning. I feel sure he would have responded with interest to much of what I have written here, even if puzzled by the provocativeness of a word like atheism. In his sermons he envisioned a society that respected the political separation of church and state while allowing its sacred and secular components to enrich one another.

But I want to explore in this chapter the cultural rather than personal dimension of his influence on me because I believe there is something in the Jewish tradition itself, stemming from the Hebrew Bible (despite its being unquestionably a theistic document), that has nurtured the ways in which I, like my literary atheists, have learned to think about God with a measure of irony. This is not to say you have to be Jewish to be a literary atheist—after all, not one of the writers discussed in Chapter Two was Jewish. But Jewish stories involving God, unlike Christian ones, *typically* feature contention between God and man, and often do not resolve this contention.

Shadows on the Hudson by Isaac Bashevis Singer offers an excellent example. The chief character thinks of himself as an unbeliever repeatedly breaking away from the Law in his personal behavior but knows that his fate as a Jew is not to ignore but to struggle with God:

> He was an unbeliever who was compelled, in times of trouble or at the sight of injustice or shame, to raise his eyes to heaven and appeal to the God whose existence he denied, and this because among Jews God was a sickness, an obsession, a mania. For a Jew, the thought that God was good and just was the quintessence of life. Whether he wanted to or not, a Jew perpetually had accounts to settle with the Almighty: he praised Him or blasphemed Him, loved Him or hated Him, but he could never be free of Him. Whatever other complexes the Jew suffered from, the God complex was his ineluctable fate: he could as little escape from Him as from his skin, his blood, his marrow.[1]

A comparable ambivalence marks Franz Kafka's view of God, as Erich Heller aptly describes it: "[Kafka] knows two things at once, and both with equal assurance: that there is no God, and that there *must* be God."[2] This is a little different from Pascal's rather similar statement, "It is equally incomprehensible that God exists and that He doesn't exist" (*Pensées* #230), because it is pitched in the key of irony. It does not balance Head and Heart but plays one against the other. So, while contending with God is part of the Christian tradition as well, the Jewish version is a peculiar kind of family feuding based on the inevitability of an ongoing, unresolvable conflict.

Some years ago I attended a ceremony at which a friend was being ordained as a rabbi. The class speaker formally addressed the teachers and said at once—without any perceptible intent to shock or dismay—"We love you and we hate you." This mixture of gratitude and rebellion was apparently understood by everyone present as a legitimate, indeed formulaic element in a traditional rite of passage. One of the reasons why a non-observant Jew like myself continues to think of himself *as* a Jew may be that the Jewish tradition is unusual in accommodating a certain ambivalence toward its own authority. Ambivalence toward even the supreme authority of God is, in fact, a crucial part of what Jacob Neusner calls the central conception of Rabbinic Judaism, the belief that scripture constitutes only a part of divine revelation so that "whatever the most recent rabbi discovers through exegesis [becomes] part of the Torah revealed to Moses." Neusner offers a dramatic possibility of such revision: "God himself, studying and living by Torah, is believed to subject himself to these same rules of logical inquiry. If an earthly court overrules the testimony...of the heavenly one, God would rejoice, crying out, 'My sons have conquered me! My sons have conquered me!'"[3] Such an idea, I think, would be hard to find in other religious traditions.

How are these testimonies of ambivalence connected to the representation of Yahweh in the Hebrew Bible?

Critical readers of the Bible over the last two hundred years have brought to light numerous textual inconsistencies and problems, accounting for them mainly in terms of linguistic and historical circumstances, such as the complexities of transmission and translation, changes of customs and conventions. What is relatively new in biblical criticism is an emphasis on ambiguity and contradictoriness as qualities of the text that are part of its network of implication and hence not inconsistent with an appreciation of its literary strength. I will specify four such approaches that will help me situate my own remarks both on Yahweh and the concept of the sacred text.

Robert Alter in *The Art of Biblical Narrative* skillfully develops the idea that the writers of the Bible, like other literary artists, "took pleasure in exploring the formal and imaginative resources of their medium." To achieve an effect, they might then aim to "produce a certain indeterminacy of meaning, especially in regard to motive, moral character, or psychology." Alter sees this new complexity as an enhancement of the sacred meaning, as if the representation of Yahweh presents no special problem for the modern secular reader. He finds common ground between the Bible and secular literature without worrying the problem of differences between them.[4]

Herbert Schneidau in *Sacred Discontent* also wants to convey to us the meaning of the text, what he calls the Bible's "fundamental message," but he finds this to be a radical criticism of culture itself, and writes of the discomforting and self-critical "Yahwist tendency to demythologize its own institutions." Schneidau carries his demythologizing argument too far (crediting the ancient Hebrews, for example, with inspiring modern science as well as anticipating our modernist belief in "the constructedness of created things"), but his aim is not to challenge the sacred; rather it is to sanctify the Bible's "discontent," to identify its spirit with the probing interest in change and originality that he finds in important secular literature. His reading is evidently more political than Alter's, but his assumptions are similar.[5]

If Alter and Schneidau do not attempt to separate the influence of the Hebrew Bible from meaning that its writers may be presumed to have shaped, Regina Schwartz, in her ambitious and disturbing Foucauldian analysis, *The Curse of Cain: The Violent Legacy of Monotheism*, does make this kind of separation. Her theme is what the text reveals about the process of "identity formation" in circumstances of scarcity, particularly the way in which this process negates "the other" and thus becomes the "origin of violence" in modern societies, influencing those who invoke one true God to support their own causes. Schwartz is hardly concerned with what the writers may have meant (at one point she raises the possibility that they may have been deploring violence by depicting it so graphically but quickly lets this drop) because contemporary political urgency is everywhere her prime concern. In her view, the very discontinuities of the text (or "ruptures" as she calls them, following Foucault) are what spur modern nationalists to create interpretations that serve their own interests.[6]

The most frequent objection that has been raised to Schwartz's book is that it ignores as sources of violence in human history both human nature itself and other poems of force unrelated to the Bible (like *The Iliad*), overrating the political power of texts in general and of the Bible in particular. My own concern in this chapter prompts me to raise another objection, her book's way of seeing the Bible's power only in terms of political influence, not in aesthetic terms at all. I feel somewhat ungrateful in doing so because her essay "Teaching a Sacred Text as Literature, Teaching Literature as a Sacred Text" formulates a point important for my argument too, namely that sacredness is conferred on a text by a particular society, and is not an inherent quality of the text itself. But her political emphasis is too exclusive. Yes, let us accept the contingency of all representation but let us value the text for its aesthetic interest as well as its political consequences. (If the aesthetic has a traceable history and is therefore in some sense an ideology, it is now so rooted in our cultural understanding that it does not function *as* an ideology, and it is not helpful to link it to a model ideology like Marxism, *pace* the pronouncements of intellectual terrorists like Fredric Jameson and Terry Eagleton.) Schwartz turns quite aside from texture to focus on influence. It is telling, I think, that she would have us read secular masterpieces in the same Foucauldian fashion. They may be taught as sacred because they are sources of immense cultural influence, not because they provide a heightened aesthetic experience.[7] Despite some superficial similarity, her position is very different from that of Harold Bloom, who finds "incoherent the judgment that some authentic literary art is more sacred or more secular than some other," for authentic art itself and not political influence is Bloom's standard of judgment. I will return to his view at the end of the chapter, in connection with the role of the reader in reformulating the concept of the sacred.

In contrast to Schwartz I would like to consider the biblical text *both* in terms of what the authors might have meant and what a modern secularist must also find there, and to make something of the incongruity between these ways of reading. Taking the reader seriously as well as the text, I will try to understand Yahweh not simply as the Bible's authors (presumably) did, nor simply from the point of view of our own age of criticism, but in both ways together, letting these ways clash as they will.

We should keep in mind, however, that incongruity is not merely the product of a modern, secular outlook, for the representation of Yahweh that the ancient Hebrews themselves give us is curiously open and contradictory. Their Yahweh is beyond us yet is inclined to change his mind as we are, incommensurate with human desire yet an inescapable if remote member of the family too. He seems in truth someone with whom his creators perpetually had accounts to settle.

The Hebrew Bible's contradictoriness is admirably conveyed by Gabriel Josipovici, in *The Book of God: A Personal Response to the Bible*, the last of my lead-in approaches. Josipovici makes a virtue of the fact that such unity as we find in the Hebrew Bible is of a loose kind, that its picture of Yahweh is marked by "contradictoriness" and its stories by ambiguity. For him, biblical narrative is "clearly meaningful, not a mere chronicle of events," but the meaning is not always clear." The Hebrew Bible only claims that history is meaningful but does not claim, like the New Testament, "to know what that meaning is." And he finds this uncertainty extraordinary for a sacred book.[8]

Josipovici perceptively contrasts these two monuments of "sacred writing" in terms of psychological openness. We are accustomed to thinking of the Hebrew Bible as more severe than the New Testament because of its emphasis on exclusivity in contrast to the Christian message of salvation available to all, Greek as well as Jew. But, he points out, "if there is a gain there is also something that is lost," for to enter the Christian family is to feel "it all rests with me; I have nothing to fall back on [if faith fails]. What this means in psychological terms," Josipovici continues, "is that the inner self becomes an object of scrutiny and that the possibility of the coexistence of contrary emotions is ruled out: love *and* hate; pain *and* trust; jealousy. But contrary emotions are what we normally experience in our lives." In the Hebrew Bible, he concludes, the wickedness of man angers and saddens the Lord but does not remove man from family and community, assumed to be inescapable.[9] So the Christian way is, in a sense, more strenuous and fearful, despite the shift of emphasis from justice to mercy, from law to salvation. Nietzsche made a similar point when he implied that the new Christian emphasis on salvation through belief in a miraculous resurrection, requiring the "abandonment of all customary modes of behavior," made the pursuit of virtue so strenuous as to be a source of great anxiety.[10]

The contrast between the two biblical texts is still clearer if we assume, as we probably should, that Paul rather than Jesus was the first Christian. Although it impossible to cite incontrovertible evidence, one may doubt that Jesus intended to found a new religion. We understand the *teachings* of Jesus as the most historical aspect of the figure indicated by that name because they are clearly extensions of the teachings of the Hebrew prophets concerning love, peace, the inwardness of morality, faith, and the unity of men under the fatherhood of God. In contrast, what we regard as the most specifically Christian element of the Gospels, the establishment of the Eucharist at the Last Supper, is likely to have been a later invention. A. N. Wilson suggests that the Jews were not likely to have put a man on trial the day of the Passover, and he reminds us that the evangelist John specifies an earlier date for the trial and crucifixion.[11]

I used to think it odd that the Gospels should have been written *after* Acts of the Apostles and the Epistles of Paul because they dramatize the living presence of Jesus whereas Paul's work reflects a time clearly subsequent to Jesus' death. The writings about and by Paul have the feel of historical documents, for they discuss practical efforts to spread the gospel and they register credibly the resistance the apostle encounters in doing so. But the evangelists, one comes to see, are assuming the existence *already* of a responsive audience and, supported by a measure of narrative confidence, are able to enhance their story with legendary material and also with detail influenced by Paul's own persuasive concentration on the crucifixion and resurrection of Jesus Christ, his intense identification with the person rather than teaching of Jesus.

Evidence of this identification may well be reflected in what the Gospels show to be Jesus' most radical departure from the Hebrew scriptures, the virtual displacement of the Father from the scene and the corresponding emplacement of the Son as the sole means of access to the Father. Matthew (11:27) and Luke (10:22) make this clear enough: "No one knows the Son except the Father and no one knows the Father except the Son," and John (14:6) is even more unequivocal: "No one comes to the Father except through me." In fact, just about the only act assigned to God the Father in the Gospels is his declaring Jesus his only begotten Son in whom he is well pleased—an adaptation of Psalm 2:7–8 in which the Lord decrees that *Israel*, represented by its king, is his begotten son. The New Testament, by virtue of focusing so intently on the single story of Jesus Christ, has lost the qualities of uncertainty and contradictoriness that Josipovici called attention to in the writings it would incorporate and replace. By virtue of declaring Christ as Messiah, the meaning of history is defined for all time. There is nothing comparable in the New Testament to the open and unpredictable interaction in the Hebrew Bible between divine and human wills.

It is often said that Yahweh cannot be discussed the way we discuss characters in novels and other literary narratives. That is true, but the chief reason it is true is not usually specified. The reasons usually given are that it was written long ago by many different people over an extended period of time, and then repeatedly and imperfectly redacted; that, unlike ancient Greek myth, biblical myth (mostly in Genesis and Exodus) is mixed freely with historical matter (and historical matter treated very differently from the way it is today); and that narrative is mixed in an encyclopedic potpourri with various other genres—codes of law and prescriptions for ritual practice, genealogies, songs, compilations of wisdom, hymns, laments, prayers, prophetic discourses, and much else. No novel that we have is quite like this. But the difference is a matter of degree, of great degree to be sure, but not a difference in kind. What makes biblical narrative decisively different from novelistic narrative is that it is regarded as *sacred*. As Aquinas said smoothly, "all is from God, all is from human authors."[12] But "from God" alters the case so much that, despite the efforts of some literary critics to discuss Yahweh as a literary character, it is not really possible to do so. Or, at any rate, it is not possible to do so without admitting considerable irony into the discussion. And the only sure way for a modern reader to exclude this irony is deliberately to proscribe it, to insist, for example, with James Kugel, author of *On Being a Jew*, that in reading the Bible we should entirely surrender our sense of human purpose to a sense of God's purpose, understanding the world entirely "in keeping with God and not the other way." "Judaism," he adds pointedly, "is about the service of God, and this is light-years away from making poems."[13] Kugel, then, has his own reasons for not believing Yahweh can be understood as a literary character. His book makes it clear that the tension between literature and religion, when religion insists on its own privileged status vis-à-vis literature, cannot be erased.

But I must return to my chief reason for thinking it is not possible to read the Bible as we read a novel, which turns on the question of what we would now call representation, a concept that its authors do not seem not to have had at their disposal. Let me put side by side the opening sentence of the Bible (the King James Version will serve) and the opening sentence of a modern novel, say *Howards End* by E. M. Forster:

> In the beginning God created the heaven and the earth.
>
> One may as well begin with Helen's letters to her sister.

The self-conscious novelist knows that his starting point must be arbitrary, but for the writer of Genesis the beginning of the story is not arbitrary: it is set down as the truth about the way things are. Similarly the novelist and his readers know that the characters are purely fictional and that their identities will be filled in as the story proceeds, whereas for the biblical writer and his audience there is nothing fictional about the name and identity of God. The essential difference, then, is that the novelist knows he is writing fiction and shares this awareness with his readers whereas the biblical writers and readers had no sense of fiction as a category separable from truth. *But what kind of fiction (hence what kind of literary character) do we have when the writer does not know it is a fiction and does not enter into a tacit contract with the reader on that basis?*

Secular modern readers know that, in order to appreciate the Bible's meaning and power, they must imagine what it is like to believe that Yahweh himself really did enter history to guide human events in certain ways. But they do not simply abandon their understanding that he is altogether a human representation of divine agency, as Kugel would have them do. Inevitably they read the biblical narrative *also* as the work of people who *wish* to represent God in this way.

It is not difficult to guess at the ancient writers' motives for representing Yahweh as they do. A homeless people surrounded by other, often hostile tribes imagine divine power concentrated in one figure who—if they trust in him—will make and renew a covenant with them to bring them to a homeland, and who—again, if they trust in him—will enable them to defeat other peoples in battle and be powerful for generations to come.

Everything depends on trust in the Lord—"trust" or "trust in" being, as one biblical scholar pointed out, a more accurate translation of the Hebrew than "believe" or "believe in."[14] In return the Israelites receive Yahweh's "steadfast love"—the phrase often used in the NRSV replacing "mercy" in other translations, and I think a notable improvement (assuming that the Hebrew permits it) because "steadfast love" connotes loyalty while avoiding the inappropriate suggestion of Christian tenderness and grace.

The actual fortunes of the ancient Israelites were of course marked by many vicissitudes, but Yahweh's loyalty must be maintained at all costs. So the biblical writers found it necessary again and again to blame the Israelites themselves for whatever went wrong. If there was a victory, it was Yahweh's doing, but if a defeat their own—most likely they were worshiping other gods or their sexual behavior was licentious. What I am getting at is that the enormous effort of fitting together or making congruent a destiny credibly directed by Yahweh and a history sufficiently consistent with collective memory to be itself credible led to all kinds of narrative gaps, attempted adjustments, unexplained connections, and uncertainties. The representation of Yahweh in particular is marked by shifting purposes, evidence of all too human parenting, and the repeated admitting of challenge and complaint from those being guided by him. This is not to underrate the narrative and rhetorical power of the Hebrew Bible, for it is laced into these characteristics. But if we do take seriously the fact that "all is from human authors," we must read the text not only by provisionally setting aside the modern secular mentality but also by directing a skeptical eye at the human motives involved in representing God's purpose.

It is commonly said, for example, that the Bible is a testament to monotheism. Certainly Yahweh insists on his supremacy: "Thou shalt have no other gods before me." But in fact this is said so obsessively that it manages to call attention to the omnipresence of rival gods. Karen Armstrong, author of *A History of God* and not exactly an unbeliever, observes strikingly that "it is very difficult to find a single monotheistic statement in the whole of the Pentateuch."[15] Jews all over the world recite the "Shema" (Deut. 6:4) as their creedal text. It is translated in the Jewish Publication Society version as "HEAR, O ISRAEL: THE LORD OUR GOD, THE LORD IS ONE." But the NRSV translation is: "Hear, O Israel, The LORD is our God, the LORD alone." And in Armstrong's own translation, the implication of anxiety about those other gods is even sharper: "Listen, Israel! Yahweh is our Elohim, Yahweh alone!"[16] Actually, I don't see why she limited her observation to the Pentateuch, for the concern about not following other gods continues to be heard throughout the Hebrew Bible. (See, for example, 2 Chron. 7:19; Isa. 17:10, 43:10–12, 44:6; Jer. 1:16.) Kugel, it may noted, devises a contorted translation that would deny the very possibility of other gods: "Understand this, people of Israel: the Lord—that is, God-in-particular—is our God; He is the only one."[17]

When we read in this way, we may see Yahweh's strangeness as a complex phenomeon. His unpredictability is not only hard to understand because he is unlike us but also questionable because he is like us as well. I will illustrate this complex combination under three headings—the ambiguities of the covenant, Yahweh as all too human parent, and, Yahweh's challengeability. This will provide a sufficiently detailed idea of the ways in which the Hebrew Bible, without losing much of its authority and strength, encourages us to think about its God ironically.

But I want to introduce this subject with a paragraph about a remarkable book that probes more boldly than any I know, and with a keener sense of the irony that must result, the challenge to the secular reader who is required to understand literally the supernatural status of Jesus Christ in particular. A. D. Nuttall in his stunning coda to *Overheard by God* fastens our attention on the claim made by Jesus in John's Gospel that he is in actual fact the incarnation of God. Nuttall approaches the reader's problem by way of a consideration of poems by George Herbert where words are invented by the poet for God as if God is actually overhearing and answering the speaker's petitions. What Nuttall calls the Herbert paradox is that the speaker claims nothing for himself, insists earnestly that he is only God's creature, while at the same time he presumes to speak for God. One cannot resolve the paradox by describing this as only a pleasant fiction, for the speaker himself, supported by an age that took its faith with utmost seriousness, will not have it so, disclaiming any belief in his own originality. Now, the situation of John the Evangelist is to some extent similar. He too is *presenting* divinity, but he diverges from Herbert in that he claims to be an actual witness of God's presence, in no way a *representer*. With relentless logic, Nuttall shows how the careful calibrations of Jesus' responses to questions asked concerning his ontological status shred every possible way of understanding that status naturalistically and allows us only to believe that Jesus is literally a supernatural being. Are there any alternatives available, then, to modern readers who come to the text with naturalistic assumptions? Only two. One is to say that Jesus was a duplicitous, cunning scoundrel—plainly an unsatisfactory inference. The other is to say that Jesus was "mad," which may seem equally unsatisfactory, although madness need not be inconsistent with moral intelligence, with goodness, and with love. "Jesus," Nuttall proposes in conclusion, "thought he was God and was really the best of men." And if nonbelievers will not accept so extraordinarily ironic a conclusion, they are compelled to accept as literal fact a supernatural Jesus.[18]

And now to return to the curious ironies engendered by the representation of Yahweh, ironies that derive from basically the same source—the difficulty of simultaneously seeing God in superhuman and also in human terms—but are more variously imbedded than in the New Testament, do not strictly call attention to the problem, and so do not drive the secular reader toward one drastic conclusion.

The Ambiguities of the Covenant

We first hear of a covenant in the story of God's relations with Noah, but its establishment is preceded by an admission ("the Lord was sorry that he had made humankind on the earth" [Gen. 6:6]) that becomes deeply ambiguous in view of his ratifying thought following the ark story: "I will never again curse the ground because of humankind, for the inclination of the human heart is evil from youth" (Gen. 8:21). Which of two contrary implications are we to favor, Yahweh's steadfast love or his lack of trust in man, the other party to the covenant?

The covenant idea is amplified in the story of Abraham, coming to involve the specific promise of a homeland and innumerable progeny. But what is surprising here is not only the Lord's teasing ways (the long deferred pregnancy of Sarai, letting Hagar first conceive a rival son, the dramatic demand for the sacrifice of Isaac) but also the declaration to Abraham "that your offspring shall be aliens in a land that is not theirs, and shall be slaves there, and they shall be oppressed for four hundred years" (Gen. 15:13). Of course the writer is concerned to adjust his knowledge of future events to the cherished idea of God's providential purpose. But four hundred years of oppression is a remarkably high price to pay for this adjustment, all the more because we know that what lies ahead is a very difficult exodus from Egypt and a protracted wandering in the wilderness, capped by the necessity for violent and bloody entry into the promised land. One is surprised by the strenuousness of the Israelites' commitment to the idea of a divinely ordained purpose, by the combination they more than tolerate of Yahweh's harshness and his loyalty.

The covenant is renewed and codified in Yahweh's extensive relations with Moses, the Old Testament counterpart to Jesus. But the mission of Moses is marked by considerably more uncertainty and ambiguity than that of Jesus. We see this readily when we compare the stories of their births and deaths, curious in the case of Moses, marvelous in the case of Jesus. It is never quite clear why Yahweh chooses Moses as his supreme servant or why he forbids him to enter Canaan after many years of faithful service, going so far as to bury him in an unmarked grave.

The comic writer Stanley Elkin captures in a stroke the ironic possibilities of the covenant idea presented in the Hebrew Bible simply by imagining God's point of view as that of a forceful but confused explainer, drolly combining divine confidence and human bewilderment:

> "So," God said, "what do you make of Me, eh? What do you make of Me now that you understand that finally it takes two to break a contract as well as make one? What do you make of Me who could have gotten it right the first time, saved everyone trouble and left Hell unstocked? Do you love Me? Do you forgive and forget as easily as I do? Do you?"[19]

Our very doubts about God's ways are here expressed, but *by* God, whose authority cannot be gainsaid.

Trust in Yahweh's ongoing purpose on behalf of the Israelites does not come to an end after the conquest of Canaan. But it does become less clear in its aim. Judges are appointed to relieve the burden on Moses, then kings are chosen and put into power, although Samuel, a man of God, speaks severely at first about the evils of monarchy, and although the first king, Saul, turns out to be someone Yahweh was sorry he had chosen (1 Sam. 15:35). The Davidic reign, the high point of the monarchy, is narrated in detail, but soon afterward and despite God's favor to Solomon, the monarchy degenerates into a moral and political failure. There is then further disintegration as a result of the conquests by Assyrians, Babylonians, and Persians. Yet, as we see in the prophetic books, the sense of an ongoing divine purpose does not die out. What happens essentially is that a messianic idea takes root, the dream of the restoration of Jerusalem and of political fortune, the promise renewed by means, perhaps, of some descendant from the line of David, its fulfillment projected into an indefinite future.

We know of course what use emergent Christianity made of the prophets' messianism. It is often said that the belief in a messiah not yet come versus belief in a messiah already come in the person of Jesus Christ is the central difference between Jewish and Christian theology. Possibly it was the Jewish idea of *deferred* messianism that, in the centuries following, allowed for the development of a looser theology and also for a more flexible mode of biblical interpretation. In the biblical commentary called midrash, although the literal meaning of the original text is not to be tampered with, the imaginative comment attached to it and itself called a midrash is equally important. As Betty Rostman put it, contributing to a volume called *Midrash and Literature*, "all is determined yet all is open."[20] Frank Kermode, contributing to the same volume, observed that "Christians...could not be so bold as the Jews; for their interpretations were always subject to censorship by the custodians of an infallible tradition that was partly independent of Scripture." He contrasted further "the rule-governed imagination" of midrash to the Christian tradition of interpretation "with its basic belief that the sense of the Jewish Bible must be sought in another book, a quite different imaginative challenge."[21]

It might be argued that the deferral of meaning implied by Jewish in contrast to Christian messianism allows for more irony regarding God and religion. Certainly Jewish humor has long exploited the gap between what one expects from the future (theologically speaking) and what one gets, as in the joke, earlier cited, about the man stationed outside the shtetl lest the coming of the Messiah be missed and who describes his job as paying poorly but "steady work." But this is a slippery argument. For one thing, there is plenty of non-Jewish irony concerning these subjects, and, for another, I would not want to defend the idea that orthodox Jews in our time are overall less fundamentalist in their thinking than orthodox Christians. Perhaps messianic yearning has been satisfied for many Jews today by the creation of the state of Israel, a fulfillment that may be altering the nature of the celebrated Jewish sense of humor.

Yahweh as All Too Human Parent

Since it appears to have been supremely important to biblical writers that they chide the moral backsliding of the people so as to fortify their trust in Yahweh's ongoing commitment to them and his interventions on their behalf, it is not surprising that they would use the most forceful rhetoric they could find to persuade the people to obey the Law. And so they turned to the language of parental threats and parental love. This connection between the father of a people and the father of a family was not lost on them, as we see in Deuteronomy 8:5: "as a parent disciplines a child so the LORD your God disciplines you." But the juxtaposition of threatening and coaxing, of the stick and the carrot, can, to an adult judgment, seem too plainly manipulative, and as a strategy it works in childrearing only because children have less developed powers of discernment and less power.

There are a number of such juxtaposed declarations on the part of Yahweh, and, although one can appreciate the writers' motives, the effect does induce in us also an ironical smile. Here is a sampling:

> I the Lord your God am a jealous God, punishing...to the third and the fourth generation of those who reject me, but showing steadfast love to the thousandth generation of those who love me and keep my commandments. (Exod. 20:5–6)

> You shall not wrong or oppress a resident alien, for you were aliens in the land of Egypt. You shall not abuse any widow or orphan. If you do abuse them, when they cry out to me, I will surely heed their cry; my wrath will burn, and I will kill you with the sword, and your wives shall become widows and your children orphans. (Exod. 22:21–24)

> [I]f you act corruptly...I call heaven and earth to witness against you today that you will soon utterly perish from the land that you are crossing the Jordan to occupy; you will not live long on it, but will be utterly destroyed....When all these things have happened to you in time to come, you will return to the LORD your God and heed him. Because the LORD your God is a merciful God, he will neither abandon you nor destroy you; he will not forget the covenant with your ancestors that he swore to them. (Deut. 4:25–31)

> And just as the Lord took delight in making your prosperous and numerous, so the Lord will take delight in bringing you to ruin and destruction. (Deut. 28:63)

> If you are willing and obedient,
> you shall eat the good of the land;
> but if you refuse and rebel,
> you shall be devoured by the sword. (Isa. 1:19–20)

These are dramatically strong threats insofar as we read them in a naïve spirit, yet manipulative insofar as we read them also with sophisticated intelligence. A good reader, I think, will try to read them straight and ironically at the same time, maintaining two levels of attention.

I do not want to slight the strength of the "straight" reading, however, which has something to do not only with our capacity for empathy (our ability, as it were, to enter into a childlike state of awe before a power greater than we can understand) but also with our text-encouraged sense of Yahweh's elusiveness and manysidedness. A contrast might be made to Allah of the Koran, who is similar in his alternate displays of cajolery and threats but who shows us very little else.

Yahweh's Challengeability

This is the most aesthetically impressive element of uncertainty in the Hebrew Bible because it is more overt than the others and hence more shaped and consciously ironic. Jack Miles in *God: A Biography* nicely praises "the profound originality of a divine-human pact in which both parties complain endlessly about each other."[22] Josipovici comments: "it is in dialogue with man that God reveals how utterly different he is from the other gods of the ancient world. He, the creator of all things, the utterly other, both talks to man and, more important, listens."[23] The editors of the NRSV, impressed by this interactive element in the book of Job, write: "A God who confesses his burdens to a human being is a God who is profoundly involved in human destiny. He is also a God who respects human independence."[24]

This dialogic aspect of the Hebrew Bible is already clear in Genesis and is continued in some form thereafter. Abraham bargains and argues with God about the destroying of Sodom (Gen. 18). Jacob wrestles for a blessing with a man who is also God, and who confers on him the name of Israel (Gen. 32). Moses pleads with Yahweh to remember his promise, and Yahweh, though at first reluctant, does so (Exod. 32:14). In Numbers 11:10, Moses complains to Yahweh, "Why have you treated your servants so badly?" and receives the reply, "Did I?" Yahweh then questions Moses, "How long will the wicked complain against me" (Num. 14:26)? For "the Lord spoke to Moses as one speaks to a friend" (Exod. 33:11). (The bit of Hebrew that sticks in my mind most firmly from *bar mitzvah* lessons, simply because it occurred so often, is *V'yomer Elohim el Moshe,* "And God said unto Moses.") Gideon in Judges questions the Lord; Samuel, David, and Elijah receive instructions from him; Jonah and Job are personally tested by him. I think Jack Miles, despite his elaborate linguistic analysis, is not convincing when he claims that Job's final submission ("I have uttered what I did not understand, things too wonderful for me, which I did not know" [Job 42:3]) "should properly be heard as irony replying to God's sarcasm," but he is right to say that Job's insistent defense of himself against his friends, based on the premise that he is a righteous man, is not undermined, and that the Lord himself in effect acknowledges that he has lost his wager with Satan.[25] When Job declares, "therefore I despise myself, and repent in dust and ashes" (42:6), he means, as the gloss on "repent" in the NRSV makes clear, only that he has changed his mind, not that he has been sinful.[26] In the prophetic books, to be sure, God's presence, earlier expressed directly either in speech or image (bush, cloud, fire or mist), is no longer direct. The prophets claim only to have an imaginative vision of God. But the pattern of give and take is not really broken, as we see in the first chapter of Isaiah (verse 18) in which the Lord is presented by the prophet as saying, "Come, let us argue it out." Much as the New Testament draws on the Hebrew Bible, this dialogic element and even the range of tones in which one addresses the Lord in the Book of Psalms (lament, prayer, hymn, thanksgiving, and so forth) are no longer in evidence.

I am certainly not claiming that the Hebrew Bible teaches us to question God's justice or disobey his law. But its remarkable ways of representing God's relations with man do dramatize contention with, not simply submission to, divine authority.

I return finally to what most decisively sets off biblical narrative from fictional and mythical narrative, especially when it involves representation of God. And that is our investing what we call Holy Scripture with the aura of the sacred, our almost instinctive belief that sacredness is inherent in it. Relatively few people today balk at the idea of human authorship, but many still read the Bible to discover what God is saying to them rather than what human authors are saying by means of that representation. Even the "secular mind" has difficulty ignoring this aura, as I discovered in finding myself reluctant to mark up my Bible, as I would any other book I own, while preparing these pages.

It does not seem possible in any imaginable future that the established distinction between sacred and secular writing will dissolve and that these categories will occupy a common aesthetic plane (as Harold Bloom would have them do) or a common political one (advocated by Regina Schwartz). Surely one reason that "secularism" has become a target of attack in contemporary social discourse is to preserve the sacred from the contamination of change. We say Sacred or Holy Scripture *tout court*. It is hardly likely that many people will prefer to say instead, "writing sacred to observant Jews, Christians or Muslims." Most people need to believe that the aura of the sacred is inherent in a form of language, even if they do not consider that this links their belief to the absolutism of divine authority. Few are ready to be won by the joys of being demystified. Indeed, even scholars hardly seem ready to question seriously the distinction between sacred and secular texts. Or so I infer from a reviewer's report on a series of biblical texts edited by a number of qualified people. In every case an editor employed the sacred-secular distinction without perceivable discomfort.[27]

From the point of view of the skeptical modern secularist, much of the difficulty here lies in our habitual association of sacredness with *writing*, a fixed form of words, rather than with *experience* that is ever-changing. To link sacred and secular under the umbrella of authentic art, as Harold Bloom does, is, I think, a step in the right direction because it is a step in the direction of the reader. This becomes clearer when Bloom describes the "radical irony" he finds in the J writer's depiction of Yahweh: "This irony is neither the contrast or gap between expectation and fulfillment, nor the saying of one thing while meaning quite another. It is the irony of J's Hebraic sublime, in which absolutely incommensurate realities collide and cannot be resolved."[28] By sublime, Bloom means above all an energetic experience of reading, one that overcomes a certain resistance and grasps a certain difficulty of meaning. It is an experience of grandeur, but it does not assign to the text the superfluous attribute of holiness.

It is fair to call this a *heightened* experience of reading, and I think it enables us to escape the bind that Schwartz's line of reasoning places us in, for it allows us to admit aesthetic value without losing sight of the contingency of representation. Of course I would like to use a word other than sacredness to describe this value, but the best I can come up with is "magic." "Magic" at least has the advantage of suggesting performance and participation and so may be applied either to aesthetic or religious experience. One could say that poetic and religious performances create something like sacred space and time but provisionally and temporarily, as does a magical performance. Such an experience, holding our attention in a spell, can be repeated, but is not immune to the erosion of time—of "slow time," the phrase John Keats used in a poem that tries to assign a permanent value to the truth of beauty and the beauty of truth without transcending the world of experience. In sum, I am suggesting that "sacred writing" is better understood as "heightened reading," a concept that does not polarize sacred and secular.

Reading the Bible, let us admit, presents a particular challenge for modern secular intellectuals. Their appreciation of imaginative power (if I may speak on their behalf) is readily aroused by the splendor of its representations of divinity. At the same time, the text's refusal, as it were, to let Yahweh *be* a representation militates against our willing suspension of disbelief, irritates that corner of our minds disposed to take an objective and hence agnostic view of the God question. I do not ask that the Bible should therefore be devalued in our eyes, but it is surely too late in the day for a reading that regards the text as exempt from interrogation. We must, as Kant said, be willing to submit the sacredness of religion to critical examination or it becomes an object of just suspicion. Which means, I think, that we must be prepared to bring into play, even in our reading of the Bible, a measure of irony, to suspect the Bible *even as* we are deeply impressed by it.

This problem should be posed in another way. Like all classics, the Bible is almost endlessly renewable. And it is so not only because scholars have devotedly studied its letter and spirit but also because it is still capable of reaching the ever-changing reader. If it were not, it would become a mere monument, respected for its historical importance but unread. But this capability of the biblical text for significant response today from the secular and skeptical reader as well as from the reader who scorns secularism means that the very distinction between sacred and secular cannot be an essential, only a superficial, aspect of the text.

Such a liberal standard for the reading of scripture is doubtless utopian. For most people, the need to enshrine this text, thereby protecting God's word and the word God, will always be stronger than the need for heightened aesthetic experience, let alone the need to avoid mocking God. But if submission to God and God's sacred word will not disappear from modern life, it follows that atheism—always, as I said at the outset, a reaction against a prevailing theism perceived as oppressive—will also not disappear. Only, let that atheism not become the dogmatic version of what it opposes. Let it not be a meaningless, simple denial of the idea of God. Let it be a complex opposition, richly imagined and sensitively alert to the turns of language and feeling. Let it be literary.

NOTES

1. Isaac Bashevis Singer, *Shadows on the Hudson*, trans. Joseph Sherman (New York: Farrar, Straus & Giroux, 1998), 375.
2. Erich Heller, "The World of Franz Kafka," in *Franz Kafka: Twentieth Century Views*, edited by Ronald D. Gray (Englewood Cliffs, NJ: Prentice-Hall, 1962), 104.
3. Jacob Neusner, *Understanding Rabbinic Judaism: From Talmudic to Modern Times* (New York: Ktav, 1974), 7.
4. Robert Alter, *The Art of Biblical Narrative* (New York: Basic Books, 1981): 46, 12, and *passim*.
5. Herbert N. Schneidau, *Sacred Discontent: The Bible and Western Tradition* (Berkeley: University of California Press, 1977): 3, 28, 232, 276, and *passim*.
6. Regina M. Schwartz, *The Curse of Cain: The Violent Legacy of Monotheism* (Chicago: University of Chicago Press, 1997): 7, 31, and *passim*.
7. Schwartz's "Statement" in *PMLA* (December 2000, vol. 15: 2041) only makes more glaring what might be called her "cultural-studies theology." Recasting "the dead God of metaphysics" as "the postmodern God," she ignores mythology, psychology, and aesthetics, and lets transcendence mean simply moving beyond self to the politically marginalized other. For her, then, the voice of God is to be identified only with the cry of the oppressed.
8. Gabriel Josipovici, *The Book of God*: 110, 275.
9. Josipovici, *The Book of God*, 147–48.
10. See Nietzsche, *Daybreak*, # 87.
11. A. N. Wilson, *Jesus: A Life* (New York: Norton, 1992), x.
12. Aquinas, quoted in the *New Revised Standard Version*, xviii. (This translation of the Bible, also called NRSV, is the one used in this chapter unless otherwise indicated.) A contemporary biographer and man of faith tries to rephrase these words of Aquinas for a modern and largely secular audience: "The Bible was of course written by human beings—it is the word of God in the words of men." See Donald Spoto, *The Hidden Jesus: A Life* (New York, St. Martin's Press, 1998), xvii. Spoto tries to follow out the consequences of his unequivocal first statement by saying that all human discourse is metaphor, but his book everywhere assumes that the Bible demonstrates *God's* agency or God's purpose, not its human representation.
13. James Kugel, *On Being a Jew* (San Francisco: Harper, 1990): 161, 44. I am somewhat unfair to Kugel because the opinions cited are conveyed through lively dialogue between a poet and a devout Jew (who, however, is given the stronger argument).
14. Richard Elliot Friedman, *The Disappearance of God* (Boston: Little Brown, 1995), 143.
15. Armstrong, *History of God*, 23.
16. Armstrong, *History of God*, 52.
17. Kugel, *On Being a Jew*, 51.
18. A. D. Nuttall, *Overheard By God: Fiction and Prayer in Herbert, Milton, Dante and St. John* (London: Methuen, 1980).
19. Stanley Elkin, *The Living End* (New York: E. P. Dutton, 1979), 143.

20. Betty Rostman, "Sacred Language and Open Text," in Geoffrey H. Hartman and Sanford Budick, eds., *Midrash and Literature* (New Haven: Yale University Press, 1988), 160.
21. Frank Kermode, "The Plain Sense of Things," in Hartman and Budick, eds., *Midrash and Literature*, 187.
22. Jack Miles, *God: A Biography* (New York: Knopf, 1995), 133.
23. Josipovici, *The Book of God*, 168.
24. NRSV, 625.
25. Miles, *God: A Biography*: 320, 314.
26. NRSV, 672n.
27. Steven Medcalf, "How shall we sing the Lord's song in a strange land?" *Times Literary Supplement* (24 December 1999), 4.
28. Harold Bloom, *Ruin the Sacred Truth: Poetry and Belief from the Bible to the Present* (Cambridge: Harvard University Press, 1989), 4.

WORKS CITED

Abbott, H. Porter. *Beckett Writing Beckett: The Author in the Autograph.* Ithaca: Cornell University Press, 1996.
———. "What Do We Mean When We Say 'Narrative Literature?' Looking for Answers Across Disciplinary Borders." *Style* 34:2 (Summer 2000): 260–273.
———. "The Evolutionary Origins of the Storied Mind: Modeling the Prehistory of Narrative Consciousness and its Discontents." *Narrative* 8:3 (October 2000): 247–56.
Abrams, M. H., ed., *Literature and Belief.* English Institute Essays (1957). New York: Columbia University Press, 1958.
Adorno, Theodor. "Commitment." In *The Essential Frankfurt School Reader.* Edited by Andrew Arato and Eike Gebhardt. New York: Continuum, 1990.
Als, Hilton. "A Critic At Large: This Lonesome Place." *New Yorker Magazine.* 29 June 2001: 82–88.
Alter, Robert. *The Art of Biblical Narrative.* New York: Basic Books, 1981.
Altizer, Thomas J. J. and William Hamilton. *Radical Theology and the Death of God.* New York and London, 1966.
Anderson, Wilda. *Diderot's Dream.* Baltimore: Johns Hopkins University Press, 1990.
Andrews, Kenneth R. *Nook Farm: Mark Twain's Hartford Circle.* Cambridge: Harvard University Press, 1950.
Angeles, Peter, ed., *Critiques of God: making the case against belief in God.* Amherst, NY: Prometheus Books, 1997.
Angier, Natalie. "Confessions of a Lonely Atheist." *New York Times Magazine.* 14 January 2001: 34–38.
Appleman, Philip, ed., *Darwin.* 2nd ed. New York: Norton, 1979.
Armstrong, Karen. *A History of God.* New York: Ballantine Books, 1991.
———. *The Battle for God.* New York: Knopf, 2000.
Arnstein, Walter L. *The Bradlaugh Case: A Study of Late Victorian Opinion and Politics.* New York: Oxford University Press, 1965.
Attridge, Derek, ed., *Acts of Literature.* New York: Routledge, 1992: 33–75.
Ayer, Alfred Jules. *Language, Truth and Logic.* New York: Dover Publications, 1952.
Barnes, Hazel E. *An Existentialist Ethics.* New York: Knopf, 1967.

Bates, Milton J. *Wallace Stevens: A Mythology of the Self.* Berkeley: University of California Press, 1985.
Beckett, Samuel. *Proust.* New York: Grove Press, 1957.
———. *Disjecta: Miscellaneous Writings and Dramatic Fragments.* Edited by Ruby Cohn. New York: Grove Press, 1964.
———. "Letters: Who is Godot?" *New Yorker Magazine.* 24 June and 1 July 1996: 3–4.
Beer, Gillian. *Darwin's Plots: Evolutionary Narrative in Darwin, George Eliot, and Nineteenth-Century Fiction.* London: Routledge and Kegan Paul, 1983.
———. *Open Fields: Science in Cultural Encounter.* Oxford: Clarendon Press, 1996.
Benn, Maurice. *The Drama of Revolt: A Critical Study of Georg Büchner.* Cambridge: Cambridge University Press, 1976.
Berkowitz, Peter. *Nietzsche: The Ethics of an Immoralist.* Cambridge: Harvard University Press, 1995.
Berlin, Isaiah. *The Sense of Reality: Studies in Ideas and Their History.* Edited by Henry Hardy. New York: Farrar, Straus & Giroux, 1996.
———. "Commentary: The Romantics and Their Roots." *Times Literary Supplement.* 19 February 1999: 13–15.
Berman, David. *A History of Atheism in Britain: Hobbes to Russell.* London: Croom Helm, 1988.
Bezanson, Walter C., ed., *Herman Melville's 'Clarel: A Poem and Pilgrimage to the Holy Land.'* New York: Hendricks House, 1960.
Blond, Phillip, ed., *Post-Secular Philosophy: Between Theology and Philosophy.* London: Routledge, 1998.
Bloom, Harold. *Wallace Stevens: Poems of Our Climate.* Ithaca: Cornell University Press, 1977.
———. *Ruin the Sacred Truth: Poetry and Belief from the Bible to the Present.* Cambridge: Harvard University Press, 1989.
———. *The American Religion: The Emergence of the Post-Christian Nation.* New York: Simon and Schuster, 1992.
———. *Omens of Millennium: The Gnosis of Angels, Dreams, and Resurrection.* New York: Riverhead Books, 1996.
———, ed., *Mark Twain: Modern Critical Views.* New York: Chelsea House, 1986.
———, ed., *Thomas Hardy: Modern Critical Views.* New York: Chelsea House, 1987.
Bradlaugh, Charles. *Humanity's Gain from Unbelief and Other Essays.* London, 1929.
Bridgewater Patrick. *Nietzsche in Anglosaxonry.* Leicester University Press, 1987.
Brodwin, Stanley. "The Theology of Mark Twain: Banished Adam and the Bible." In *The Mississippi Quarterly.* XXIX, No. 2 (Spring 1976): 167–89.
———. "Mark Twain and the Myth of the Daring Jest." In *The Mythology of Mark Twain.* Edited by Sara deSaussure Davis and Philip D. Beidler. Birmingham: University of Alabama Press, 1978: 136–57, 173–77.
———. "Wandering Between Two Gods: Theological Realism in *A Connecticut Yankee in King Arthur's Court.*" *Studies in the Literary Imagination.* 16:2 (Fall 1983): 57–82.
———. "Mark Twain in the Pulpit: The Theological Comedy of *Huckleberry Finn.*" In *One Hundred Years of 'Huckleberry Finn': The Boy, His Book, and American Culture.* Cen-

tennial Essays. Edited by Robert Sattelmeyer and J. Donald Crowley. Columbia, MO: University of Missouri Press, 1985: 371–85.

———. "Mark Twain's Theology: The Gods of a Brevet Presbyterian." In *The Cambridge Companion to Mark Twain*. Edited by Forrest G. Robinson. New York: Cambridge University Press, 1988: 220–250.

Brombert, Victor. *In Praise of Antiheroes: Figures and Themes in Modern European Literature 1830–1980*. New Haven: Yale University Press, 1999.

Bruce, Steve. *The Rise and Fall of the New Christian Right: Conservative Protestant Politics in America 1978–1988*. Oxford: Clarendon Press, 1988.

Buckley, Michael J., S.J. *At the Origins of Modern Atheism*. New Haven: Yale University Press, 1987.

Burke, Kenneth. *The Rhetoric of Religion: Studies in Logology*: Boston: Beacon Press, 1961.

Butler, Jon. *Awash in a Sea of Faith: Christianizing the American People*. Cambridge: Harvard University Press, 1990.

Bryden, Mary. *Samuel Beckett and the Idea of God*. New York: St. Martin's Press, 1998.

Camus, Albert. *The Rebel: An Essay on Man in Revolt*. Translated by Anthony Bower. New York: Vintage, 1962.

Caputo, John D. *The Prayers and Tears of Jacques Derrida: Religion without Religion*. Bloomington: Indiana University Press, 1997.

Carlyle, Thomas. *Sartor Resartus*. Edited by Kerry McSweeney and Peter Sabor. Oxford: Oxford University Press, 1987.

Coleridge, Samuel Taylor. *The Major Works*. Oxford: Oxford University Press, 2000.

Coles, Robert. *The Secular Mind*. Princeton: Princeton University Press, 1999.

Cowley, Malcolm, ed., *The Portable Hawthorne*. New York: Penguin, 1976.

Crews, Frederick. "Saving Us from Darwin." *New York Review of Books*. 4 October 2001: 24–27 and 18 October 2001: 51–55.

Crocker, Lester G. *Diderot's Selected Writings*. Translated by Derek Coltman. New York: Macmillan, 1966.

Cupitt, Don. *The Religion of Being*. London: SCM Press, 1998.

Daiches, David. *God and the Poets*. Oxford: Clarendon Press, 1984.

Damasio, Antonio. *Descartes' Error: Emotion, Reason, and the Human Brain*. New York: Putnam, 1984.

———. *The Feeling of What Happens: Body and Emotion in the Making of Consciousness*. New York: Harcourt Brace, 1999.

Danto, Arthur C. *Jean-Paul Sartre*. Modern Masters Series. New York: Viking, 1975.

———. *Connections to the World: The Basic Concepts of Philosophy*. Berkeley: University of California Press, 1997.

Dawkins, Richard. *The Selfish Gene*. New edition. New York: Oxford University Press, 1989.

———. *The Blind Watchmaker: Why the Evidence of Evolution Reveals a Universe without Design*. New York: Norton, 1996.

Delbanco, Andrew. *The Real American Dream: A Meditation on Hope*. Cambridge: Harvard University Press, 1999.

Dennett, Daniel C. *Consciousness Explained*. Boston: Little Brown, 1991.

Derrida, Jacques. *Politics of Friendship*. Translated by George Collins. London : Verso, 1977.

———. *Margins of Philosophy.* Translated by Alan Bass. Chicago: University of Chicago Press, 1982: 207–81.

———. *Specters of Marx.* Translated by Peggy Kamuf. New York: Routledge, 1994.

———. "How to Avoid Speaking: Denials." Translated by Ken Frieden. In *Languages of the Unsayable: The Play of Negativity in Literature and Literary Theory.* Edited by Sanford Budick and Wolfgang Iser. Stanford: Stanford University Press, 1987.

Descartes, René. *The Philosophical Writings of Descartes.* Translated by John Cottingham, Robert Stoothoff, and Dugald Murdoch. Vol. 1. London: Cambridge University Press, 1985.

Diderot, Denis. *Oeuvres complètes.* Edited by J. Assézat and M. Tourneux. Paris, 1966.

———. *Diderot: Interpreter of Nature: Selected Writings.* Translated by Jean Stewart and Jonathan Kemp. Westport, CT: Hyperion Press, 1937.

Diderot, Denis. *Correspondance de Diderot 1713–1757.* Paris: Éditions de Minuet, 1955.

———. *Jacques the Fatalist and His Master.* Translated by Michael Henry. New York: Penguin, 1986.

Didion, Joan. "God's Country." *New York Review of Books.* 4 October 2000: 68–76.

Duckworth, Colin, ed., *En attendant Godot.* Modern World Literature Series. Walton-on-Thames, Surrey: Thomas Nelson, 1985.

Durkheim, Emile. *The Elementary Forms of The Religious Life.* Translated by Joseph Warren Swain. New York: Free Press, 1965.

Eagleton, Terry. "Giants Refreshed: Matthew Arnold." *Times Literary Supplement.* 21 January 2000: 14.

Einstein, Albert. *Ideas and Opinions.* New York: Crown, 1956.

Eldredge, Niles. "More Corn from Kansas." *Times Literary Supplement.* 18 February 2000: 9.

Eliot, T. S. *Selected Essays.* London: Faber and Faber, 1972.

Elkin, Stanley. *The Living End.* New York: E. P. Dutton, 1979.

Epstein, Helen. "The Fly in the DNA." *New York Review of Books.* 24 June 1999: 14–18.

Febvre, Lucien. *The Problem of Unbelief in the Sixteenth Century: The Religion of Rabelais.* Translated by Beatrice Gottlieb. Cambridge: Harvard University Press, 1982.

Fellows, Otis. *Diderot.* Twayne updated edition. Boston: G. K. Hall, 1988.

Feuerbach, Ludwig. *The Essence of Christianity.* Translated by Marian Evans. New York: 1885.

Feynman, Richard. *The Meaning of It All: Thoughts of a Citizen Scientist.* Reading, MA: Helix Books, 1998.

Fish, Stanley. "Condemnation Without Absolutes." *New York Times.* 15 October 2001: A19.

Fodor, Jerry. "Workings of the Spirit." *Times Literary Supplement.* 29 January 1999: 20.

Foot, Michael and Isaac Kramnick, eds., *The Thomas Paine Reader.* London: Penguin, 1987.

Forster, E. M. "What I Believe." In *Two Cheers for Democracy.* San Diego and London: Harcourt Brace, 1966.

Freud, Sigmund. *Civilization and Its Discontents.* Translated by James Strachey. New York: Norton, 1962.

Friedman, Richard Elliot. *The Disappearance of God.* Boston: Little Brown, 1995.

Furbank, P. N. *Diderot: A Critical Biography.* New York: Knopf, 1992.

Gallup, George, Jr. and Jim Castelli. *The People's Religion: American Faith in the 90s.* New York: Macmillan, 1989.

Gay, Peter, ed., *Voltaire's Philosophical Dictionary.* 2 vols. Translated by Peter Gay. New York: Basic Books, 1962.

Ginzburg, Carlo. *The Cheese and The Worms: The Cosmos of a Sixteenth Century Miller.* Translated by John and Anne Tedeschi. Baltimore: Johns Hopkins University Press, 1980.

———. *Wooden Eyes: Nine Reflections on Distance.* Translated by Martin Ryle and Katie Soper. New York: Columbia University Press, 2001: 156.

Glanz, James. "Nobelist Ponders God, Truth and 'Final Theory.'" *New York Times.* 25 January 2000: F2.

Gould, Stephen Jay. "Viewpoint." *Time Magazine.* 23 August 1999.

Gordon, David J. *Iris Murdoch's Fables of Unselfing.* Columbia, MO: University of Missouri Press, 1995.

Gunn, Dan. "The beam of Sam's light." *Times Literary Supplement.* 15 January 1999: 3–4.

Haack, Susan. *Evidence and Inquiry: Towards Reconstruction in Epistemology.* Oxford: Blackwell, 1993.

———. "Commentary: Staying for An Answer." *Times Literary Supplement.* 9 July 1999: 12–14.

Hamburger, Michael. Introduction. In *'Leonce and Lena, Lenz, Woyzeck'* by Georg Büchner. Translated by Michael Hamburger. Chicago: University of Chicago Press, 1972.

Hand, Seán, ed., *The Levinas Reader.* Oxford: Blackwell, 1989.

Hardy, Florence Emily. *Life of Thomas Hardy.* New York: St. Martin's Press, 1962.

Hardy, Thomas. *Thomas Hardy: The Complete Poems.* Edited by James Gibson. New York: Macmillan, 1976.

———. *The Complete Poetical Works of Thomas Hardy,* vol. 5. Edited by Samuel Hynes. Oxford: Clarendon Press, 1995.

Hart, Kevin. *The Trespass of the Sign.* London: Cambridge University Press, 1989.

Hartman, Geoffrey H. and Sanford Budick, eds., *Midrash and Literature.* New Haven: Yale University Press, 1988.

Hauser, Ronald. *Georg Büchner.* Boston: Twayne, 1974.

Heidegger, Martin. *Nietzsche.* Translated by David Farrell Krell. Vol. 1. San Francisco: Harper and Row, 1961.

———. *Being and Time.* Translated by John Macquarrie & Edward Robison. Harper and Row, New York, 1962.

———. "Letter on Humanism." Translated by Edgar Lohner. In *Philosophy in the Twentieth Century.* Edited by William Barrett and Henry D. Aiken. Vol. 3. New York: Random House, 1962: 270–302.

———. *An Introduction to Metaphysics.* Translated by Ralph Manheim. New Haven: Yale University Press, 1987.

Heller, Erich. "The World of Franz Kafka." In *Franz Kafka: Twentieth Century Views.* Edited by Ronald D. Gray. Englewood Cliffs, NJ: Prentice-Hall, 1962: 99–122.

Hill, Robert W., Jr., ed., *Tennyson's Poetry.* New York: Norton, 1971.

Himmelfarb, Gertrude. "Deity and Doubt." *Wall Street Journal Bookshelf.* 15 June, 1999.

Holbach (Paul Henri Thiry, baron d'). *Système de la nature ou des lois du monde physique et morale*. 2 vols. Hildesheim: Georg Olms, 1966.

Hollander, Robert. "Lecture Thirteen: Justice and Poetry: Dante's Book of the Dead." *The Great Courses on Tape: The Bible and Western Culture, Part II*. Springfield, VA: The Teaching Company, 1998: 4–5.

Holt, Jim. "Infinitesimally Yours." *New York Review of Books*. 20 May 1999.

Hume, David. *Writings on Religion*. Edited by Antony Flew. La Salle, IL: Open Court, 1995.

Hunter, Michael. "The Problem of Atheism in Early Modern England." In *Transactions of the Royal Historical Society*. Fifth Series, No. 35. London, 1955: 135–57.

———, and David Wootton, eds., *Atheism from the Reformation to the Enlightenment*. Oxford: Clarendon Press, 1992.

Huxley, Thomas Henry. *Christianity and Agnosticism: A Controversy. Consisting of papers by Henry Wace, D. D., Prof. Thomas H. Huxley, The Bishop of Peterborough, W. H. Mallock, and Mrs. Humphry Ward*. New York, 1889.

James, William. *The Varieties of Religious Experience*. London: Longmans, Green: 1928: 485–527.

———. *Principles of Psychology*. Cleveland: World Publishing Company, 1948.

———. *The Will to Believe and other essays in popular philosophy*. Edited by Frederick Burkhardt, Fredson Bowers and Edward Madden. Cambridge: Harvard University Press, 1995.

Janofsky, Michael. "Colorado Asks: Is 'In God We Trust' a Religious Statement." *New York Times*. 3 July 2000: A9.

Jarraway, David R. *Wallace Stevens and The Question of Belief: Metaphysician in the Dark*. Baton Rouge: Louisiana State University Press, 1993.

Johnson, Dirk. "Schools Seeking to Skirt Rules That Bar Ten Commandments." In *New York Times*. 27 February 2000: Sec. 1:24.

Josephs, Herbert. *Diderot's Dialogue of Gesture and Language*. Columbus, OH: Ohio State University Press, 1969.

Josipovici, Gabriel. *The Book of God: A Response to the Bible*. New Haven: Yale University Press, 1988.

Jung, Carl Gustav. *Psychology & Religion*. New Haven: Yale University Press, 1966.

Kant, Immanuel. *Kant: Selections*. Edited and translated by Theodore Meyer Greene. New York: Charles Scribner's Sons, 1929.

Kaufmann, Walter. *Nietzsche: Philosopher, Psychologist, Antichrist*. 4th edition. Princeton: Princeton University Press, 1974.

———, ed., *Existententialism from Dostoevsky to Sartre*. Revised and expanded. New York: Penguin, 1975.

Kermode, Frank. *The Sense of An Ending*. New York: Oxford University Press, 1967.

Knowlson, James. *Damned to Fame: The Life of Samuel Beckett*. New York: Simon and Schuster, 1996.

Köhler, Joachim. *Nietzsche & Wagner: A Lesson in Subjugation*. Translated by Ronald Taylor. New Haven: University Press, 1996.

Kors, Alan Jay. *Atheism in France 1650–1729: The Orthodox Sources of Disbelief*. Princeton: Princeton University Press, 1990.

Kristeva, Julia. *Revolution in Poetic Language*. Translated by Margaret Waller. New York: Columbia University Press, 1984.

Küng, Hans. *Does God Exist? An Answer for Today*. Translated by Edward Quinn. Garden City: Doubleday, 1980.

Kugel, James. *On Being a Jew*. San Francisco: Harper, 1990.

Lathem, Edward Connery and Lawrance Thompson, eds., *Robert Frost: Poetry and Prose*. New York: Holt, Rinehart and Winston, 1984.

Lawrence, D. H. "Study of Thomas Hardy." In *Phoenix: The Posthumous Papers of D. H. Lawrence*. Edited by Edward McDonald. London: Heinemann, 1936.

Lear, Jonathan. *Open-Minded: Working Out the Logic of the Soul*. Cambridge: Harvard University Press, 1998.

———. *Happiness, Death, and the Remainder of Life*. Cambridge: Harvard University Press, 2000.

Levin, Harry. *The Gates of Horn: A Study of Five French Realists*. New York: Galaxy Books, 1966.

Lewontin, Richard. *It Ain't Necessarily So: The Dream of the Human Genome and Other Illusions*. New York: New York Review Books, 2000.

Lilla, Mark. "The Politics of Jacques Derrida." *New York Review of Books*. 25 June 1998: 36–41.

———. *The Reckless Mind: Intellectuals in Politics*. New York: New York Review Books, 2001: 164–90.

Lindenberger, Herbert. *Georg Büchner: Modern Critiques*. Carbondale, IL: Southern Illinois University Press, 1964.

Lipset, Seymour Martin. *American Exceptionalism: A Double-Edged Sword*. New York: Norton, 1996.

Lockerbie, D. Bruce. *Dismissing God: Modern Writers Struggle Against Religion*. Grand Rapids, MI: Baker Books, 1998.

Lowe, David and Ronald Meyer, eds., *Dostoevsky's Letters*. Ann Arbor, MI: Ardis Publishers, 1988.

Lukács, Georg. *The Meaning of Contemporary Realism*. Translated by John and Necka Mander. London: Merlin Press, 1962.

MacIntyre, Alasdair C. "Existentialism." In *Sartre: A Collection of Cri-tical Essays*. Edited by Mary Warnock. Garden City, NY: Anchor, 1971: 23–39.

McEwan, Ian. *Enduring Love*. London: J. Cape, 1997.

Magnus, Bernd and Kathleen M. Higgins, eds., *The Cambridge Companion to Nietzsche*. London: Cambridge University Press, 1996.

Marion, Jean-Luc. *God Without Being*. Translated by Thomas Carlson. Chicago: University of Chicago Press, 1982.

Marsden, George M. *Understanding Fundamentalism and Evangelicalism*. Grand Rapids, MI: William B. Eerdman's, 1991.

Marty, Martin E. *Religion and Republic: The American Circumstance*. Boston: Beacon Press, 1987.

Mason, John Hope. *The Irresistible Diderot*. London: Quartet Books, 1982.

Medcalf, Steven. "How shall we sing the Lord's name in a strange land?" *Times Literary Supplement.* 24 December 1999: 3–6.

Menand, Louis. *The Metaphysical Club: A Story of Ideas in America.* New York: Farrar, Straus & Giroux, 2001.

———. "T. S. Eliot." *The Cambridge History of Literary Criticism.* Vol. 7. Cambridge: Cambridge University Press, 2000.

Midgley, Mary. *Science and Poetry.* London : Routledge, 2001.

Miles, Jack. *God: A Biography.* New York: Knopf, 1995.

———. "Belief by the Numbers." Compiled by Russell Shorto. *New York Times Magazine.* 7 December 1997: 60.

Mill, John Stuart. *Collected Works: Essays on Ethics, Religion, and Society.* Edited by F. G. L. Priestley. Toronto: Toronto University Press, 1969: 423–489.

Montaigne, Michel de. *The Complete Essays of Montaigne.* Translated by Donald M. Frame. Stanford: Stanford University Press, 1965.

Mossner, Ernest Campbell. *The Life of David Hume.* Second edition. Oxford: Clarendon Press, 1980.

Mueller, Carl Richard. *Georg Büchner: Complete Plays and Prose.* New York: Hill and Wang, 1963.

Murdoch, Iris. *Sartre: Romantic Rationalist.* Revised edition. New York: Viking, 1987.

———. *Existentialists and Mystics: Writings on Philosophy and Literature.* Edited by Peter Conradi. London: Chatto and Windus, 1997.

Nagel, Thomas. *The View from Nowhere.* New York: Oxford University Press, 1986.

———. *The Last Word.* New York: Oxford University Press, 1997.

Nehamas, Alexander. *Nietzsche: Life as Literature.* Cambridge: Harvard University Press, 1985.

———. *The Art of Living: Socratic Reflections from Plato to Foucault.* Berkeley: University of California Press, 1998.

Neusner, Jacob. *Understanding Rabbinic Judaism: From Talmudic to Modern Times.* New York: Ktav, 1974.

Neusch, Marcel. *The Sources of Modern Atheism.* Translated by Matthew J. O'Connell. New York: Paulist Press, 1982.

Newton, Roger G. *The Truth of Science: Physical Theories and Reality.* Cambridge: Harvard University Press, 1997.

Niebuhr, Gustav. "Baptists' Ardor for Evangelism Angers Some Jews and Hindus." *New York Times.* 4 December 1999: A10.

Nietzsche, Friedrich. *Werke in drei Baenden.* Vol. 3. Edited by Karl Schlecta. Munich: C. Hanser, 1954–56.

———. *Beyond Good and Evil: Prelude to a Philosophy of the Future.* Translated by Walter Kaufmann. New York: Vintage, 1966.

———. *Thus Spake Zarathustra: A Book for All and None.* Translated by Walter Kaufmann. New York: Penguin, 1966.

———. *The Birth of Tragedy* and *The Case of Wagner.* Translated by Walter Kaufmann. New York: Vintage, 1967.

———. *Twilight of the Idols and The Anti-Christ*. Translated by R. J. Hollingdale. Baltimore: Penguin, 1968.

———. *The Will to Power*. Translated by Walter Kaufmann and R. J. Hollingdale. New York: Vintage, 1968.

———. *The Gay Science: with a Prelude in Rhymes and an Appendix of Songs*. Translated by Walter Kaufmann. New York: Vintage, 1974.

———. *Ecce Homo: How One Becomes What One Is*. Translated by R. J. Hollingdale. Harmondsworth, England: Penguin, 1979.

———. *Philosophy and Truth: Selections from Nietzsche's Notebooks of the Early 1870s*. Edited and translated by Daniel Brezeale. Atlantic Highlands, NJ: Humanities Press, 1979.

———. *The Portable Nietzsche*. Edited and translated by Walter Kaufmann. New York: Viking Penguin, 1982.

———. *Human, All Too Human: A Book for Free Spirits*. Translated by R. J. Hollingdale. London : Cambridge University Press, 1986.

———. "History in the Service and Disservice of Life." In *Unmodern Observations*. Edited by William Arrowsmith. Translated by Gary Brown. New Haven: Yale University Press, 1990: 87–145.

———. *Daybreak: Thoughts on the Prejudices of Morality*. Translated by R. J. Hollingdale. Cambridge: Cambridge University Press, 1982.

———. *Twilight of the Idols*. Translated by Duncan Large. Oxford: Oxford University Press, 1998.

Nuttall. A. D. *Overheard By God: Fiction and Prayer in Herbert, Milton, Dante, and St. John*. London: Methuen, 1980.

O' Connor, Flannery. *3 by Flannery O'Connor*. New York: Signet, 1962.

Orel, Harold, ed., *Critical Essays on Thomas Hardy's Poetry*. New York: G. K. Hall, 1995.

Outram, Dorinda. *The Enlightenment*. Cambridge: Cambridge University Press, 1995.

Polkinghorne, John. *Belief in God in an Age of Science*. New Haven: Yale University Press, 1998.

Popkin, Richard H. *Scepticism in the Enlightenment*. Dordrecht/Boston/London: Kluwer Academic Publishers, 1997.

Porter, Roy. *Gibbon: Historians on Historians*. New York: St. Martin's Press, 1988.

Price, Victor. Introduction. In *Danton's Death, Leonce and Lena, Woyzeck by Georg Büchner*. Translated by Victor Price. Oxford: Oxford University Press, 1971.

Prengeman, Leo. "Absent Fathers, Ambiguous Father: Walker Percy and the Scandal of Christendom." Dissertation. City University of New York Graduate Center , 1999.

Remnick, David. "A Critic at Large: In the Capital of Words: *When Alfred Kazin came to the city and discovered America*." *New Yorker Magazine*. 22 June 1998: 136–42.

Ricks, Christopher. *Beckett's Dying Words*. New York: Oxford University Press, 1993.

Ricouer, Paul. *Figuring the Sacred: Religion, Narrative, and Imagination*. Translated by David Pellauer. Edited by Mark I. Wallace. Minneapolis: Fortress Press , 1995.

Robertson, J. M. *A History of Freethought in the Nineteenth Century*. London, 1929.

Rolston, Holmes, III. *Genes, Genesis and God: Values and Their Origins in Natural and Human History*. Cambridge: Cambridge University Press, 1999.

Rorty, Richard. *Contingency, Irony, and Solidarity*. Cambridge and New York: Cambridge University Press, 1990.

———. "Beliefs: Interview with Richard Rorty." *Science New York Times*. 11 July 1998: B6.

Ruse, Michael. *Can A Darwinist Be A Christian?* London: Cambridge University Press, 2000.

Russell, Bertrand. *Why I Am Not a Christian and Other Essays*. New York: Simon and Schuster, 1957.

———. *Collected Essays 1943–1949*. New York: Arno Press, 1972.

Safranski, Rüdiger. *Martin Heidegger: Between Good and Evil*. Translated by Ewald Oser. Cambridge: Harvard University Press, 1998.

———. *Nietzsche: A Philosophical Biography*. Translated by Shelley Frisch. New York: Norton, 2002.

Santayana, George. *Interpretations of Poetry and Religion*. Edited by William G. Holzberger and Herman J. Saatkamp, Jr. Cambridge: MIT Press, 1989.

Schneidau, Herbert N. *Sacred Discontent: The Bible and Western Tradition*. Berkeley: University of California Press, 1977.

Schwartz, Delmore. "Poetry and Belief in Thomas Hardy." In *Hardy: A Collection of Critical Essays*. Edited by Albert J. Guerard. Englewood Cliffs, NJ: Prentice-Hall, 1963: 123–34.

Schwartz, Regina M. *The Curse of Cain: The Violent Legacy of Monotheism*. Chicago: University of Chicago Press, 1997.

———. "Teaching a Sacred Text as Literature, Teaching Literature as a Sacred Text." *Profession*. New York, MLA, 1998: 186-98.

———. "Statement." In *PMLA*. Vol. 15 (December 2000): 2041.

Scruton, Roger. *Kant*. Past Masters. Oxford: Oxford University Press, 1982.

Seymour-Smith, Martin, ed., *The Mayor of Casterbridge* by Thomas Hardy (including General Preface to the Wessex Edition of 1912). London: Penguin, 1985.

Sherman, Carol. *Diderot and the Art of Dialogue*. Geneva: Librairie Droz, 1976.

Shermer, Michael. *How We Believe: The Search for God in an Age of Science*. New York: W. H. Freeman and Company, 1999.

Silberstein, Laurence J., ed., *Jewish Fundamentalism in Comparative Perspective: Religion, Ideology, and the Crisis of Modernity*. New York: New York University Press, 1993: 27-41.

Singer, Isaac Bashevis. *Shadows on the Hudson*. Translated by Joseph Sherman. New York: Farrar, Straus & Giroux, 1998.

Smith, Christian. *American Evangelicalism: Embattled and Thriving*. Chicago: University of Chicago Press, 1998.

Spoto, Donald. *The Hidden Jesus: A New Life*. New York: St. Martin's Press, 1998.

Stack, George J. *Nietzsche and Emerson: An Elective Affinity*. Athens, OH: Ohio State University Press, 1992.

Steiner, George. *Real Presences: Is there anything in what we say?* London: Faber and Faber, 1989.

Stephen, Leslie. *An Agnostic's Apology and Other Essays*. New York: 1893.

Stevens, Holly, ed., *Wallace Stevens: Letters*. New York: Knopf, 1966.

Stevens, Wallace. *Collected Poetry & Prose*. Edited by Frank Kermode and Joan Richardson. New York: Library of America, 1997.

Sugrue, Michael. *The Great Courses on Tape: The Bible and Western Culture*. Springfield, VA: The Teaching Company, 1998.
Talbot, Margaret. "A Mighty Fortress." *New York Times Magazine*. 27 February 2000: 36.
Taylor, Mark C., ed., *Critical Terms for Religious Studies*. Chicago: University of Chicago Press, 1998.
Tocqueville, Alexis de. *Democracy in America*. Edited by George Lawrence, translated by J. P. Mayer and Max Lerner. New York: Harper and Row, 1966.
Turner, James. *Without God, Without Creed: The Origins of Unbelief in America*. Baltimore: Johns Hopkins University Press, 1985.
Twain, Mark. *The Autobiography of Mark Twain*. Edited by Charles Neider. New York: Harper and Row, 1975.
———. "Reflections on Religion." Edited by Charles Neider. *The Hudson Review* 16:3 (Autumn 1963): 329–52.
———. *Mark Twain's 'Mysterious Stranger' Manuscripts*. Edited with an introduction by William M. Gibson. Berkeley: University of California Press, 1969.
———. *Pudd'nhead Wilson*. New York: Signet, 1980.
———. *Letters from the Earth: Uncensored Writings of Mark Twain*. Edited by Bernard De Voto. New York: Harper Perennial, 1991.
———. *The Bible According to Mark Twain*. Edited by Howard G. Baetzhold and Joseph B. McCullough. New York: Simon and Schuster, 1995.
Unamuno, Miguel de. *The Tragic Sense of Life*. Translated by J. E. Crawford Flitch. London: Macmillan, 1926.
Updike, John. "Reflections: The Future of Faith." *New Yorker Magazine*. 29 November 1999: 84–91.
Vahanian, Gabriel. *The Death of God: the culture of our post-Christian era*. New York: G. Braziller, 1961.
Vartanian, Aram. "Diderot: A Dualist in Spite of Himself." In *Diderot: Digression and Dispersion: A Bicentennial Tribute*. Edited by Jack Udank and Herbert Josephs. Lexington, KY: French Forum Publishers, 1984: 250–58.
Vendler, Helen. *On Extended Wings: Wallace Stevens's Longer Poems*. Cambridge: Harvard University Press, 1971.
———. *Words Chosen Out of Desire*. Knoxville, TN: University of Tennessee Press, 1984.
Ward, Graham, ed., *Theology and Contemporary Critical Theory*. New York: St. Martin's Press, 1996.
———, ed., *The Postmodern God: A Theological Reader*. Oxford: Blackwell, 1997.
Ward, Mrs. Humphry. "The New Reformation: A Dialogue." In Huxley, *Christianity and Agnosticism*: 284–312.
Weinberg, Steven. "Five and a Half Utopias." *Atlantic Monthly*. January 2000: 112–15.
———. "The Future of Science and the Universe." *New York Review of Books*. 15 November, 2001: 58–63.
Wheatcroft, Geoffrey. "Politics Without Piety." *New York Times*. 9 September 2000: A15.
White, Micah. "Atheists Under Siege." *New York Times*. 21 June 1999: A15.
Whitehead, Alfred North. *Adventures in Ideas*. New York: Macmillan, 1933.
Williams, Hugo. "Commentary." *Times Literary Supplement*. 26 February 1999: 10.

Williams, James D. "Revision and Intention in Mark Twain's 'A Connecticut Yankee.'" In *American Literature* 36 (1964–1965): 288–97.

Wilson, A. N. *Jesus: A Life*. New York: Norton, 1992.

———. *God's Funeral*. New York: Norton, 1999.

Wilson, Arthur M. *Diderot*. Oxford: Clarendon Press, 1972.

Wilson, E. O. *Consilience: The Unity of Knowledge*. New York: Vintage, 1998.

Wilson, James Q. *The Moral Sense*. New York: Free Press, 1993.

Wittgenstein, Ludwig. *Lectures & Conversations on Aesthetics, Psychology and Religious Belief*. Compiled by Yorick Smythies, Rush Rhees, and James Taylor. Edited by Cyril Barrett. Berkeley: University of California Press, 1972.

———. *Tractatus Logico-Philosophicus*. Translated by D. F. Pears and B. F. McGuiness. Revised 2nd ed. New York: Humanities Press, 1972.

Wolosky, Shira. *The Negative Way of Language in Eliot, Beckett, and Celan*. Stanford: Stanford University Press, 1995.

Wood, James. *The Broken Estate: Essays on Literature and Belief*. New York: Random House, 1999.

———. "Writing Under God." *The New Republic*. 26 February 2001: 28–32.

Wright, Robert. "The Accidental Creationist." *New Yorker Magazine*. 13 December 1999: 56–65.

INDEX

A

Abbott, H. Porter, 55n46, 111, 114–15, 116–17, 158
Abraham (biblical), *see* Covenant
Abrams, M. H., 22–23, 135, 167, 168
Adorno, Theodor, 114
Alter, Robert, 175
Altizer, Thomas J. J., 57n100
Anaxagoras, 1
Agnosticism, dogmatism of, 25, 33–36; objectivity of, 2–3, 4, 23, 36
Angier, Natalie, 168n37, 171n98
Aquinas, *see* Thomas Aquinas
Armstrong, Karen, 53, 129, 159, 170n95
Aristotle, 1, 13, 14, 148
Arnold, Matthew, 23, 24, 95, 133–34
Ashcroft, John, 164
Auden, W. H., 30, 140
Augustine, Saint, 37, 112, 113
Ayer, A. J., 21

B

Bacon, Francis, 12, 13, 63, 164
Barnes, Hazel E., 38, 50
Barth, Karl, 4, 38, 39, 44, 130–31
Bates, Milton, J., 123n125

Bayle, Pierre, 15
Beckett, Samuel, 110–17; exemplary irony of, 5; relation of to other literary atheists 6, 52, 59, 75, 101
Beer, Gillian, 31, 94, 99, 136
Behe, Michael, 147
Belief, subjectivity of, 3, 4, 26–27, 34; *see also* Poetry and Belief
Benn, Maurice, 72
Bentham, Jeremy, 26, 65
Berg, Alban, 73
Bergson, Henri, 32, 106
Berkowitz, Peter, 80
Berlin, Isaiah, 20, 48, 152
Berman, David, 17
Bezanson, Walter C., 29
Bible, Old versus New Testaments of, 82, 177–79, 182–85; representation of Yahweh in, 16, 94, 130, 174–89
Blake, William, 2, 21, 132
Bloom, Harold, on American Religion, 165; on the Bible, 176; on James, 145; on Romanticism, 22, 27, 131–32; on sacred texts, 188, 189; on Stevens, 104–05, 123n125
Bologne, Jean-Claude, 111, 116
Bradlaugh, Charles, 24, 35, 87, 141
Bridgewater, Patrick, 123n125
Brodwin, Stanley, 87–88, 90, 121n76

Brombert, Victor, 69
Brooks, Cleanth, 134–35, 136
Browning, Robert, 23, 24, 27, 28, 95
Bruce, Steve, 170n93, 171n103
Bryden, Mary, 111, 112–13, 114, 116
Buber, Martin, 4
Büchner, Georg, 18, 59, 68–74
Büchner, Ludwig, 74
Buckley, Michael J., 12–13, 17, 53n3
Bultmann, Rudolf, 131
Burke, Kenneth, 127
Bush, Douglas, 135
Bush, George W., 166
Butler, Jon, 161, 171
Butler, Samuel, 32

C

Caldwell, Pastor, 166
Calvin, John, 13
Camus, Albert, 5, 141
Caputo, John D., 51, 52
Carlyle, Thomas, 23, 25–26, 27
Catholicism, 4, 40–42, 159, 164
Charron, Pierre, 12
Chaumette, Pierre, 18
Chesterton, G. K., 161
Christ, *See* Jesus Christ
Christianity, relation of to atheism, 2, 5, 11–13, 30–31, 36
Churchland, Paul, 155
Clifford, W. K., 23, 24, 33, 104
Coleridge, Samuel Taylor, 20, 24, 107, 128, 133, 135–37
Coles, Robert, 144, 163
Comte, Auguste, 23, 94, 138
Covenant (biblical), 183–85
Corbin, Henry, 145
Crane, Hart, 60
Crews, Frederick, 169n49
Cupitt, Don, 50
Curran, Stuart, 27

D

Daiches, David, 25, 136
Damasio, Antonio, 130, 156, 157
Dante Alighieri, 130, 149
Danto, Arthur C., 49, 76
Danton, Georges Jacques, 72
Darwin, Charles, 25–26, 31–33, 64; and Freud, 148; and Hardy, 94, 96, 101–02; and Nietzsche, 74–75, 77, 81, 119n31; *see also* Darwinism
Darwinism, 31–34, 59, 94, 101, 119n31, 148, 152
Davidson, Donald, 20
Davies, Paul, 149
Dawkins, Richard, 31, 32, 151, 152–54, 156
Deism, 12, 15–16, 18, 60, 62, 86
Delbanco, Andrew, 144
Democritus, 1, 115
Dennett, Daniel C., 151, 154, 155–56
Derrida, Jacques, and Marx, 21; and institution of literature, 138; and Nietzsche, 87, 115; and Steiner, 128–29; and theology, 37, 39, 46–52
Descartes, René, 2, 12, 13–15, 60, 63
Determinism vs. Free Will, 63–67, 71, 152–53
De Voto, Bernard, 90
Dewey, John, 126, 138, 144, 168
Diderot, Denis, 59, 60–68; and Büchner, 71; and 18th c. atheism, 2, 14, 18; and Voltaire, 17, 118n3; and E. O. Wilson, 152
Didion, Joan, 170
Dionysius, *see* Pseudo-Dionysius
Donald, Merlin, 158
Donne, John, 136, 137
Dostoevsky, Fyodor, 27, 29, 30–31
Duckworth, Colin, 111
Durkheim, Emile, 139, 163
Duvall, Robert, 165

E

Eagleton, Terry, 134, 137, 167, 168, 176
Eckhart, Meister, 37
Einstein, Albert, 14, 129, 150
Eisenhower, Dwight D., 160
Eldredge, Niles, 147, 169
Eliade, Mircea, 163
Eliot, George, 22, 23, 76, 133
Eliot, T. S., 28, 134–36, 167n21
Elkin, Stanley, 184
Emerson, Ralph Waldo, 20, 24, 29, 80, 106, 132
Enlightenment, relation of to atheism, 2, 5, 12, 19–20, 131, 138, 152
Epicurus, 1, 71–72, 82, 83, 108
Erasmus, Desiderius, 108
Evangelicalism, 159–60, 163–66, 170n95
Evolutionary biology, 150, 151–55, 158

F

Falwell, Jerry, 164
Febvre, Lucien, 11
Feuerbach, Ludwig, 21, 22, 23, 74, 86
Feynman, Richard, 144–46, 151, 156–57
Fichte, J. G., 68
Fish, Stanley, 3
Flaubert, Gustave, 24
Fodor, Jerry, 131–32, 158
Forster, E. M., 128, 167, 179–80
Foucault, Michel, 51, 85, 176
Free Will, *see* Determinism
Freud, Sigmund, 37, 46–48, 140; and Darwin, 148; and Dennett, 156; and Hardy, 100; and James, 142; and Nietzsche, 74, 82–83
Friedman, Richard Elliot, 191
Frost, Robert, 7, 105, 130

Fundamentalism, 143, 160, 164–65
Furbank, P. N., 64, 67

G

Gallup, George, Jr., 162, 171n98
Geulincx, Arnold, 115
Gibbon, Edward, 160
Gibson, William M., 92
Ginzburg, Carlo, 3, 12
Gladstone, William, 27
Goethe, J. W. G., 14, 80
Gosse, Philip, 31
Gould, Stephen Jay, 148, 151, 157
Graham, Billy, 159, 160, 165
Greek religion, *see* Paganism
Greene, Graham, 40–42

H

Haack, Susan, 145
Hamburger, Michael, 73
Hardy, Thomas, 94–102, 153; and Diderot, 68; and Huxley, 33; and literary atheists, 59; and Stevens, 103
Harrison, Frederic, 35
Hart, Kevin, 51
Hart, Ray L., 36
Hartmann, Eduard von, 94
Hauptmann, Gerhard, 72
Hauser, Ronald, 70
Hawking, Stephen, 149–50
Hébert, Jacques, 18
Hegel, G. W. F., 20, 22, 23, 47, 68
Heidegger, Martin, 38, 49–50, 78, 85, 148–49
Heine, Heinrich, 13, 46
Heller, Erich, 45, 47, 174
Helvétius, Claude Adrien, 62, 65
Herbert, George, 13, 182
Higgins, Kathleen M., 119n30

Himmelfarb, Gertrude, 139
Hitler, Adolf, 140, 163
Hobbes, Thomas, 12, 14, 135
Holbach, Baron d', 17–18, 20, 62, 67
Hölderlin, Friedrich, 60
Hollander, Robert, 130, 167
Hook, Sidney, 39
Howe, Irving, 99
Howells, William Dean, 86, 93
Humanism, 22, 23, 38, 48–50, 65, 141, 152; *see also* Secularism
Hume, David, 12, 14, 16–17, 143, 151; and Hobbes, 135; and Kant, 19, 20, 21; and Shelley, 27
Hunter, James Davison, 170n95
Hunter, Michael, 53n3
Huxley, Thomas Henry, as agnostic, 25, 33, 35, 153; as Darwinist, 32; influence on Hardy, 94–95; influence on James, 104

I

Ingersoll, Robert, 24, 141
Islam, 2, 4; the Koran, 186; *see also* Mohammed

J

James, Henry, 23
James, William, 6, 129; influence on Stevens, 104–06; views on religious belief, 26–27, 33, 55n44, 142, 145
Jameson, Fredric, 176
Jarraway, David R., 105
Jaspers, Karl, 50, 79
Jastrow, Robert, 149
Jefferson, Thomas, 161
Jesus Christ, belief in, 12, 30, 34, 139, 166; biblical image of, 82, 127, 65, 178–84

John, Saint, 130, 178, 182
Johnson, Lyndon B., 160
Johnson, Phillip, 147
Johnson, Samuel, 131, 135
Josephs, Herbert, 63
Josipovici, Gabriel, 159, 177, 178–179, 181, 187
Joyce, James, 24
Judaism, 1–2, 4, 45–46, 52, 164; ambivalence in, 173–74; and Hebrew Bible, 178–79, 184–85, 191n13
Jung, Carl, 80

K

Kafka, Franz, 40, 45–46, 174
Kant, Immanuel, and modern atheism, 2, 5, 19–21, 36, 37; and moral law, 47, 139, 140; and Nietzsche, 76, 81; and perspective, 48, 64; and religion, 189–90
Kaufmann, Walter, 119n30, 129
Kazin, Alfred, 145, 163
Keats, John, 112, 189
Kennedy, John F., 160
Kermode, Frank, 106, 108, 110, 133, 185
Kierkegaard, Søren, 29, 38, 44
King, Martin Luther, Jr., 4
Klein, Melanie, 129
Knowlson, James, 111
Köhler, Joachim, 120n61
Kors, Alan Charles, 13
Kristeva, Julia, 137
Kugel, James, 179, 180, 181, 191n13
Küng, Hans, 129
Kushner, Tony, 143

L

Lacan, Jacques, 49

La Mettrie, Julien Offray de, 18, 62
Lange, F. A., 74
Lawrence, D. H., 60, 99
Lear, Jonathan, 48, 148
Leavis, F. R., 121n86
Lenz, J. M. R., 73
Lessing, G. E., 20
Levin, Harry, 138
Levinas, Emmanuel, 39, 52
Levine, George, 101–02
Lévy-Strauss, Claude, 50
Lewes, G. H., 23
Lewontin, Richard, 150, 155
Lilla, Mark, 52, 58
Lincoln, Abraham, 160
Lindenberger, Herbert, 69, 70
Lipset, Seymour Martin, 161–62, 171
Locke, John, 12, 15
Lockerbie, D. Bruce, 136–37
Lucretius, 1
Lukács, Georg, 114
Lyell, Charles, 31

M

McEwan, Ian, 142–43
MacIntyre, Alasdair C., 49
Madison, James, 161
Magnus, Bernd, 119n30
Mahar, Margaret, 98–99
Mailer, Norman, 60
Marcel, Gabriel, 50
Marion, Jean-Luc, 38–39, 130, 131
Maritain, Jacques, 4
Marlowe, Christopher, 11–12, 53n3
Marsden, George M., 164
Marty, Martin E., 161, 162
Marx, Karl, and Büchner, 68; and Derrida, 21, 52; and Diderot, 63; and Feuerbach, 22; and Freud, 47; and religion, 17–18, 23, 138, 176
Mason, John Hope, 63
Materialism, relation of to atheism, 11, 13–15, 18, 60, 62–63, 72, 74
Mazzini, Giuseppe, 23
Melville, Herman, 27, 28–30
Menand, Louis, 55n44, 167–68n21
Merimée, Prosper, 60, 124n139
Meslier, Jean, 16
Midgley, Mary, 6
Miles, Jack, 171n98, 187
Mill, John Stuart, 23, 25–26, 65, 94–95, 129
Millard, Kenneth, 98
Milton, John, 2, 12, 13, 71, 101, 149
Mohammed (prophet), 139
Montaigne, Michel de, 12, 13, 22, 62, 135, 167
Moral judgment, absolute vs. relative aspects of, 3, 21, 48, 76–79, 139; conscience in relation to, 47–48, 82–83, 140–41; metaphysical basis of, 7–8, 20, 76, 139, 141
Morrell, Roy, 122n105
Moses (biblical), 128, 139, 183–84, 187
Mossner, Ernst C., 54n20
Murdoch, Iris, 40, 43, 48, 50, 56
Musil, Robert, 24
Mysticism, 37, 116, 129
Myth, relation of to God, 41, 131–33, 146, 149

N

Nagel, Ernest, 39
Nagel, Thomas, 150–51, 154–55
Naigeon, André, 18
Nashe, Thomas, 11
Negative Theology, 37–40, 51–52, 116
Nehemas, Alexander, 3, 79–80, 85
Neusner, Jacob, 174
Newman, John Henry, 34, 129
Newton, Isaac, 12–15, 17, 19, 31, 63
Newton, Roger G., 156
Nietzsche, Friedrich, 74–85, 169n49,

177; influence of on Dennett, 156; on Heidegger, 38; on Nagel, 155; on Nehemas, 3; on Rorty, 3, 25; on Stevens, 108, 123n125; relation of to atheists, 59; to Arnold, 134; to Beckett, 115, 17; to Diderot, 65, 68; to Feuerbach, 22; to Josipovici, 177; to Kierkegaard, 29; to Mill and Carlyle, 26; to Twain, 86
Nihilism, 49–50, 78–79, 83
Nixon, Richard M., 160
Novak, Michael, 163
Nuttall, A. D., 182

O

O'Connor, Flannery, 40–42, 128, 167
Ong, Walter, J., 136–27
Outram, Dorinda, 14–15
Overbeck, Franz, 83

P

Paganism, 1–2, 71–72; 103, 136
Paine, Thomas, 18, 71, 86
Paley, William, 17
Pascal, Blaise, 13, 61, 174
Pater, Walter, 23
Patterson, Paige, 166
Paul, Saint, 7, 82, 128, 178
Percy, Walker, 50
Perspectivism, 3–4, 6–7, 20, 64, 76–80 *see also* Philosophy
Philosophy, and perspectivism, 36, 39, 65, 151, 154–56
Pike, Burton, 119n31
Pinker, Steven, 67
Plantinga, Alvin, 15
Plato, 1, 43, 48, 148
Plotinus, 37
Poetry and Belief, question of, 7, 59–60, 105, 125–37, 167n21

Poincaré, Jules Henri, 151
Polkinghorne, John, 149, 169
Pope, Alexander, 71
Positivism, 21, 34–36, 39, 131
Price, Victor, 69
Protagoras, 1
Protestantism, 4, 11,19, 43–45, 85, 59, 161, 164
Proust, Marcel, 24, 113
Pseudo-Dionysius, 37

R

Raleigh, Walter, 11, 53n3
Religious experience, 144–45, 150
Richards, I. A., 134, 135
Richardson, Joan, 106
Ricks, Christopher, 116
Ricoeur, Paul, 132–33, 146, 167
Rilke, Rainer Maria, 60, 133
Robertson, J. M., 32
Robertson, Pat, 164
Robespierre, Maximilien, 18, 69
Rolston, Holmes, III, 31, 147, 153
Romanticism, relation of to modern atheism, 2, 5, 19–22, 121, 152; religious displacements of, 22–25, 27, 131–32
Rorty, Richard, on Freud, 47–48; on Kant, 19–20; on Nietzsche, 79; on relativism, 3, 20–21; on religion, 25, 138, 140
Rostman, Betty, 185
Rousseau, Jean-Jacques, 19, 70
Rubenstein, Richard L, 57n100
Ruse, Michael, 147, 169
Ruskin, John, 23
Russell, Bertrand, 35–36

S

Sacred Writing, 175–77, 188–90

Sade, Marquis de, 60, 124n139
Safranski, Rüdiger, 38, 65, 77–78
Santayana, George, 104–05, 129–30
Sartre, Jean-Paul, 37, 38, 43, 46, 48–50
Saussure, Ferdinand de, 50
Schleiermacher, Friedrich, 20
Schneidau, Herbert, 133, 175
Schneider, Alan, 112
Schopenhauer, Arthur, 71, 74, 76, 81–84, 94, 101
Schroeder, Gerald, 149
Schwartz, Delmore, 134
Schwartz, Regina M., 57n89, 175–76, 188, 189, 191n7
Science, relation of to religion and the arts, 6, 7, 26, 33, 126, 146, 151–58
Scott, Eugenie, 31–32
Scott, Walter, 90
Scriven, Michael, 39
Secularism, 127, 138, 141–44, 158–66, 173; secular vs. sacred, 147, 163, 180–83, 188–90
Sedgwick, Adam, 32
Seymour-Smith, Martin, 98
Shakespeare, William, 12, 78, 101
Shaw, George Bernard, 31, 32, 62, 147
Shelley, Percy Bysshe, 25, 27, 60, 69, 94
Shermer, Michael, 25, 169
Singer, Isaac Bashevis, 152, 173–74
Smith, Christian, 164–65
Socrates, 1
Solomon, Robert C., 77
Spencer, Herbert, 31, 32, 33, 94–95, 147
Spinoza, Baruch, 12, 14, 22, 66, 129
Spoto, Donald, 191n12
Stack, George J., 81
Steiner, George, 128–29
Stendhal, 81
Stephen, Leslie, 25, 34–35, 94–95
Stevens, Wallace, 102–110; relation of to atheists, 59, 113; views on poetry and belief, 7, 24, 130, 131

Strauss, D. F., 31, 74
Swinburne, Algernon, 23, 28, 60, 94
Swinburne, Richard, 44

T

Taine, Hippolyte, 138
Tate, Allen, 134, 135
Taylor, Mark C., 36
Teilhard de Chardin, P., 31, 133, 147, 167
Teleological thinking, 32, 79, 146–50
Tennyson, Alfred, 23–4, 27–8, 95, 153
Theology, anthropomorphism in, 14, 37–38, 96; Death-of-God style of, 22, 50, 78–79, 101, 110; sophistication in, 5, 6, 21, 39–41, 129, 133, 139–40; science mixed with, 25, 146–50, 169n49; arguments of, 12, 13, 17, 19, 21; see also Negative Theology
Thomas Aquinas, Saint, 130, 179
Thomson, James, 60
Tillich, Paul, 38, 131
Tipler, Frank, 149
Tocqueville, Alexis de, 161, 162
Tolstoy, Leo, 4
Truth, religious versus poetic, 6–7, 22, 126–27, 130–31, 133–36, 145–46
Turner, James, 53n3
Twain, Mark, 33, 59, 68, 85–94, 103
Twichell, Joseph, 86, 93

U

Unamuno, Miguel de, 4
Updike, John, 40, 43–45, 164

V

Vahanian, Gabriel, 57n100

Vartanian, Aram, 63, 66
Vendler, Helen, 106, 109
Voltaire, 12, 14, 15–16, 61, 68, 70

W

Wagner, Richard, 80, 82
Ward, Graham, 49, 167
Ward, Mrs. Humphry, 23
Weidig, Ludwig, 69
Weil, Simone, 111
Weinberg, Steven, 140, 148, 152
Weiner, Jonathan, 152, 155
Wheatcroft, Geoffrey, 171n 99
Whitehead, Alfred North, 90
Whitman, Walt, 24, 29, 102, 106, 138
Wilde, Oscar, 23
Williams, James D., 90
Williams, William Carlos, 102
Wilson, Arthur M., 65
Wilson, A. N., 139, 178
Wilson, E. O., 21, 64–65, 140, 146, 151–54, 156
Wilson, James Q., 140–41
Winters, Ivor, 136
Wittgenstein, Ludwig, 3, 46, 48, 129, 146, 149
Wolosky, Shira, 112, 116–17
Wood, James, 44–45, 125, 137, 168
Woolf, Virginia, 24, 34–35
Wootton, David, 53n2
Wordsworth, William, 20
Wright, Robert, 148

Y

Yahweh, *see* Bible
Yeats, W. B., 23, 60, 84

Z

Zola, Emile, 69